BLACK ROCK DESERT

Ladder Creek Mt Observation

D E

Black Rock Sp.

Mt Namany River

Upper Mud Lake

Three Springs

Mountain Sp.

Hun

Boiler or Steamboat Springs

1495

Lower Mud Lake

Fremont's Route 1845

U O

V

T

WINNEMUCCA LAKE (MUD LAKE)

Humboldt Lake

Mud L.

Volcanic Hill

Hot Sp.   Sulphur Wells

Sink

PYRAMID LAKE

DESERT

BIG BEND OF TRUCKEE R.

Area of 1860 Battles

Reese's New Route to C

J R

Willow Sp.

R

Little Meadows

T   H

25 Mile Desert

E

M. Desert   Volcanic Rocks

Ragtown

River

Sink of Carson River

Springs

R

Carson

Carson Lake

Salt Lake

RSON CITY

Sonora Emigrant Road

Hot Sp.

Walker's R.

Proposed Route   New

S

Basaltic Hills

Range

Low Pass

West Fork

Basaltic Cañon

Range

WALKER'S VALLEY

D1165725

Range o

Dry Lagoon

SAND IN A WHIRLWIND

FEROL EGAN

SAND IN A WHIRLWIND

The Paiute Indian War of 1860

Foreword by A. B. Guthrie, Jr.

Doubleday & Company, Inc., Garden City, New York, 1972

ISBN: 0-385-01814-2
Library of Congress Catalog Card Number 72-79385
Copyright © 1972 by Ferol Egan
All Rights Reserved
Printed in the United States of America
First Edition

This book is for
George R. Stewart and Charles L. Camp
who know and love
the Great Basin

CONTENTS

PART II

THE GATHERING FURY 1860

PART III

THE COST OF VIOLENCE 1860

PART IV

SAGEBRUSH SOLDIERS 1860

PART V

AN END TO GLORY 1860

The tourist making the long, summer-hot drive across northern Nevada will strike the town of Winnemucca. If he inquires, he may be told that the town was once a wagon stop on the Overland Trail that became a trading center for nearby mines and ranches. Further inquiry may elicit the information that the town owes its name to the Indians, in particular to Chief Winnemucca of the Paiutes, about whose life maybe fusty historians can tell. What then of Numaga? The townsman probably will shake his head. No such place on the map. No place in memory for him, the once-celebrated war chief of the tribe.

A further drive to the west and north will take the tourist to Pyramid Lake, the heartland of the Paiutes, the focus of struggle between invaded and invader, the spiritual and by preference physical home of War Chief Numaga.

It is appropriate here to ask and answer the question: Who were the Paiutes? The mountain men of the fur hunting days spoke of them and their neighbors as Diggers because they fed on roots and insects and fish, red-blooded game being scarce. They didn't take into account, these fur-seekers, that the Paiutes had adjusted to cruel changes of weather over the centuries or that their habitat was compressed and restricted by human forces outside it.

The Paiutes never acquired the reputation of the Blackfeet, Sioux, and Cheyenne. They were not by nature fighting men, as the Blackfeet were. They had no Sitting Bull or Crazy Horse to make them famous, nor any such blazing event as the Battle of the Little Bighorn, nor such a celebrated adversary as General George Armstrong Custer. They fought, they had to fight finally, and they lost.

They had their Numaga. They had their courage, their battles, and they have their sizable place in the history of the West.

It is time that their piece in the sad pattern of race against race is presented and placed, as it is here in Ferol Egan's sturdy prose.

Egan's sympathies are with the Indians, as they should be. Yet he writes with moderation, even a compassion, that removes his book from the charge of blind partisanship. The whites had their problems, their painful decisions, some of them implicit in hard and cruel circumstances, others forced on thoughtful and conscientious men by Indian haters and hotheads. And he recognizes the impersonal irony of events, the habit that comparatively minor incidents have of pushing decisions to great and tragic conclusions.

Given the circumstances, history would probably repeat itself. Yet I dare hope it's beneficial to see again, as Egan makes us see, that greed has no honor, that historically the Indian has had no rights against a sentiment superior in strength if not in right.

A. B. Guthrie, Jr.

The Indian Wars of the American West hold a strange fascination for the world. No doubt, part of this is derived from movies, part from fiction and folklore, and a very small part from objective histories of what took place, why it happened, and who was there.

Certainly, the pinnacle of Indian glory in these battles belongs to the Sioux; and it finds its greatest fame in one bloody June day of 1876 when Chiefs Sitting Bull and Crazy Horse led a combined force of warriors from more than one tribe in a single action that created both legend and history by giving George Armstrong Custer and the 7th Cavalry their final moments in the Battle of the Little Bighorn. Yet this was no more than one battle in the concluding struggle between Indians and whites for control of the Indian lands of the trans-Mississippi West. In a very real sense the true beginning of this greatest of all land grabs started with the Lewis and Clark Expedition, as this was the advertisement that caught the fancy of a westward-moving, frontier people. It was the bait that pulled them into one Indian sanctuary

after another—regions "protected" by treaties with the
United States. This was the birth of a Manifest Destiny
concept that would find a champion in John C. Frémont,
take a deadly toll in Indian and white lives, and reduce
the Indians to a vanishing people by the start of the
twentieth century.

Many histories of this period are filled with clichés.
If the Indians won, it was a massacre. If the whites won,
it was a glorious victory. Other histories give the impression that only such tribes as the Sioux, Cheyenne,
Blackfeet, Nez Percé, and Apache resisted white invasion.
Combined with these impressions are the names of a
few outstanding chiefs such as Red Cloud, Sitting Bull,
and Crazy Horse of the Sioux; Chief Joseph of the Nez
Percé; and Mangas Coloradas and Geronimo of the
Apache. These names and the battles in which they fought
give most readers the impression that only a few tribes in
the American West bothered to fight for their homes,
and that only these tribes had great chiefs. Such was not
the case.

Sixteen years before the Little Bighorn and before the
rise to fame of other western tribes and their warrior
chiefs, peace-loving Chief Numaga of the Paiutes led a
combined army of his own men, warriors from other
Paiute tribes, Bannock warriors, and Shoshoni warriors in
a remarkable defense of the Paiute desert home in the
Great Basin of what was then Utah Territory. Like other
great Indian leaders who had to function within the most
democratic of societies, Chief Numaga could not control
all his men at all times. Still, he was able to hold them
together for a last-ditch stand against the encroachment
of white invaders who marched from the diggings at the
Comstock Lode and headed toward Pyramid Lake with
the idea of settling the "Indian question" for the last

time. What the whites had not counted on was the skill of Chief Numaga and the willingness of his warriors to fight to defend their homeland—a combination that was so effective that it terrified all of Utah Territory and Northern California. It brought all work in the Comstock Lode to a frightened standstill, halted the Pony Express, the stagecoaches, and all other travel on the California Trail across the Great Basin.

This war between whites and Paiutes is a good example of what can happen when a powerful people assume that they can easily push a small group of people out of their homes and carry on "business as usual." And it is the story of what the price of victory cost the Paiutes then and what it continues to cost them to this day.

ACKNOWLEDGMENTS

Much of the material that was used in writing this history came from unpublished diaries, reminiscences, and letters. Government documents, newspapers, and important secondary sources were very helpful. However, the country itself played a key role. To write about the struggle for this stretch of earth, it was necessary to know the land— how it looks at different times of the day and the year, how it appears to a man on foot or horseback, and what the weather is like in the various seasons.

Many institutions and individuals helped in the making of this book, and I should like to thank them for their generosity and interest. Libraries, historical societies, museums and their staffs are the backbone of scholarship, and in the end they are the silent contributors to any work of history. And I acknowledge my debt to the following: The Bancroft Library, University of California; Nevada State Historical Society, Reno; Special Collections Department, University of Nevada Library, Reno; The Nevada State Museum, Carson City; Nevada State Library, Carson City; California State Library, Sacramento; Society of California Pioneers, San Francisco; Sutro Library, San Francisco; California Historical Society, San Francisco; and the Bureau of Outdoor Recreation, San Francisco.

I was also most fortunate to have some individuals give unstintingly of their time, knowledge, and labor. These people deserve special thanks, and I hope the book meets the expectations of: Mrs. Marion Welliver, former Director of the Nevada State Historical Society; Mrs. Eslie Cann of the Nevada State Historical Society; Mrs. Pamela Crowell, Accessions and Research, The Nevada State Museum; Mr. Richard Dillon, Head Librarian, Sutro Library; Mr. Luther Nichols, my editor; and especially my wife, Marty, who is my listener, copy editor, typist, and a source of steady encouragement.

Ferol Egan

Berkeley, California
January 1972

PROLOGUE

The Long Passing of Time

The first Indians knew the country when there was plenty
of food and water. They lived in natural caves and rock
shelters above the shores of ancient Lake Lahontan—
a massive inland lake that stretched over more than
eight thousand square miles of what is now northwestern
Nevada and northeastern California. Fed by water from
melting glaciers and Sierra Nevada rivers, the lake fingered
in and around the north-south mountain ranges of the
Great Basin in the shape of a giant petroglyph. There
was always enough rain to keep the grass green for
bighorn sheep, mule deer, and elk, while the lake provided an unlimited supply of fish, and served as a nesting
place each year for great flights of water fowl. But in
the long drift of time more than ten thousand years
passed. New tribes immigrated into the country, and the
weather changed season after season.[1]

At first, changes were hardly noticed. An old man
sitting in the shade of a rock overhang looked at the
clear sky. He commented upon how little rain, how warm
the summer, how much harder the hunt. Little things,

small things mentioned by an old man. Nearby, young men listened politely. But when they were away from the old man, they laughed, dismissed what he had said, and agreed it was only a bad season.

More time passed. Season ran into season. Generations lived and died, and no book of records was handed down to the young. There were strange carvings on the rocks in some places, but these had been made by earlier tribes. The latecomers could not read their meaning.[2] All they had were vague memories kept alive by the ancient ones. Stories told by the fireside, but stories that changed as memories faded in the long passing of time. There was no memory any more of easy hunting. Now old men only knew that the land had always been dry, that it had always been hard to find enough to eat. But the seasons were getting drier, and the span of a man's life could be marked by the new beach lines of the dying desert lake.

All the while, all through the years of change, the Indians adapted to the seasons. They no longer depended upon hunting for most of their food. They became excellent fishermen, and they called themselves the People. But this band of Northern Paiute[3] who lived close to Pyramid Lake were also called Kuyuidokado or Fish Eaters. A name they shortened to Cui-ui and gave to the large suckerfish descended from ancestors that swam in the Pleistocene water of Lake Lahontan.[4]

Once a year the Pyramid Lake Paiutes caught the strange looking cui-ui suckerfish as it swam up from the depths of the lake and into the Truckee River to spawn. Then in the spring and fall they netted and speared the two runs of spawning salmon trout. The spring cutthroats were smaller and called tamaagaih, but in October the fishermen caught the large hoopagaih with the brilliant red marking on its throat as though it had been slashed by an obsidian blade.[5] While the men fished, the women cleaned and filleted their catch, and dried and smoked them as part of their winter food supply.

No source of food was overlooked. Bow and arrow hunters patiently crept close enough to pronghorns, big-horn sheep, and mule deer to send killing arrows into the prey before it bounded away. Camouflaged men crouched in the cold water of the tule marshes and snared unwary ducks and geese. Rabbit drives involved all the People. The frightened rabbits were driven from their sagebrush hiding places by a line of walkers who made noise and headed the fleeing animals toward an arc of a large net. Here the trapped rabbits were quickly clubbed to death to provide meat for food and skins for robes.[6]

Along with hunting and fishing, the Paiutes worked together in picking pine cones from the squatty piñon pines for their year's supply of pine nuts. The women and girls gathered grass seeds and carried them to camp in tightly woven burden baskets, and they waded waist deep into the cold water of the marshes to rob nests of eggs and to pick the sweet tule shoots. They dug for roots with sharpened sticks, and collected and roasted grasshoppers and other insects.[7]

More seasons passed, and the climate became drier and drier. All but a few of the great desert lakes became mud-hardened playas. Some lakes even turned into shallow bogs of salty water with the rank odor of alkali and sulfur. During these centuries of changing climate the Paiute fish eaters of Pyramid Lake were settled by the fresh water of the lake and the Truckee River. Here, where the meadows had green grass in the spring, there was more food than in other regions of the water-starved Great Basin.

Away from the water was the desert. As far as a man could see there were only long stretches of lonely distance. Most of the land was covered with sagebrush and greasewood on the flats and up on to the foothills where the piñon pines grew, and some regions were so dry that only the blinding whiteness of alkali or sand could be seen. Yet close to this wind-driven wilderness, this barren land of many basins there was the upthrust of the Sierra Nevada to the west, and separating the many basins were the tall north-south mountain ranges whose peaks were islands in an ocean of dead land.

Often during the hot summer months, the Paiutes left their basket-shaped dwellings, their karnees made of willow limbs and bundled grass. Sometimes they journeyed across the Sierra Nevada and traded with the California Miwoks. At other times they traveled to Lake Tahoe. Here in the Washo[8] country they camped, and enjoyed the cool breeze that whistled down the gulches and canyons and rattled the quaking aspen and cottonwood leaves into green waves of movement. Hunters stalked deer, grouse, and quail; and fishermen caught mountain trout from the icy water—fish with hard flesh, speckled backs, and rainbow stripes on their sides.

Through the long span of time the Paiutes and other Great Basin tribes had learned how to live in their desert home, had learned how to use everything they could find to sustain life. The different tribes respected their territorial boundaries for hunting and fishing, and only crossed into these regions with permission. Thus they avoided organized warfare. For in a land where the act of living was a daily battle there was no time to fight other foes. So the peaceful years flowed into each other, and all time was one.

Only certain events marked interruptions in the regular

cycle of seasons: birth and death, a winter of deep snow, a summer of burnt grass, a trading trip across the tall western mountains, a fall of many rabbits. Then, from the direction of sunrise came strangers—men with white eyes, hair on their faces, and buckskin covering their own sand-colored skin.

Warily, the People crept closer to these strangers, and most first meetings were peaceful. Through sign talk and a few words of neighboring tribes that some of the strangers knew, it was learned that they were lost and needed directions. Squatting next to each other, the brown and sand-colored men talked, and the brown men scratched maps in the dirt to guide these wanderers on their way.

Time as the white man marked it was like the strange rock carvings to the People of the Great Basin, who measured years by events and seasons. Yet there are records of their first meetings. In 1841, Paiutes along the Humboldt River met the Bidwell-Bartleson party of emigrants. As John Bidwell pointed out in his journal, these were friendly Indians. One of the tribe even went out of his way to overtake their party, "bringing the piece of tobacco which he had found at our latest camp and surrendered it."[9]

Three years later John C. Frémont and twenty-four men worked their way south from Oregon. On January 10, 1844, the explorer and Kit Carson reached the summit of the desert mountains at the northern end of the home of the fish eaters. Astounded by his first view of the lake Frémont wrote:

> It broke upon our eyes like the ocean. The neighboring peaks rose high above us, and we ascended one of them to obtain a better view. The waves were curling in the breeze, and their dark-green color showed it to be a body

of deep water. For a long time we sat enjoying the view, for we had become fatigued with mountains, and the free expanse of moving waves was very grateful. It was set like a gem in the mountains, which, from our position, seemed to enclose it almost entirely.[10]

After this first view from the pass, Frémont and his men traveled south toward the mouth of the Truckee River. When he saw the great rock that rises some three hundred feet from the water like a massive arrowhead maker's tool, he thought it was close to an exact outline of the great pyramid of Cheops. "This striking feature suggested a name for the lake, and I called it Pyramid Lake."[11]

Having named their lake, Frémont next met the Paiutes living near its shores. The weary explorer and his men were treated to a feast of salmon trout. As they rested and talked, the explorer asked for directions, and the fish eaters were most helpful:

They made on the ground a drawing of the river, which they represented as issuing from another lake in the mountains three or four days distant, in a direction a little west of south; beyond which, they drew a mountain; and further still, two rivers; on one of which they told us that people like ourselves traveled.[12]

The invasion of the Great Basin had just started, and it was still possible for the Indians and the sand-colored strangers to meet in peace. But as the seasons passed, there were more and more white eyes. Some came on foot, some on horses, some in traveling houses, and some even camped in the meadows at the foot of the tall western mountains.

By 1859, the Indians were no longer happy to greet these strangers. Now they knew these men called themselves Americans, and always seemed to be saying, "goddamn, son-of-a-bitch." But what really worried the People of the Great Basin was that these Americans were no longer just passing by. Some came and made their homes in the great meadows, and others returned from across the tall western mountains to dig holes in the ground.

Some of these Americans were good men who learned the language of the Paiutes and the Washos, and treated them as brothers. But others were like rattlesnakes and not to be trusted. These white eyes shot the People whenever they got a chance. They cut down the pine nut orchards to use in the holes they dug or to burn in their fires. They even drove their horses and cattle to the grassland around Pyramid Lake. Then like a coyote trickster, they stole women, used them, and sent them back to the People with an evil spirit that sickened any man who touched them.

In the seasons of one man's life the way of the Great Basin People changed. Their very existence was threatened by the sand-colored Americans. At first, these white eyes were no more worry than a single cricket, but then they became a wind-blown swarm of crickets that destroyed everything in its path.

Tribes in all directions sent word of their concern to the Paiutes at Pyramid Lake. The time had come to do something about these Americans. The days of peace were coming to a close. The tinder was in place beneath the kindling of bad feelings. All that was needed was a spark of violence.

PART I

A SEASON OF DISCONTENT

1859-60

CHAPTER 1

An Occurrence at Black Rock Canyon

The weather was cold for late April, colder than usual. Snow still lingered on the northeastern flanks of the Sierra Nevada just above Honey Lake Valley and the small settlement of Susanville in Utah Territory. Even a three-day ride into the northeastern desert had not made it any warmer for the men. It was not a comfortable season to be camping out in the lonely vastness of the Black Rock Desert. But though he was a pioneer trailblazer, a man who knew this land better than most, Peter Lassen was not able to resist the possibility of sudden riches. Despite all the disappointments, the old optimism was still with him.

Lassen knew he had wasted too many years and too much energy on the frontier without much to show for it. This silver strike in the Great Basin was another chance, perhaps a last chance. He hadn't made it as a landowner or merchant, though he had tried more than once in California before the discovery of gold. And like his former employer, Captain John Sutter, he had failed to strike it rich during the Gold Rush. Yet silver was something new, something he hadn't thought about, much less counted on. But the discovery of the Comstock Lode was all the talk of the sparse population in the sagebrush country, and Lassen wanted to stake his claim early. For, once the snow melted in the high country passes, there would be a rush of miners from California's Mother Lode, where the easy pickings had ended.

As the fifty-nine-year-old Dane and his fellow prospectors sat around their campfire on the chilly evening of April 25, 1859, he might have worried about the possibility of such a small party being attacked by Indians. If so, he showed no sign of it. Instead, he talked easily to young Edward Clapper and Lemericus Wyatt, the sixty-year-old, broad-shouldered farmhand, handyman, and carpenter.

The plan from the start had included their rendezvousing with Captain William Weatherlow's larger party. Lassen had assured the others that there would be no difficulty in doing this even though they were a few days behind the Weatherlow party. But this was their second day at Black Rock Canyon, and there was no sign of the other men. Worse than that, now that Clapper had made a scouting trip to Mud Lake and back, it was very hard for a man to rest easy. All he had found were the footprints of two white men and the tracks of shod horses. Such signs could mean the Weatherlow party had been ambushed. They talked all this over with Lassen; and in the end, he convinced them "the advance party were over the mountains at another camping place."[1] Come morning, they'd ride over there and join forces with them.

Lassen's decision eased the tension. Neither Clapper nor Wyatt could hide their feelings. They had not liked this camp from the beginning. While they admitted that having a small creek of sweet running water was an advantage, this hadn't removed their major concern. Camping in a box canyon was too much of a trap. Yet Lassen had persisted. He considered the three high lava cliffs as walls of defense. Any foe would have to come straight at them across the flat, open alkali plain. All this sounded fine, but there was a flaw. Both sides of the canyon floor had thickets of greasewood and tall sagebrush, and clusters of quaking aspens. There was more than enough cover for a man to ease a horse by if he happened to be clever enough.

But hell, everything was going to be all right. They'd spend one more night by themselves, no more than that. Feeling easier, the men relaxed by the fire. Tomorrow would be another day on the road to riches. It only made good sense that more men working together would increase the chances of striking a silver lode.

Completely at rest, all worries buried, Clapper and Wyatt were startled when Lassen quit talking and peered beyond the rim of light from their campfire.

They stared in the direction of the canyon mouth only to hear a sound behind them. Then from out of nowhere, as though he had always been there, the men saw an Indian on horseback. He was slowly, cautiously circling their camp, drifting in and out of the firelight like an apparition. Clapper and Wyatt reached for their rifles, but the Indian vanished into the darkness. When he reappeared, he was on foot, and he was standing at the edge of the firelight—standing and waiting.

Clapper and Wyatt waited for Lassen's command. Instead, they heard him speak to the visitor in Paiute. As the old man talked, they looked around for more Indians and got ready for an attack. Neither man had lived among the Indians as had Lassen. And though they knew the Dane was Chief Numaga's friend, they weren't sure that the young Indian standing before them was Paiute. He hadn't answered yet. Maybe he was with a hunting party of Pit River Indians from across the Sierra Nevada—the same tribe that had been defeated by Lassen, Weatherlow, and other men from Honey Lake Valley along with the help of Chief Numaga and his warriors.

Finally, the young man answered Lassen in Paiute. More conversation followed, until the old man persuaded the Indian to join them beside the fire. The men watched carefully as the Paiute walked across the clearing. He moved as though he were gliding. When he reached the fire, he gracefully settled into a cross-legged sitting posture and began to speak.

While the two men talked, Lassen's companions waited for a translation. But the tension had eased, and they were no longer so disturbed. They relaxed and listened to the foreign sounds of the Indian's speech. Still, everything was going to be all right. The man was a Paiute, and Paiutes were friendly. So they sat and listened to the mixture of sounds: the deep-in-the-throat speech, the running creek water, and the wind-rustled leaves of the quaking aspens. Then these safe sounds were suddenly shut off by the loud report of a rifle—the noise bouncing back and forth off the canyon walls.

Before anyone moved, the visitor said, "Paiute."

"Where?" Lassen asked.

"From our camp."

"How many men hunt with you?"

"Five more."

The tight expression of Lassen's face relaxed. He rapidly translated so that the others would know who had fired the shot, and that everything was all right.

The men listened, but they were not as sure about this as their leader. Yet one thing was very clear. If the Indians were up to something, they were sure as hell risking the life of the man sitting beside the fire.

When no more shots followed, the men settled down again. Obviously, the Indian had told the truth. There was nothing to worry about.

The conversation continued for a while longer. Then the young hunter got up, said good-by, and eased back into the darkness, where he mounted his horse and rode away. The men listened intently, but once he was outside the perimeter of their camp, they could not even hear the movements of his horse. Yet there were perfectly good reasons for this. The soil was soft in the meadow grass beside the creek, and the hunter's horse was not shod. But it didn't put a man's mind to rest. If one Paiute could do this, what was to keep a war party of Pit River Indians from doing the same thing? There, by God, was the real worry, and there was no escaping it until they got together with the Weatherlow party.

For now, for this one night they'd have to accept the conditions of their position. Knowing this, the men stretched out their bedrolls on the ground near the glowing coals and fading warmth of the campfire. The night air was cold in this high desert country, and overhead the bright stars were like pure silver specimens that had been removed from the dull, blue ore. In the morning, they'd break up camp, locate the others, and get on with the business of getting rich.

2

Before daylight, the men shivered beneath blankets covered with frost. All that remained of the night's fire was a pile of gray ashes, glowing coals, and a thin streamer of smoke hanging in the stillness of dawn like a giant spider's thread. The men moved around in their blankets, tossing about in that half-world between sleep and full awareness. Then the quiet of first light was shattered with the echoing shock of a rifle shot.

Lassen and Wyatt were out of their blankets before the last re-echo of the shot had faded into the air. They had to pick up their gear and supplies and get out of this trap. Wyatt moved from one thing to another, frantically trying to decide what to grab first. *Blankets, they'd need their bedrolls!* Wyatt turned around, and for the first time, he realized that Clapper was still asleep —asleep with all this noise. He reached down to shake him, missed his shoulder, and touched his face. My God! His fingers felt something warm and sticky, and when he pulled his hand back it was covered with blood. Feeling sick about what he knew he would find, he rolled Clapper's limp body over. There was no longer any question about the reason for the rifle shot. Clapper had been shot through the temple. The blood was still pumping out of the small entry wound, and the other side of his head had a larger hole where the bullet had smashed out of his skull and scattered blood, brains, and bone fragments.

Stunned and sick, Wyatt turned and looked at Lassen. Somehow, if there was any chance at all, he knew the old mountaineer would get them out of this canyon alive.

"I'll watch for Indians while you gather up things,"[2] Lassen said.

Working rapidly, moving as fast as he could, Wyatt grabbed things at random. *Food! They'd need food!* He reached for the food packs. As he hefted them across his broad shoulders, he saw the tools: axes, picks, shovels, cooking pots and pans. He picked up all he could hold, moving from one thing to another, piling item on top of item, and resting all of them on his large hands and arms, until he had to cradle them against his chest. When he could not bend over for any more, he started for the small grove of quaking aspens where the frightened horses were pulling at the picket ropes, trying to break away.

Seeing that the nervous horses would get loose at any moment, Wyatt began to run. The distance wasn't far, but the frosty and slippery grass made it hard for him to keep his balance. Hanging tightly to his heavy load, he stumbled along as best he could in his awkward gait. As he neared the horses, he realized Lassen wasn't right behind. He yelled for him to run for it while there was still time.

When he didn't answer, Wyatt stopped. He looked back, and "Uncle Pete" was still standing in the open. With one hand, he was shading his eyes against the glare of the first sunlight striking the volcanic glass in the canyon walls as he searched for Clapper's killer. In his other hand, he held his rifle ready for use.

Again Wyatt shouted for him to run. But almost as the words left his mouth, they were lost in the air as another shot filled the canyon with its reverberating shock. To Wyatt's horror, Lassen clutched at his chest. For a moment, it was all frozen in Wyatt's mind. *It wasn't possible! None of it could really be happening!* Then the nightmare became reality. Lassen fell backward as though the echoing report of the shot had roped his legs and jerked them out from under him.

Wyatt dropped everything he was carrying. He ran back across the clearing. When he reached Lassen, he knelt and gently raised him from the ground. Lassen's face was as white as the alkali desert. But his eyes were not glazed, and he was still breathing. As Wyatt watched him try to speak, his eyes darted wildly. Wyatt thought he heard him say, "They have killed me."[3] That was all he said. Anything else was lost as he gasped for air. His body shuddered, and before Wyatt could catch him, Lassen slid from his grasp. He fell face down on the ground, gave a spasmodic jerk, and was gone.

Frantically, Wyatt got up and ran for the horses. As he neared them, the frightened animals reared back, pulled their picket ropes loose, and stampeded past him. Running desperately, his lungs burning for air, Wyatt trailed after the horses as they ran toward the mouth of the canyon. In all the confusion, he heard another shot. Almost in the same instant one trouser leg flapped violently, nearly tripping him. But there was no searing pain, no sudden shock of wound to topple him to the ground.

Now he ran wildly, crazily. He ran with a speed born of fear and desperation. At the canyon's entrance, he plunged through a low line of sagebrush, and stumbled onto the alkali plain.

Hope of survival vanished as he stared ahead. Out on the white alkali plain, a cloud of moving dust hid the runaway horses that were his only hope of staying alive. Then before his disbelieving eyes, "the form of his own fine black pacing horse suddenly appeared. The animal had faced about, apparently struck by some sudden impulse."[4] And it galloped back toward him as though it had been ordered to do so.

Wyatt watched the horse draw closer and closer. When it was almost upon him, he stepped aside. With a kind of agility he had never known in his whole life, he grabbed the horse's flowing mane with one hand, the halter with his other hand. Jumping upward, using all his strength, he pulled himself astride, and headed the horse out across the glistening alkali flat.

He gripped the horse's withers by tightly squeezing

his legs inward, and he reached down and grabbed the dragging picket rope to use as a rein. From that point on, the miles and hours ran into each other. Whenever the horse slowed to a walk, Wyatt looked behind with dread. But nowhere in the vast plain was there any sign of pursuers. Still, he was not certain of his direction. All he truly knew was that he had to travel over one hundred miles to the southwest. There, if he didn't get lost, he would find safety in Honey Lake Valley and Susanville. Other than that, he knew he was alive, and that Clapper and Lassen were dead. Ahead of him was a long ride for his life.

CHAPTER 2

A Desert Mystery

After four long, weary days and nights, Lem Wyatt and
his exhausted black horse reached Susanville. The old
man had never been much of a horseman, but somehow
he had managed to ride nearly 140 miles without a saddle
and with only a picket rope for a rein. His knees and
calves were rubbed raw from gripping the horse's withers,
and his hands were rope-burned. Every inch of his body
was one solid ache. Yet before he rested, he told the
tragic story of Peter Lassen's death at Black Rock
Canyon.

The reaction of the other settlers in Honey Lake Valley
came swiftly. While Lem Wyatt couldn't read or write,
he had never been a man to stretch the truth. Besides,
all any doubter had to do was look at Wyatt. His worn-
out legs were still shaky from having been cramped like
a vise for so many hours; his eyes were bloodshot from
too much sun and too little sleep; his skin was afire with
sun and wind burn, and his clothing and skin had a
fine coating of alkali dust and sand. A man in Wyatt's
condition had to be telling the truth: Edward Clapper

and Peter Lassen had been murdered by Indians, and Lemericus Wyatt was lucky to be alive.

Now there was even more to worry about. Wyatt had not seen any sign of Captain William Weatherlow's party. If the Indian raiders who ambushed Lassen were hitting all whites in the desert, the chances of survival for Weatherlow and his companions were very dubious, at best. Betting on the slim chance that at least some of them were alive, the settlers quickly formed a relief party. Armed and ready for trouble, they rode northeast into the desert. They were on their way to help the living, to bury the dead, and to kill the Indians who had made Black Rock Canyon into a death camp.

2

Two days out of Susanville, the relief party met Captain Weatherlow and his men. They had run short of supplies and were on their way home. When told of the tragedy, they were astounded and then enraged. The two parties discussed all the possibilities as to who might have killed Lassen and Clapper. Then they joined forces and rode into the desert.

When they reached the death camp, things were just as Wyatt had described them. Clapper was sprawled half on the ground, half on his bedroll. His distorted head was caked with dried blood, flies and yellow jackets were crawling all over the openings in his skull. Lassen's body was close to the fire pit, and insects crawled all over him. Neither corpse had been mutilated, but the warm midday sun had aided the process of decomposition. Both bodies were much too rank to carry back to Susanville. Covering their mouths and noses with bandanas or whatever cloth was handy, the burial detail worked rapidly as they placed Lassen and Clapper in graves near the site of their last camp.

While the men finished burying the dead, the rest of the party searched for clues that might indicate who had murdered their friends. Time, though, was on the side of violence. All tracks—man and horse, Indian and white— were already too old to be of help. Some things were obvious: shod horse tracks and leather boot tracks near the Lassen camp, and unshod horse tracks and Paiute moccasin tracks near the canyon mouth. None of these things were of value. They only gave veracity to Wyatt's story of the two friendly camps. Yet one thing was out of joint at the white camp. It had not been completely plundered. If Indians had murdered these men, why had they overlooked some of the supplies? This was a mystery that later bothered Indian Agent Major Frederick Dodge, who commented upon "the fact that two sacks of flour, some dried beef, blankets, and part of a keg of whiskey, were found."[1]

But the men who buried Lassen and Clapper were strangely silent about this. Either they did not think it unusual for raiders not to take all the plunder, or they considered the possibility that the killers were in too much of a hurry to be bothered. Whatever the men thought, however, never appeared in any recorded document, or simply vanished in the passing of time. What is known is that once they had prayed over the fresh graves, they were in a hurry to return to Susanville. Any trail the killers might have left was much too old for them to follow even if they had been lucky enough to find it. For the moment, the Honey Lake men had accomplished one job—the burial. The other job—the capture of the killers—was not possible. Things simply hadn't worked out all the way for them. Having done what they could do, they rode out of Black Rock Canyon and headed southwest, knowing the other half of their task might never be completed.[2]

3

By the time the combined party returned to Susanville, the small frontier community was fired up for retribution. Past friendship and help from the Paiutes was overlooked in a mad frenzy of hate. The old American feeling about Indians surfaced. Biblical revenge was altered to suit the rage. Any eye—especially an Indian eye—that was handy would serve the cause of revenge, would help to ease the community anger at the death of Peter Lassen. He had been murdered in Paiute country, the reasoning went, therefore the Paiutes had to be guilty—not just one Paiute, but all Paiutes.

Captain William Weatherlow observed the excitement and hate among the settlers of Honey Lake Valley, and it made him sick. He called upon them to stop and consider what they were about to do. Everybody, he reminded them, had signed a treaty with the Paiutes. Justice for both peoples was to be the same. Had they forgotten that? Chief Numaga and his warriors had helped them to defeat the Pit River tribe that had caused them much harm and grief. Was this to be overlooked? Most of all, though, Peter Lassen and Chief Numaga had always been close friends. They had been friends long before many of them had come to this valley. Was this to be tossed aside as though it had never existed? Then he asked them if the Paiutes in the valley had become warlike. The answer was given slowly and with hesitation, but the truth came out. No, the Indians were as friendly as they had always been. They gave no indication of

even knowing of Lassen's death. At this point, Weatherlow suggested that this was hardly the behavior of a
band of killers.

The reply from the settlers was immediate. If the
Paiutes didn't commit this murder, then who did?
Weatherlow was ready for this question. As he said in
a later interview, "I attributed it entirely to the Pit River
tribe which the whites had fought and defeated and who
frequented the Black Rock Country in small bands."[3]

While Captain Weatherlow's reasoning about the murder of Peter Lassen and Edward Clapper had the ring of
logic behind it, one man did not accept his theory. This
was the recently appointed Indian Agent, Major Frederick
Dodge. When news of the killing traveled south to his
home at Genoa[4] in the Carson Valley, he saddled his
horse and rode to Susanville.

During his short stay in Honey Lake Valley, Major
Dodge interviewed Lemericus Wyatt, Chief Numaga, and
members of the relief party who had buried the dead.
From the latter he learned of the untouched supplies
they had found at the Black Rock Canyon camp. To
Dodge, this was hardly normal procedure for an Indian
raiding party. Everything pointed away from Indians and
toward white men—possibly individuals who had trailed
Lassen to this lonely canyon for the specific purpose of
murdering him. As for the slaying of Clapper and the
attempt on Wyatt's life, that was easy to explain. The
killers wanted no potential witnesses. By murdering all
the men, the whole affair would automatically become
an Indian massacre.

Major Dodge's theory even had a motive for Lassen's
murder. Namely, the old Dane had many enemies among
men who had suffered a great deal when they had taken
Lassen's Trail—a shortcut, an easy path across the north-

ern reaches of the Great Basin that took so long to cross that it was cynically called Lassen's Horn Route, "with the implication that it was as bad as going around Cape Horn."[5]

By word of mouth and by letters, Major Dodge's theory spread, and it was given more than casual credence. Newspapers on both sides of the Sierra Nevada picked it up. While in Honey Lake Valley, it became the kind of news that attracted immediate attention because of its sensational attributes. "At first a good many believed it, but in a short time very few put any faith in the story."[6] However, Captain William Weatherlow was openly upset. To him, Major Dodge's notion cast a dark shadow in his party's direction. As Captain Weatherlow put it, "This was a charge of the most unwarrantable nature against four white men who were the only ones within hundreds of miles of the place where the massacre took place, and I as their leader and commander called Major Dodge to an account personally for the charge."[7]

If such an apology was ever given, Captain Weatherlow never heard of it. But two things were quite clear to him. Major Dodge never returned to Honey Lake Valley before he rode to the East, where he ultimately was killed in the Civil War, and the emotional cries of outrage against the Paiutes for Lassen's death gave way to dispassionate reason as the settlers concluded that Chief Numaga's tribe had had nothing to do with the tragedy at Black Rock Canyon.

A few persons persisted in believing Major Dodge's theory about white assassins, but most of Honey Lake Valley's residents thought otherwise. To them, it made more sense to assume that the killers had been renegade Indians, or that they had been warriors from the Pit River tribe, who had very good reasons for hating Peter

Lassen. Still, the events surrounding the old trailblazer's death continued to have a desert strangeness about them, a kind of mirage quality. For it wasn't until November 1859 that three citizens of Susanville rode back to the death camp to recover the bodies. Yet when they returned, they carried only Peter Lassen's remains. Their failure to bring home Edward Clapper's corpse seemed peculiar to many of the settlers, and there was a good deal of protest regarding it. But despite the questions and the bickering, there were no volunteers ready to saddle their horses and make the long ride to Black Rock Canyon.

There were too many reasons for remaining home. An earlier, colder winter than anyone could remember had already started. There was talk of Indian trouble to the south in the area around the new mining camps of the Comstock Lode. There was no getting away from it: things were changing too fast, and the first rush of miners from California was already affecting the friendly relationship the whites had enjoyed with the Paiutes and Washos. What the hell! Clapper wasn't going anyplace anyway.[8] They'd get his body when things were calmer. Meanwhile, it would be wise to keep a watch for trouble and be ready for action.

CHAPTER 3

The Victims of Justice

Major William Ormsby was cut out for the frontier West. He was alive with energy, filled with ambition, and sparked with vision. Eagle Valley and the small settlement of Carson City in western Utah Territory struck him as the very right place to be located. He believed that his friend Abraham Curry was absolutely right. This new town on the road to the Comstock Lode was destined to be the capital of a new state. There was no getting around it. Abe Curry had used his head when he had hired young Jerry Long—a prospecting surveyor—to lay out the town in a proper fashion: complete with wide streets and a large plaza for the future capitol grounds. What bemused Ormsby was the fact that Long had so little faith in the town that he turned down a block of prime land across from the plaza for a smaller payment in cash for his services.

To prove his own belief in what he considered an emerging seat of power, the enthusiastic Ormsby built a solid establishment which the *Territorial Enterprise* of September 17, 1859, described as "an adobe house 45×50 feet, and two stories high."[1] The Ormsby House was designed as both a residence and a place of business. Here was the future for a lively pioneer. Let the miners come and go. The men would need a warm, comfortable lodging as they passed through town; and many of them would be delivered right to Agent Ormsby's front door and lobby as they traveled via the Pioneer Stage Company. Miners would always be in need of supplies, and Ormsby would be ready for them. Mining was a gambler's game, but providing services and goods to miners was a surefire path to riches.

Things were going to be better than they had ever been for the Ormsby family, and curly-haired William could bounce his young daughter on his knee and tell his wife, Elizabeth, all about the great opportunities for them. They were going to be important people in this new country. Why, there was nothing to worry about, not even the Indians. For Ormsby had made friends with Poito, whom the whites called Chief Winnemucca,[2] and as a favor to the Paiute chief he had agreed to have his daughters—Thocmetony, called Sarah by the whites, and her younger sister—live with them to learn the language and ways of the whites. Oh, he had heard about the death of Peter Lassen and Edward Clapper during the past spring. But that had happened in the Black Rock Desert, a long way to the north. Old Lassen, of all people, should have known better than to travel with a small party in that desolate region where renegade Indians were always causing trouble. Carson City, though, was another matter. Yes, sir, this was the place to put down roots and watch the trees grow.

2

In the late fall the weather turned much colder than any of the whites had experienced in this sagebrush country that they were beginning to call Washoe. There were snow flurries, icy mornings, frosted ground that was rock hard, and a chilling wind that swept down from the Sierra Nevada peaks and made a man's lungs burn and ache. But trouble was not limited to weather. Word came that two miners—McMullen and MacWilliams—had been murdered while on their way to California for supplies. Worst of all, the men who found the bodies reported that the killing had been done by Indians.

When asked how they could be sure, they replied: "We know, because it was done with arrows."[3]

Thirty volunteers rode into the mountains for the bodies of the murdered men. They found them in what was obviously their first overnight camp beside the steep, switchback trail. The dead were not scalped or mutilated. But their wounds still contained the fatal arrows, which the volunteers brought back along with the bodies. There didn't seem to be much doubt. McMullen and MacWilliams had been ambushed by Indians. Yet something was wrong. Something was not quite right. Both men had been carrying money for supplies. But the money was not with their bodies. This was a nagging question, for why would Indians have taken the money? It would have made sense if the clothing and supplies had been stolen, but money was one thing the Indians had not yet learned to use. Still, the fact remained. Only the money was missing from the last camp of McMullen and MacWilliams.

The very idea of Indian trouble put the sparse popula-

tions of the new towns on edge. Logically, the problem should have been handled by Indian Agent Major Frederick Dodge and his friend and frequent interpreter Warren Wasson. But Ormsby was too excited to wait for either man to hear of the mountain murders. Possibly because Chief Winnemucca's daughters were living in his home he considered it his responsibility to settle this affair. Whatever his reasoning might have been, one thing remains clear. Major Ormsby took it upon himself to send word to Chief Winnemucca of what had happened and to request his assistance in finding the guilty parties.

3

Two days after Ormsby's message reached Chief Winnemucca at Pyramid Lake, the citizens of Carson City were startled by the sudden appearance of one hundred mounted Paiute warriors and their two leaders: Chief Natchez, Sarah's brother, and her cousin, War Chief Numaga.

Wearing rabbit skin robes as protection against the cold, the warriors must have looked like a strange breed—a cross between man and bear. They entered Carson City from the northeast and rode down Carson Street. As they passed the town's first hotels, boarding houses, saloons, and stores, they were watched by apprehensive whites: men who stared at long hair swinging back and forth across fur covered backs, men whose sweaty hands made sure that pistols and rifles were ready—just in case.

But most of all, they watched one Paiute who sat tall and bolt upright on his pony. This was Chief Numaga and to the whites who watched him, here was no ordinary man. He was at least six feet tall, had broad shoulders, a thick chest, and made an imposing figure. To the whites, he was a man to be reckoned with. Men who caught his glance, stared as Numaga's dark eyes watched both sides of the street. They looked at the Paiute chief's broad forehead and high straight nose that gave him the appearance of a creature as much eagle as man. His very presence created visions of epic heroes.

When the warriors reached the Ormsby House, the major, his wife, and Winnemucca's daughters were waiting outside to greet them. And while Ormsby did not know the Paiute language, two things made it possible for him to speak in his own tongue. Sarah already had more than an elementary grasp of English, and Chief Numaga had learned a fair amount of the language during the seasons he had worked as a field hand for the Mission Fathers in California's Santa Clara Valley.

In his blunt, excited way, Major Ormsby either ignored formality or did not know the proper form for the beginning of such a discussion. Numaga and Natchez were not asked to join him in a customary smoking ceremony so that each man could take time to look into the other's face and see his heart. Nor did Ormsby inquire as to the health of ancient Chief Truckee or even Chief Winnemucca's welfare. He spoke not about the unusual cold weather, and did not ask about the hardships the early winter had brought. Nervously, Major Ormsby handed the fatal arrows to Chief Numaga and abruptly asked if he knew which tribe had made them.

Chief Numaga knew at a glance, and he told Ormsby the arrows had been made by Washos. Still, he must have wondered why it was so important for Ormsby to know about the makers of arrows. But even as Numaga watched and wondered, the tall white man, whose chin was covered with a brush line of black whiskers, wasted very little time. Ormsby looked at Natchez and Numaga, and said:

"Will you help us to get the Washoe chief to come in and give up the men who killed the two white men?"[4]

Considering what Major Ormsby had asked, it is a wonder that Numaga and Natchez did not take it as a gross insult. Not only had Ormsby failed to give any indication of proper form in greeting them, but also had added this touch of ignorance. If he had known anything at all about the Paiutes and Washos, Ormsby would have realized that peace existed between the two peoples only because the harsh land of the Great Basin did not permit the luxury of constant warfare. Yet the wish for peace was so much a part of their culture that Numaga and Natchez overlooked Ormsby's barbarous behavior and gave polite and serious consideration to his incredible request.

While Ormsby waited, the chiefs talked over what he had asked. Finally, much to Ormsby's relief, Chief Numaga informed him that they would do what they could to help find the killers of the two white men.

Following this agreement to help the whites, Chief Numaga carefully selected five of his best warriors, men who were not apt to let emotions dictate their moves, and told them they were to ride to the camp of Captain Jim of the Washos. Numaga made it quite clear that their task was extremely delicate, and that they were not to become involved in a fight. The orders were very specific. They were to inform Captain Jim about the killings, ask him to give up the guilty men, and come with them to Carson City, where they would be treated fairly and judged the same as any white man.

After receiving their orders, the five warriors rode their ponies out of town. As they moved out of sight, the rest of the Paiutes made camp for the night. They picketed their ponies in the many vacant lots, made fire pits for the night, and unpacked their supplies. That evening was a strange one in this frontier community. A large bonfire was built in the plaza,[5] and townsfolk and Paiutes mingled together. While the whites stood and watched, the Indians performed a war dance, or so young Sarah Winnemucca called it. And the dance was as exciting for the girls as it was for the townspeople, for as Sarah wrote, it was "the first one I had ever seen."[6]

Shuffling, then raising their knees high and coming down with a thump on the earth, the dancers pounded out the rhythm with their feet. The glow of the bonfire outlined their moving figures, framed them between red-orange flames and the dark blue of the cold night sky. And they chanted: "Hey yah, hey yah, hey yah." Their heads moved up and down, back and forth, and their bodies swayed to the beat and tempo of their own movements.

Whites watching them stood silently, almost nervously at the beginning, but as the dance picked up movement, as the shadows of the moving men took on a mystic aspect, the warriors were no longer Paiute warriors who had rode their ponies down Carson Street and camped for the night. Now their identity was lost in sounds and movements, shapes and sights as old as mankind. Here was all of man's past caught up in a ritual dance around a fire, a dance that kept back the demons of the night. Here were painted faces hiding reality for the moment. Here was the regalia for remembrance of things past and for things unknown. Round and round the fire they danced and danced, chanted and chanted.

Thoroughly caught up by the moving bodies, the pulse beat sound, the mystery of something not known, not understood, Major Ormsby's wife was fascinated. This proper woman, the major's lady, whom he alone called Lizzie, nudged young Sarah Winnemucca, and the chief's daughter saw the wild curiosity in her eyes, and heard her ask: "Where is Natchez? Where is Natchez?"[7]

He was there somewhere. He was one of the figures of the dance, but he was not to be seen as a single man. He was part of the dance, part of that time when man wore a mask to ward off the spirits of darkness as he danced to his gods. And Sarah could not tell the major's wife which dancer was her brother, nor could any of the others standing and watching as the dancers chanted: "Hey yah, hey yah, hey yah."

When the last dancer had halted the movement of the others with a solid stomp on the pounded surface of the earth, there was a silence of a cold night, a stillness of an icy, windless planet spinning beneath and in and around the endless backdrop of stars in the desert's winter sky to hold the attention of the watchers and dancers, of white men and Indians. It was as though all sound, save the last cracking, burning sagebrush and logs, and the breathing of the people reflected in the dying light of the fire had vanished with the final echo of the dancers' chanting. Then the silence was broken. First, by the lonely barking and yipping of coyotes; next, by the voice of Major Ormsby, who had stepped into the fading light of the fire and said: "We will sing the Star-Spangled Banner."[8]

And when it was all over, when the years had made that evening a fading memory for those still alive, a much older Sarah Winnemucca described its ending. Referring to Chief Truckee, she wrote: "It was not a bit like the way my grandfather used to sing it, and that was the first time I had heard it sung by the white people."[9]

The following morning the ground was white with frost, but there was no sign of a storm. Warriors hunched their shoulders underneath their rabbit skin robes and moved in close to the fire pits. Using willow sticks with looped ends, the men lifted egg-size rocks from the coals and dropped them into watertight cooking baskets to heat pine nut soup.

Before the sun neared its midday peak, the five Paiutes rode back into Carson City. With them were Captain[10] Jim and some eight or nine other Washos. But it was Captain Jim who drew the most attention. He was one of the largest men that any of the Paiutes or whites had ever seen. His rounded face made his big head appear even larger than it was, and he stood well over six feet tall. Yet most of his massive size was concentrated in his broad upper body. Like the Paiutes, he wore a rabbit skin robe as protection against the cold. However, from his neck hung five or six strands of an intricate necklace made of small bones and connected in such a fashion that it looked very much like the rib cage of some strange animal. Though his short, heavy legs were bare, his wide feet were covered with light-colored buckskin moccasins that were beautifully decorated with small trade beads and porcupine quills in the V shapes of flying geese.[11]

By the time the riders reached the Ormsby House, the news of their arrival had flown before them like leaves in a sudden wind. Major Ormsby, the self-appointed leader of Carson City's citizens, was waiting for them; and he wasted no time in getting right down to business. Once again, he held out the fatal arrows, and he asked Captain Jim if he knew who made such arrows.

Speaking slowly, as though he thought it might help the nervous white man to understand, Captain Jim said, "You ask me if these are my people's arrows. I say yes."[12]

Major Ormsby looked at Numaga and Natchez. He told them what he wanted of Captain Jim, and they translated the order: ". . . he must bring the men and all the money, and they shall not be hurt, and all will be right."[13]

There simply wasn't going to be due process of law. The Washos—at least some Washos—were guilty, and had to be guilty of this crime. After all, Washo arrows stood as the evidence. What more was necessary? The right of injury, of protection from villainy, and even of vengeance belonged to the whites; for whites had been killed by Washo arrows. Ormsby left no room for discussion, no consideration of the possibility that the Washos just might be innocent.

Captain Jim listened to this outright accusation of his people. Still, he remained calm while the man with eyes the color of Tahoe treated him as though he might be guilty of this crime. Then, the Washo leader tried once again.

> "I know my people have not killed the men, because none
> of my men have been away; we are all at Pinenut Valley,
> and I do not know what to think of the sad thing that has
> happened."[14]

While it was true that there had been a history of conflict between the Washos and Paiutes, this—of all moments—was the time for the tribes to help each other against a common threat. Instead, War Chief Numaga informed Captain Jim that he had ten days in which to bring in the guilty men. If he did not do this, Paiute warriors would fight the Washos to help their white friends.

With nowhere to turn for help, Captain Jim and his men agreed to do as they were ordered. Their faces mirrored the sadness they felt as they left Carson City to bring back the already convicted Washos.

But even as the Washos were moving out of sight, it was obvious to Sarah Winnemucca that her brother Natchez and many of his warriors did not like Chief Numaga's decision to back the whites. They openly expressed their feelings, and said that only the passing of time would finally clear away all doubts and tell whether or not the Washos had killed the two white men.

4

Five days of the allotted ten passed. On the sixth day Captain Jim returned to Carson City. With him were three warriors, their mothers, and one young, childless wife. News of their arrival quickly spread throughout the small town. Men came on the run. In a very short time the frightened young Washos were bound at the wrists and locked up in a small house that was to be their jail.

That night the Washo chief, the mothers of the young men, and the lonely wife camped by themselves. As they heard the nearby Paiutes discussing whether or not the Washos had really killed the white men, Captain Jim and the women prayed to their gods for help.

On the following day, the prisoners were brought out of their temporary jail. Most of Carson City's residents were there to stare at them. Major Ormsby questioned the men through Chief Numaga, but while this took place, town hotheads and professional Indian haters shouted catcalls, referred to the prisoners as Diggers, bug eaters, dirty bastards, killing sons-a-bitches, and every other vile thing that came to mind. Boys took up the taunting, mimicking the men, then they laughed and began to throw stones at them. The men encouraged the boys, and the mood of the mob focused into a fury of hate. The emotional pitch became that of a ritual stoning, a crucifixion, or a typical American lynch mob. Excitement mounted, and cruel laughter greeted shouting men who yelled, "Hang the red devils right off."[15]

With varying intensity the crowd kept up its clamor for the lives of the Washos well into the late afternoon. Then about three o'clock, the harsh and abrasive cries were replaced by the threat of action as thirty-one whites, each carrying a gun, marched down Carson Street toward the captives. When Chief Numaga and Natchez saw these men, they ran to meet them to make sure that justice, not murder, was their intention.

As the Paiute chiefs ran, one of the Washo women became hysterical. To her, the outcome of this meeting was preordained. She screamed with anguish, "Oh, they have come to kill them!"[16] This broke all bonds of emotional control the other women had been maintaining, and they began to cry and wail as they protested what they thought was about to happen. Over and over, they said their men were not killers, that they had been at the Pine Nut Valley camp when the whites were supposed to have been killed, and that Captain Jim had brought them to Carson City only because they had no fathers to speak out for them, and because they had no children who would need fathers.

The young wife ran to War Chief Numaga. She threw herself at his feet, and she implored him to save her husband, crying out:

> "Oh, you are going to have my poor husband killed. We were married this winter, and I have been with him constantly since we were married. Oh, Good Spirit, come! Oh, come into the hearts of this people. Oh, whisper in

their hearts that they may not kill my poor husband! Oh, good chief talk for him. Our cruel chief has given my husband to you because he is afraid that all of us will be killed by you, 'and then she raised up her head and said to the Washoe chief,' You have given my innocent blood to save your people."[17]

Even as the wife begged for her man's life, the whites moved in closer. As she watched them, her eyes darted around as though she were a trapped rabbit in a net listening to the approaching hunters and struggling to break loose and make one last try for the open ground and escape.

All of it was fast becoming a nightmare, a scream in the night without anyone to hear. Sensing what might take place, Chief Natchez moved toward the Washo women. In a calm voice, a soothing voice intended to give comfort and to ease their mounting excitement, he tried to assure the women that the white men had only come to take the men to jail, that they had not come there to kill them.

Yet his words fell on ears stricken dumb with grief. Then as the armed whites took the men by their arms and began to lead them away, one of the women cried out, "See, they are taking them away."[18]

The combination of armed whites and their own terrified women was far more than the prisoners could bear. In a sudden move, they broke away from their captors and ran toward the open meadow and the faraway cottonwoods of the Carson River like dog-driven deer.

Almost as a reflex action, the whites raised their rifles and took aim. Before anyone could cry halt, white puffs of powder smoke hung in the cold air of the late afternoon, followed by the echoing sound of shots.

Two men fell in mid-stride, and the other stopped. Before a second round was fired, he turned and faced the riflemen, his hands raised upward. The hard-faced men held their rifles steady and casually motioned for him to come back.

The Washo women screamed and ran past the line of riflemen to their wounded men. Dropping to the ground, they clutched the men tightly to themselves, moaned and cried, and rocked back and forth while the blood from the bullet wounds spurted and soaked their clothing and bare skin.

The scene was etched in young Sarah Winnemucca's memory forever. She and her sister were stunned and sick. And though the two men lived throughout the long night, and their women held them close, their bodies became cold with death as the morning sun began to rise. The exhausted women threw themselves on the men when they realized they were dead. They sobbed and wept until Sarah thought they would never stop. The "weeping was enough to make the very mountains weep."[19]

Crying with grief, Sarah ran to Mrs. Ormsby. She clung tightly to her, and told her that she believed the Washo women. She thought they had told the truth; their men were innocent, and now they had been killed for something they had not done.

Mrs. Ormsby looked down at her, and with all the conviction of the self-righteous, she said: "How came the Washoe arrows there? . . . the chief himself has brought them to us, and my husband knows what he is doing."[20]

There was not going to be an error. There couldn't be a mistake. Guilt was not to be carried in the hearts of the staunch, law-abiding citizens of Carson City.

But Captain Jim heard the heartbroken women curse

him and the Paiute chiefs for allowing innocent men to be killed. And even as they cursed him, the whites led the remaining warrior away for a trial[21] to be held in California, where, as they told Captain Jim, the man would receive justice. But the word was without meaning to the Washo chief, and there is no record of its being translated for him. All that remains are Captain Jim's words as the women accused him of betrayal.

With tears running down his broad cheeks, he faced them and said to the sky itself, "It is true what the women say,—it is I who have killed them. Their blood is on my hands. I know their spirits will haunt me, and give me bad luck while I live."[22]

Justice had come to Carson City, and the first victims were to be burned in the custom of their people. That much was done in the spirit of truth.

CHAPTER 4

Storms of Sorrow

All the others were gone. Only Chief Natchez, his two sisters, and some warriors rode away from Carson City as the first big storm of winter broke. They were late because Sarah's younger sister was sick. She had become ill the day that she saw the Washos shot down like fleeing rabbits that had been caught in a net. Natchez did not wish to leave his sisters in the white town; so he and his men camped close to the Ormsby House for two weeks, by the white man's calendar, until his younger sister was able to travel.

War Chief Numaga and all the other Paiute warriors had departed this place of betrayal and death two days after the Washo women had wailed and rocked back and forth with the bleeding bodies of their dying men. While no written record tells of Chief Numaga's feelings, it is not difficult to imagine that his mood was a combination of anger, disgust, and shame. By request from Major Ormsby, the Paiutes had intervened. Chief Numaga had done so to keep peace with the white settlers, who had promised justice. He had given his word to Captain Jim of the Washos that no harm would come to his men. But the whites had betrayed his trust. Now his word was without meaning. All this, and more, must have run through his mind as Numaga and his men rode back to Pyramid Lake.

But the journey home was not over for Natchez and his sisters. They rode their ponies through wind-driven snow that stung their faces with icy flakes that made their skin burn and ache. Forcing their ponies upward through the deepening drifts, they headed into the Pine Nut Mountains. The higher they climbed, the harder it was to travel. The wind shrieked off the sawtooth peaks of the Sierra Nevada, whirled across the frozen, eastern meadows, and swirled and curled upward until its full fury enveloped the Pine Nut Mountains. Forced by cold, blinding winds, and numb, weary bodies to call a halt, Chief Natchez decided they would have to stay in the mountains—close to the new mining camp of Virginia City—and wait for a change in the weather.

Here in the mountains where they often harvested pine cones from the squatty piñon pines, they quickly made temporary brush shelters for protection. Then they waited for the blizzard to blow past and into the eastern desert. While they watched for a break in the weather, a tall figure appeared at the edge of their camp. His sudden appearance startled everyone, and they waited to see if the man truly existed, or if he were a snow-covered spirit standing like a sign in a dream.

While they waited, the man moved forward until he was beside their fire. He was tall and very big, and his heavy body was protected by a snow-covered rabbit skin blanket tightly wrapped around him. And now in the light of the fire, now as the snow melted and ran down his broad face like great streams of tears, everyone in camp knew that he was Captain Jim of the Washos.

Before Natchez even asked why he was in their camp, why he had risked his life in such a storm, the chief began to explain in his deep voice. He had been in Carson City, and he had heard that they were on their way home by way of the Pine Nut Mountains. He had walked for a long time without stopping, and he had climbed through deeper and deeper snow drifts. But there was something they had to know.

Captain Jim waited until there was a lull in the wind. Slowly, making each word count, he told them that the real killers of McMullen and MacWilliams had been captured and hanged. Then he caught his breath, paused, and told them that the men were not Indians. They were other white men.

When Natchez asked where he had heard all this, Captain Jim replied that he had been told so by none other than Major Ormsby. Then the Washo chief said, "I have to ask you to pay me for the loss of the two men."[1]

Natchez was silent for a long time. When he spoke, his voice was controlled as he slipped back into an ancient pattern of Paiute paternalism. Despite all that had happened, despite their own role in the death of the Washos, Natchez and the other Paiutes hesitated to accept any portion of blame. The old heritage of Paiute domination over the peaceful Washos was not easily dismissed. Chief Natchez was insulted by Captain Jim's request for payment. The Washo chief had forgotten his position. It was not his right to give an order or make a demand on any Paiute.

"It is you," Natchez said, "who ought to pay the poor mother and sister and wife . . . you gave them up yourself. We only did our duty. . . ."[2]

While Captain Jim listened politely to what Natchez said, he did not give up. Instead, he persisted. He refused to be ignored because of old customs, and he remained at the Paiute camp all that night. As the winds whipped the brush shelters, he hunched his big shoulders beneath his rabbit skin robe, crouched by the fire, and kept it burning during the night.

At daybreak the storm passed into the eastern desert. Chief Natchez ate, and once again talked to Captain Jim. Now, though, his attitude was different. All that night, Natchez had thought about the terrible events that had taken place, and he knew in the gray of dawn that his own part in the death of the Washos was not without guilt.

Taking ten warriors, and giving Captain Jim a pony to ride, Natchez and the men rode to Carson City. Here, the Paiute chief learned that whites had committed the murder over money won in a game of cards. In his own mind, Natchez must have thought of the dead Washos and their grief-stricken women. But there was nothing he could do now, not even allowing Captain Jim to ride a pony for the first time since the Paiutes had become horse warriors and had defeated the Washos so badly that they were able to tell them they were never to ride again,[3] could blow away the storm clouds of grief that had gathered at Carson City in the name of justice.

2

During November of 1859 snowstorms became the usual weather for the Great Basin. In between the arctic blizzards that rushed over the Sierra Nevada on winds that cut through clothing and made death by freezing a daily possibility, there were lapses for a day or even three days when a man could look upward and see the glare of the sun in a sky that was like a reflection of all the high country lakes in the Sierra Nevada. But even during those days, the sun was without warmth, and the temperature varied between freezing and well below zero.

In December, the Honorable Isaac Roop—newly elected Governor of the unrecognized Territory of Nevada—journeyed from his Susanville home to Carson City. When he crossed the Truckee Meadows, he was shocked at the terrible toll the bitter cold was taking from the Washos. Interviewed by the *Territorial Enterprise* in their new office at the Ormsby House,[4] Governor Roop described what he had seen:

> The Indians in Truckee Meadows are freezing and starving to death by scores. In one cabin the Governor found three children dead and dying. The whites are doing all they can to alleviate the miseries of the poor Washoes. They have sent out and built fires for them, and offered them bread and other provisions. But in many instances the starving Indians refuse to eat, fearing that the food is poisoned. They attribute the severity of the winter to the whites. The Truckee River is frozen over hard enough to bear up loaded teams.[5]

The blizzards played no favorites. While the Washos were hit hard, the Paiutes also suffered greatly. And the miners didn't have much more protection than the Indians. The bearded whites, who were gophering into Sun Mountain (present Mount Davidson); and the pigtailed Chinese, who were working placer claims along the Carson River, began to cut more and more piñon pines for firewood. Never once did they think that they were destroying the pine nut orchards of the Paiutes and Washos.

All they worried about was their own condition as they burned chunks of small logs in their stoves and open fires. When they began to run short of wood, they searched through the blinding gusts of snow and found enough sagebrush to keep the fires burning.

There was no letup, no sudden warm wind to bring an end to the cold. Even work became impossible as a man's hands were quickly frostbitten if he tried to dig into the frozen earth. The intense cold penetrated everything, and drove men back to incomplete shelters they had hastily thrown up. In Virginia City there were only two solid houses. All the rest was a shack town, a tent town, a town of hovels, a town where some men even huddled for warmth in "shallow pits partly covered over with boards and earth."[6]

While the miners tried to keep warm, they ate greasy bacon, and rationed the last of their coffee and tea. Still, storms raged. One after another they swept across the mountains, and dropped layer after layer of wind-driven snow. It was as though a new Ice Age had found the right time, the correct cycle for a beginning.

Cattle, horses, donkeys and other animals forced to stand in the open and endure the freezing wind and driving blizzards died of cold and hunger. And as the men waited for the coming of spring, the snow reached depths of five and six feet in the Pine Nut Mountains, and cut off all communication and travel in the one mile between the mining camps of Gold Hill and Virginia City.[7]

The winter of 1859–60 appeared to be endless. The snow piled higher and higher, and the wind blew constantly. Yet some parties of anxious miners managed to cross the Sierra Nevada from California. These men came on snowshoes and pulled sleighs of supplies up the western slopes all the way from Placerville. When they topped the last ridge, and looked back at Lake Bigler (present Lake Tahoe), they got aboard their sleighs and rode them down the slopes to Genoa. Here they rested for three days before pressing on to the Comstock Lode.

In late February of 1860 the snowshoe-wearing newcomers had joined the other men at Virginia City in their wait for the storms to cease. But the wait was not easy. Samuel Young, who had fought his way across the mountains, pointed out that he and his companions slept in a tent and were forced to endure the snow-laden gales. On a night typical for that winter, their tent was buffeted by severe winds that whipped down Sun Mountain.

> About 12 at night blew down a pair of rafters & stove pipe, tore the canvas roof of the tent in two. We got up & went to stone building, Gambling Saloon, & sat by the stove until four o'clock in the morning. Wind lulled. We went back to tent turned in our blankets. In the morning got up covered with snow next day mended tent in a snow storm. Nearly froze our fingers.[8]

Each day men would awake with the wish for a clear sky and an end to the storms. But each day there was more and more snow. Endless cascades of white flakes filled the air and floated to the ground in a ceaseless vision of white. Worst of all, winter's grip on the Great Basin carried the coldness of death. Men became sick overnight, raved with fever, and died without ever again seeing the sun. Though nobody mentioned it, the notion of punishment, of payment for having defiled the untouchable, must have been in more than one man's mind as they placed companions in the hard, frozen earth. Perhaps, one man among all the chilled and hungry miners might even have considered that there was something

more than primitive superstition in the Indians' belief
that the endless storms were a white man's curse.

3

While the miners were enduring the icy beginning of
1860 as best they could, the destiny of many of them
was already taking shape elsewhere. The events that
would affect their lives with violence and sorrow were the
final blows of a bad winter that would set the stage for a
springtime flooded with hate.

Shortly after the start of the year, Chief Natchez, his
sisters, and his warriors arrived at their Pyramid Lake
home. But their homecoming was not a happy time, for
Chief Truckee—the aged patriarch, the man who knew
Captain Frémont, the friend of the whites—was dying.
To get word of this tragedy to the scattered Paiutes, men
went out and built "the signal-fires of death on every
mountain-top."[9]

The Paiutes came from nearby camps and from distant
camps. They rode through the falling snow and the cold,
cutting winds to gather around Chief Truckee. At the
dying man's request, one of his white friends, a man
called Snyder,[10] was sent for; and he, too, rode to Pyramid Lake to stand alongside Truckee in his final moments.

Chief Truckee's hair was as white as the underfeathers
of the pelicans that nested on Pyramid Lake's Anaho
Island. His face was creased and weathered like old bark,
and his thin fingers were gnarled and twisted like the
limbs of a very ancient tree. In a soft, high voice he
called out to those gathered beside his rabbit skin bed.
His first words were directed to Snyder:

"I am going to die. I have always loved you as if you were my dear son; and one thing I want you to do for me."[11]

Snyder and all the others in the crowded karnee stood close to Chief Truckee. They listened intently as he asked the white man to take Sarah and her younger sister to the mission school at San Jose, California.[12] For as he explained in his fading voice, he wished them to learn more about the ways of his white friends.

When Snyder said that he would do this for his old friend, Chief Truckee reached up and grasped his hands and held them as he told him farewell for the last time. Then he said, "I want to talk to my own people."[13]

Speaking very slowly, conserving his strength for his last moments, Chief Truckee counseled his son, Chief Winnemucca. White-haired Truckee's lips barely moved as he spoke, but he told his son to look after his People and continue to be a good father. When the old chief finished, his strength was exhausted, and he fell into a deep sleep.

All during the long night the people in the crowded karnee stood vigil. Late the next morning an Indian doctor was called into the karnee to see if he could bring the old man back from his deep sleep. Chanting and praying, the doctor laid his hands on Truckee's frail body, but the chief continued to sleep. He did not awake that day, and slept on into the night. Shortly after midnight, he turned and twisted. He opened his eyes and called to Chief Winnemucca, "Son, where are you? Come and raise me up—let me sit up."[14]

Chief Winnemucca gently lifted him so that he could look around. Truckee's eyes suddenly were brighter than they had been in many seasons. He gazed around the karnee, and he called for Winnemucca's wife and the children. When everyone had gathered around him, he told them that he was tired, but that soon he would be happy. Once again he spoke to Winnemucca:

> "Now, son, I hope you will live to see as much as I have, and to know as much as I do. And if you live as I have you will some day come to me. Do your duty as I have done to your people and to your white brothers."[15]

The dying man was exhausted from the effort it had required to speak. He closed his eyes and relaxed. Thinking that Chief Truckee had died, the women cried and moaned and swayed back and forth. But the shrunken, white-haired man opened his eyes once more. With a final struggle, he managed to say, "Don't throw away my white rag, friend; place it upon my breast when you bury me."[16] And though his lips moved again, no sounds were heard. Yet all the people in the karnee believed their chief had cried out as he entered the Spirit-land.[17]

The death of Chief Truckee was a final blow to the Paiutes. It was the end of a way of life, the culmination of a bad winter plus an ever increasing white population that threatened to destroy their hunting, fishing, and gathering economy, and by so doing, destroy all of them.

Even Sarah Winnemucca, young as she was, fully realized the vital role her grandfather had played as a buffer between the whites and the Indians.

> "I crept up to him. I could hardly believe he would never speak to me again. I knelt beside him, and took his dear old face in my hands, and looked at him quite a while. I could not speak. I felt the world growing cold; everything seemed dark. The great light had gone out.

I had father, mother, brothers, and sisters; it seemed I would rather lose all of them than my poor grandpa. I was only a simple child, yet I knew what a great man he was. I mean great in principle. I knew how necessary it was for our good that he should live."[18]

But death, that single, barking coyote in the middle of the night, would not wait. He howled in the cold desert night, and the great leader, the friend of both races, was called away. His belongings were gathered. He was wrapped in his finest rabbit skin robes, and he was placed in the sage-covered earth.

After he was buried, six of his best ponies were led to the side of his grave. Here, the animals were killed so that Chief Truckee would have good ponies to ride on his journey to Spirit-land.[19]

PART II

THE GATHERING FURY

1860

CHAPTER 5

Rewards of Intolerance

Jack Demming, according to many neighbors, was a first-rate son-of-a-bitch. He came West with all his prejudices intact, and did his very best to keep them pure.

In the fall of 1858, Jack Demming laid claim to a stretch of land in Willow Creek Valley. Here, ten miles from Honey Lake Valley, he built a rough log cabin the next year. With this start of his ranch headquarters completed, he sent East for his brother Dexter, and got ready to reach out for the American Dream of carving a personal empire out of the wilderness. The flaw in his dream, the cancer in his frontier outpost was a very old one in Indian-white relations: Jack Demming hated Indians, and he was very open in his hatred.

The settlers around Honey Lake Valley and Susanville knew about Jack Demming's attitude toward Indians. They couldn't help but know, for he openly bragged that whenever he caught an Indian traveling by himself, he cut another notch on his rifle stock. His hatred of Indians, all Indians, was a very pure brand of bigotry, for he made no exceptions. Thus it was not at all unusual that this streak of intolerance surfaced at an Indian dance near Susanville in the early part of 1860.

The dance was for pleasure, a friendly meeting between white men and Indians. But Jack Demming's behavior at this affair was neither friendly nor tolerant. During the dance, he focused all his malicious attention and cruel remarks on an Indian who was wearing a high-crowned Mexican hat. All evening, Demming made fun of the man's hat. Finally, as the joke wore thin among the other whites, Demming decided to liven the occasion. He casually walked over to the dancing Indian, reached upward, and with a quick yank jerked the man's hat down over his eyes.

The crowd laughed as the Indian struggled to pull his hat up. When he finally managed to get it loose, he glared at Demming, "but there were so many white men present that he did not dare do anything then."[1]

Nobody worried. Nobody cared. After all it was just a joke, only a practical joke. But practical jokes often have a vicious intent, and such intentions sometimes backfire with their own vicious results. This may have run through the minds of many who saw this act of cruelty, for Jack Demming had never done one thing to warrant the respect or friendship of the Indians. This incident at a friendly dance was a final invitation to disaster. Before the first month of 1860 ended, all of Jack Demming's intolerance and inhumanity came home to haunt him.

2

The deep snow made traveling very hard work, even with a pair of snowshoes, and Jack Demming was sweaty and weary after trudging all the way from the ranch to Susanville. He had come to town for supplies that were needed to make fence rails, and it had been his intention to transact his business and get on home. But he had misjudged how long it would take him to make the journey on snowshoes, and the sun was already setting when he had picked up what was needed. Yet he still needed to find a grindstone to sharpen his axes, and that was at Toadtown. There was no other choice. He was forced to remain in Susanville for the night.

On Friday the thirteenth, Demming was out of bed early, and quickly snowshoed to nearby Toadtown. Along with his axes and rifle, he carried a pack of supplies on his back. He stopped at Fred Hines's place, where he used his small grindstone and honed the bits. When he finished the slow work, it was already late in the afternoon, and Hines encouraged him to stay overnight. But he wanted to get back to Willow Creek Valley. He visited with Hines for a short time, looked over his library, and borrowed two books: *Lorenzo Dow's Sermons* and *Dr. Kane's Arctic Explorations.*[2] Placing the books in his pack, Demming told Hines good-by and started for home. He moved as fast as he could in the deep snow, for he knew Dexter would be waiting, and probably worrying and wondering why a trip for supplies was taking so long.

It was late afternoon, and the first shadows of darkness were spreading across the valley when Jack slowly climbed the knoll on which the cabin was built. But even before he neared the door, things didn't look right to him. There was no smoke curling upward from the chimney, and everything was much too quiet. This time of day Dexter would be getting supper ready. There would be the clatter of pots and pans, maybe even the sound of Dexter whistling one of the tunes he played on his fiddle.

Jack eased forward, and close to the house he saw a single set of snowshoe tracks leading toward the front door. This made him feel better, for he knew Dexter "had just made a pair of snowshoes,"[3] and that he had intended to practice using them. Yet the tracks did not go all the way. Before they arrived at the door, they came to an abrupt halt. To his horror, Jack saw the snow around the last set of tracks was blotched with small and large bloodstains. It was a pattern of death, the kind of pattern a man would expect to find if he had shot a deer with a full load of buckshot.

Demming knelt and removed his snowshoes and pack. Then, holding his rifle ready for action, he cautiously walked to the cabin door. He pushed it open, jumped aside, and waited. When he heard no sound of movement, he walked inside. The homemade furniture was there, and so was the cold fireplace. Everthing else was gone: food, blankets, clothing, Dexter's fiddle, the other rifle, the shotgun, and all the ammunition—including the buckshot. And Dexter was nowhere to be seen.

Frantic now, and fearing disaster, Jack ran outside and headed for the corral. But it was no use, the two horses were gone. Hoping his brother might only be wounded and not able to move, he called out his name. Time after time, he yelled. But there was no answer. All he heard in the cold air was the echo of his own voice. Knowing he couldn't look for Dexter alone, he moved the supply pack next to the door, quickly strapped his snowshoes back on, and headed for Toadtown.

Traveling with speed born of desperation, he arrived in Toadtown well after dark, just as most people were turning in for the night. Without pausing to catch his breath, he told everybody in the small settlement what he had found at Willow Creek Valley.

Nobody held out much hope for Dexter's life, and there wasn't much they could do that night. If he were still alive, chances were it would mean that some Indians were holding him captive. Come morning they would get a search party together and try to find him. If they were lucky, he would only be stiff and sore from a flesh wound, or he might even have a broken bone or two. If they weren't lucky, then, by God, they would chase down the Indians who had cashed in Dexter's chips.

Early next morning nine Toadtown settlers and Jack Demming started for Willow Creek Valley. But Demming was the only member of the party who had snowshoes. The lack of proper gear for the others turned the progress of the men into a hard, slow pace. In many places the snow was so deep that a trail had to be broken before they could move ahead. Hour after weary hour passed, and instead of taking Demming's usual three or four hours to get to his ranch, the men didn't arrive at the cabin until nearly sundown.

The first thing Jack Demming noticed at the cabin was that his supply pack was missing. Obviously, the Indians had heard him yelling for his brother, and had come back after him. Only his frantic departure for Toadtown and the quick, falling darkness had saved him.

A thorough search of the whole cabin produced what the men feared. In a very small cellar was the stripped body of Dexter Demming. There wasn't any doubt as to what had happened. While Dexter had been practicing with his snowshoes, Indians had raided the cabin. From all appearances, Dexter had been on his way back to the cabin when the raiders bushwhacked him with his own shotgun. Then they had stripped his body and tossed it into the cellar.

Some of the men wanted to go after the Indians right away. One of them, William Dow, said that the Indians were so loaded down with plunder that they couldn't be far away. He figured that they simply had to be camped in some nearby gulch or grove of trees where there was shelter from the night wind. It was his argument that if they headed out in a hurry, they would no doubt overtake the Indians by dawn and capture or shoot the whole lot before they even had time to climb out of their rabbit skin robes.

But cooler and wiser heads prevailed. All the men were tired from the hard day's work of beating a path through the snow. They were hardly ready for a cold night of forced marching. Besides, Jack Demming was worn out—physically and emotionally. If they did start after the Indians right away, they would have to leave men to take care of Jack; and that would make the pursuit party much too small for safety. No, it would be better if they rested for the night. That way, they could bury Dexter, and everyone could sleep in a warm cabin.

With that settled, the men looked around for a shovel or a pick to dig a grave. But the raiders had taken everything. "All they could find to work with was a small piece of iron and a board."[4] Using these improvised tools, they hacked away at the exposed ground in the cellar. The frozen earth was so hard that the best they could do was to scrape out a very shallow grave.

One of the Toadtown party had thought to bring a blanket with him, and the men used it to wrap Dexter Demming's body. They apologized to Jack for not having dug a deeper grave. He told them that it would do for the winter, for when the spring thaw came, he intended to give his brother a proper burial in another place on their ranch. The burial party went along with Jack's wishes, and they covered Dexter Demming as best they could, said a prayer over his temporary grave, and retired for the night.

The next morning the men again discussed the pros and cons of chasing after the Indians. All the arguments of the previous evening still held true: Jack was in no shape for such a pursuit; the snow was deep, and the icy wind was the kind that easily caused frostbitten hands and feet. All things considered, it would be wiser to hurry back to Toadtown. After that, they could inform Governor Isaac Roop and all the citizens of the communities in the unofficial Territory of Nevada of what had taken place. Most of all, they could let Captain Weatherlow and his sixty Honey Lake Rangers give chase to Dexter Demming's killers.

3

The news of Dexter Demming's death was a shock wave that hit all the settlers around Honey Lake Valley. It had been no more than two months since men had gone out to Black Rock Canyon, exhumed Peter Lassen's body, and brought it back for a decent burial. Now they were once again forced to face the fact that in a period of nine months seven settlers had been killed by Indians.[5]

Violence was gathering momentum, and there wasn't much they could do about it. For the last two years they had lived in peace with most of the local Indians, and they certainly had not had trouble with the Paiutes. Whites and Indians had agreed by treaty to the principle of equal justice for all. Thieves and killers, white or Indian, were to be turned over to the authorities. Almost as if they wanted to prove their good intentions, the Paiutes under War Chief Numaga had fought side by side with the whites against the raiding parties of Pit River Indians from across the Sierra Nevada. Everything had been done to keep peace, to make sure that all men

could live free of fear in the northwestern part of the
Great Basin.

But tensions were mounting, and they had been since
the first rush of silver miners had streamed across the
Sierra Nevada. There were ruthless killings of innocent
Indians, wanton destruction of trees, plants, and game
that constituted the basic supply of Indian food; and the
pressure of a devastating winter of ice and snow that
brought an unusually high death rate to the very young
and the very old.

The design of disaster was sketched in snow and blood.
Fear replaced trust. Friendship gave way to hostility.
The time of pastoral peace had vanished in a whirlwind
of misunderstanding. Frightened Indians and whites
needed a scapegoat. Being neighbors, they sadly used
each other.

The excited settlers of the Honey Lake region wasted
no time in contacting Captain William Weatherlow. As
he later wrote in a government report, they came to him
and "demanded that I should take my company which
was still under organization and march out . . ."[6] against
the Paiutes.

Calmly, Captain Weatherlow told the hotheads that
they had no proof that the Paiutes had committed this
murder. It could easily have been the act of a Pit River
raiding party, for they often hunted the Willow Creek
area north of Honey Lake. Furthermore, he stated that
he first wanted to see War Chief Numaga, whom he called
Young Winnemucca,[7] and speak to him before he took
any course of action. Then he reminded the jittery men
that a treaty existed between the Paiutes and them—a
treaty the Paiutes had never broken.

There was a good deal of grumbling over Captain
Weatherlow's reluctance to lead the Honey Lake Rangers

against the Paiutes. But he made it quite clear to the would-be Indian fighters that he was not about to be a party to such a wild scheme. Unhappy at his reaction, Governor Roop and the citizens promptly held a meeting. After much discussion, Governor Roop requested that Captain Weatherlow send Lieutenant U. J. Tutt and fifteen rangers to track the killers in the snow and find out if they were Paiute or Pit River Indians.

Jack Demming was out for revenge. He had never liked Indians; and the murder of his brother only proved he had been right in his thinking all the time. He quickly volunteered and was accepted as a member of Lieutenant Tutt's command.

They traveled on foot through the snow, and the going was hard, miserable work. Signs of the raiding party took them northeast of Honey Lake Valley. On their first night out, they took shelter at the abandoned "Rice cabin about a mile north of the place where the murder had been committed."[8]

The next day was no easier than the first. They continued northeast, moving wearily and making little mileage. The only thing that kept them going was the knowledge that the Indians were traveling even slower than they were, for all signs indicated that the raiders did not know they were being followed. By nightfall, the men of Lieutenant Tutt's command had reached the mountains overlooking the southeastern end of Horse Lake. Here they made camp for the night.

Early in the morning, on their third day away from Honey Lake, they caught up to the Indians at Snow Storm Creek. But the Indians had already spotted Lieutenant Tutt and his men, and had withdrawn to a handy rock pile where they neatly fortified themselves. "There they had a good natural fort and they had the two Demming guns, or perhaps more, and some ammunition, and the white men were out on the flat without any shelter."[9]

As Lieutenant Tutt and his men got within shooting range, "the Indians stood up on the rocks and made insulting gestures and dared them to come on, and when a man came close enough they took a shot at him."[10]

For several hours the Honey Lakers tried to coax the Indians into the open. Two volunteers even crawled within range of the rock fortress, but the back-up men failed to carry out their part of the scheme—remaining well out of harm's way. This left the volunteers without any protection, and they had to get out of their position on their own. One man ran as fast as he could, but the other—a man called Spencer—was so angry about the performance of his companions that "he deliberately got on his feet, threw his gun over his shoulder, and strolled away with his nose in the air as carelessly as though there was not an Indian within a hundred miles of him."[11]

Fortunately for Spencer, the Indians did not decide to take a shot at him, for he was an easy target as he casually strolled away from the perimeter of their rock fortress. When he reached the others, Lieutenant Tutt had already decided that it would cost too many lives to dislodge the Indians. Besides, he and some of the others knew from the catcalls of the Indians that the raiders were part of Smoke Creek Sam's band of Paiutes—a band that had broken away from the control of Winnemucca and Numaga.

Back at the spot where the raiders had stopped for the night, the Honey Lakers found all the evidence they needed to convince them that Smoke Creek Sam's warriors were responsible for Dexter Demming's death. There were the two axes Jack had left at the cabin door, the supplies he had carried from Susanville and Toadtown for splitting rails, Dexter's fiddle, food, clothing, blankets, the two horses, and even the borrowed books from Fred Hines's library. The only things that were missing were the firearms that the Paiutes took with them to the rocks, and Dexter Demming's life.

The killers were cornered, but so were the Honey Lake Rangers. To charge the rock pile was out of the question, but to freeze and starve the Paiutes out of their fort was an equally bad solution. One glance at their own food supply told them that they had enough to get home, no more than that. And one glance at the sky made it only too clear that a big storm was gathering in the high mountains.

The choice was not theirs to make. It had been made for them by the land itself. The hard journey of Lieutenant Tutt and the rangers had accomplished one thing: it had told them who had killed Dexter Demming. Knowing at least that much, they started back to Honey Lake Valley. The final decision about what to do next would have to be made by Governor Roop, Captain Weatherlow, and all the other leading citizens of the Honey Lake country.

CHAPTER 6

Too Many Hurts for Too Many Years

Confirmation of fear carries a strange excitement, and the news Lieutenant Tutt and his men brought back to Honey Lake Valley served such a purpose. No longer could the accusing fingers be held off. No longer was a treaty between Indians and whites worth anything. Here was proof of Paiute treachery. This time Captain Weatherlow and his friends would not be able to protect their redskin friends. This time the double-crossing Indians had been caught with the goods. And men talked with the fury of hate in their voices as they condemned the Paiutes.

There was Toadtown talk, Susanville talk, talk between ranchers and prospectors come to town for supplies, talk held back for months—maybe longer—and now it was talk to be heard, talk that would become action.

Captain Weatherlow heard it all. He listened patiently, and held back his temper. These were people he had known for a long time. He knew these same people had often shared their food with Washos and Paiutes, and they had been happy to sign a treaty with the Indians. But the death of close friends had shut their eyes to anything except revenge. They thought they had been lied to about all the murders, for they had been told these killings had been the wanton acts of Pit River raiders. Now they knew otherwise, or so they thought. Now the proof had been obtained, and the proof told them one thing: all this time they had been tricked into believing the Paiutes were innocent; all this time they had been willing to accept the theory that the murder of their friends had been done by Pit River Indians. The time had come to forget made-up stories. For the truth was in the open, and it wore the war paint of a Paiute warrior.

A meeting was held in Susanville, and cries of outrage greeted Governor Roop and Captain Weatherlow. The waiting was over. It was time to give the Paiutes a taste of blood. By God, the Honey Lake Rangers had their work cut out for them. The Paiutes were camped at Pyramid Lake, and they had damned well earned the sound of shot and the smell of powder.

One after another the Honey Lakers had their say. It was as democratic as Fourth of July oratory for everybody except the Paiutes, and nobody got around to inviting them. Anger poured out in a steady stream as the good citizens said everything they had been holding back for a long, long time. The cry was for blood, Paiute blood.

Captain Weatherlow patiently and calmly listened and waited. When the first flush of vituperation had passed, he tried to explain that to go chasing Indians with his band of rangers might well prove fatal to men who were already in the vicinity of the Paiute stronghold. After all, "at that time there were three thousand head of stock at Pyramid Lake protected by only a few herders."[1]

But there was no worry about the cattlemen, and the citizens of Honey Lake Valley made their feelings clear. If the herders wanted to take a chance by running their cattle on Paiute land, then they'd damned well better be ready to accept the risk without crying.

Again Captain Weatherlow tried to point out the dangerous situation that a show of force would create for men that everyone at the meeting knew. These weren't strangers they were talking about. These were men they had broken bread with, men they had tipped the jug with. These were friends they were proposing to risk.

Trying to make the picture as clear as possible, trying to avoid needless bloodshed, he continued to argue his case: "There were settlers located in small valleys remote from each other and distant from the settlements at Honey Lake . . . small parties of prospectors were scattered through the mountains in every direction, all of whom would be hopelessly exposed and murdered if I made an attack upon the Indians."[2]

But even as he made his case, he was only buying time, and not much of that. It was already common knowledge that Chief Numaga was very unhappy about the way his people were being treated by cattlemen. He had complained to Indian Agent Major Dodge, and he had even gone to Virginia City to state the grievances of the Paiutes. As was later pointed out in a letter to Frederick W. Lander,[3] Chief Numaga had tried to get the whites to hear his side of things. Herders had driven cattle all over Paiute grazing land, letting their livestock eat grass for Paiute ponies. Worst of all, these cattlemen had even accused the Paiutes of rustling, and threatened violence if Chief Numaga did not bring in cattle that they claimed were missing from their herds. They told the chief that they would "bring down a heap of white men from Virginia City and kill all the Indians at Pyramid Lake."[4]

The tempo of violence was building for both whites and Paiutes. A steady run of inhuman treatment and stupid inconsideration of the Indians by the growing white population had brought a furious retaliation by small Paiute raiding parties. Things were resting at a very precarious point. Yet, knowing all this, knowing that their own lives would be in jeopardy, Captain William Weatherlow and Thomas J. Harvey abided by Governor Roop's request for them to ride to Pyramid Lake to have a friendly talk with War Chief Numaga. But it was hardly a friendly talk that the settlers requested.

"Ask Chief Numaga about the murders," they said; "ask him why he and his people don't live up to the treaty they signed with the Honey Lakers."

At best, Weatherlow and Harvey had volunteered for a journey better suited to Don Quixote and Sancho Panza. At worst, they were about to make a horseback ride to martyrdom.

2

The snow was deep, and the horses made very slow time. Weatherlow and Harvey found the cold days running together into a much slower trip than they had anticipated. What could have been a long day's ride, or no more than two days of riding from Honey Lake to Pyramid Lake turned out to be a miserable three-day journey.

As they neared the lake they saw the Needle Rocks on the northwestern shoreline. These wind-worn outcroppings of tufa reached skyward like giant bone awls. Then far to the northeast they saw Frémont's Pyramid standing like a fantastic wedge. Beyond that was Anaho Island—where the great pelicans nested in the spring. But what caught their attention most of all was the sudden sight of the lake itself. After days of riding through snow-

covered alkali desert and sagebrush, here was a piece of
the ocean, a part of the sky neatly nestled among the
snow-covered desert mountains. It was a sight to be dis-
believed, for no body of water such as this had any right
to exist in this land of sagebrush and piñon pine, of
white-rumped antelope and big-eared jackrabbits. Yet
even though they had seen the lake before, the first view
of it once again, the sudden sight of this great body of
water in a land without water, was still an incredible
vision. It was not something a man grew accustomed to,
for it defied all custom and betrayed the senses. The
water was green, then blue, and the white-capped waves
broke with a steady rolling motion against the long, curling beach lines. Both men shaded their eyes and squinted.
The reflection of sunlight off the snow-covered hills and
the shimmering water was like a glare of light from a
country of brilliant lights.

The men rested their horses and stared at the great
lake. They were so fascinated with its sudden appearance,
so absorbed by its beauty that they did not hear the
approaching Indians. Before they realized that there was
any other person within sight, Weatherlow and Harvey
were surrounded by thirty well-armed and mounted
Paiute warriors. The Indians quickly relieved them of
their firearms, took them prisoner, and escorted the Honey
Lakers to their camp.

All that cold, long night the men were kept under
close guard. During their nervous wait they realized that
they had been captured by Smoke Creek Sam and his
band, and they listened as their fate was openly discussed around the campfire. As far as most of the Indians
were concerned, there was no reason to let them remain
alive. But their lives were spared through the interven-
tion of a young warrior. This member of the war party

was known as Pike to the white men, and it was their good fortune that it had been Thomas Harvey who had raised the young man. Even so, Pike had a great deal of talking to do in order to save both men. For while Smoke Creek Sam was willing to give Harvey his life and his freedom, Captain Weatherlow was another matter. Yet, Harvey refused to go without Weatherlow; and Pike persisted to the point where the Indians held another council. When it ended, they "gave the two men their property and told them to go."[5]

The way to Chief Numaga's camp at the southern end of Pyramid Lake was blocked. Smoke Creek Sam would not listen to the Honey Lakers' request for permission to ride to it. His orders were right to the point, and his men made it quite clear. "They told us in plain terms that we should not see him but must go back to Honey Lake if we valued our lives."[6]

The day was overcast and gray, and the chill west wind whipped off the Sierra Nevada, swept along the freezing flats and desert hills, and carried the cold of high country snow drifts. The men pulled their heavy coats up high, jerked their hats low on their foreheads, and hunched down as they tried to protect their faces against the wind-driven snow, ice, and fragments of sagebrush that were caught up in a swirl and slapped into them, stinging and cutting the exposed skin.

They retreated slowly, following the route they had taken from Honey Lake. After they had traveled a few miles beyond Smoke Creek Sam's camp, the wind suddenly stopped blowing; and a dense mountain fog enveloped them. Luck had taken a turn in their favor, for this was what the Paiutes called a pogonip[7]: the damp, ground-hugging clouds of fog; the killing air that hid the sun, kept light away from the frozen earth, and brought the coughing sickness that made the body sweat and shake, shake and sweat, until only water remained in the lungs, and all breathing stopped. Even the bravest warrior would not leave his karnee and the warmth of the fire and his rabbit skin robes to travel through the cloudy wet death.

Taking advantage of the pogonip, Weatherlow and Harvey turned their horses to the southwest. Figuring that the Indians would not move around in the dense fog and that the damp clouds would muffle the sounds of their horses, the Honey Lakers carefully circled around Smoke Creek Sam's camp. When they thought they were far enough away from it, they turned their horses to what they hoped was a southerly direction, and slowly rode toward the Truckee River.

Hours later, they rode through the tall, snow-covered sagebrush and saw the line of cottonwoods and quaking aspens that marked the river. The pogonip lifted as quickly as it had dropped down upon them, and they followed the northeast course of the river toward the southern end of Pyramid Lake. As they neared the lake, Captain Weatherlow wrote, "we found camps of Indians scattered along at intervals but they refused to give us any information as to the whereabouts . . ."[8] of Chief Numaga.

Passing by camp after camp, the men saw smoke swirls drifting upward from small openings in the basket-shaped karnees. Dogs barked at them, small children and women peeked out from behind grass mats that covered entrances to karnees, and they saw picketed Indian ponies—their ribs showing from a hard winter of little feed—and the stare of silent men.

On they rode toward the wide mouth of the Truckee River, where the icy waters of Lake Tahoe, the creek and spring water of the Sierra Nevada, and the run-off water from melting snowpacks flowed together and spread out across the sandbar and entered Pyramid Lake. Here, close to the river's mouth, they found the camp of War Chief Numaga.

Standing tall and proud, broad-shouldered Numaga was waiting in front of his karnee. He motioned for them to come toward him. Then he invited the men into his karnee, and spread out a rabbit skin blanket to sit on.

Both men acknowledged the chief's welcome, but there the social amenities ended. Curtly and without any consideration of the fact that neither Chief Numaga nor his warriors had been seen by Lieutenant Tutt and his pursuing force, Captain Weatherlow forged ahead as though Numaga were directly responsible for the actions of raiders from Smoke Creek Sam's band. "We told him our errand," he wrote, "and . . . demanded of him the delivery of the murderer or murderers of D. E. Demming in accordance with the terms of the treaty between his people and the whites."[9] Almost in the same breath, he then asked Chief Numaga to bring the other chiefs at Pyramid Lake and return to Honey Lake Valley with them and "settle our difficulties amicably."[10]

Fortunately for Weatherlow and Harvey, Chief Numaga was more interested in maintaining peaceful relations with the whites than in giving full vent to his anger. A man with less control of his temper might well have decided the Honey Lakers represented a last insult in a long, hard season of insults, robberies, and murders by the invading whites.

However, the end of peaceful coexistence was not far off, and Chief Numaga made this point quite clear. For while he agreed that the terms of the treaty did allow the whites to ask him to turn over any Paiutes who had broken the peace, he refused to admit or deny that any of his people had killed Dexter Demming.

Captain Weatherlow continued to ignore the touchy situation he was in, and kept asking Chief Numaga to follow the terms of the treaty. Numaga took as much of this as he could. Finally, he began to show signs of anger. He even went so far as to "decline to interpose his authority to prevent his people from committing depredations upon the whites."[11]

Trying to get some sort of agreement, some kind of dialogue, some indication that all chances for peace were not gone, Captain Weatherlow then asked Chief Numaga "to appoint some future time for visiting us."[12] But Numaga had run out of patience. He looked at the two men sitting on his rabbit skin robes, and he very coldly said "that he would not come at all, but that the people of Honey Lake must pay to his people $16,000 for their land."[13]

Here was a puzzle for the Honey Lakers. They knew that the Paiutes did not value anything in terms of dollars and cents. This simply was not their way. All of this indicated that possibly some white man had given them this figure as a bargaining term. If so, who was the man? Was it the German, Snyder, who had long been a friend of the late Chief Truckee, or was it some other white man who had decided to use the Paiute grievances as a means to the acquisition of money for himself?

Up to that time, Chief Numaga had been "willing that the whites should occupy the valley."[14] His only request was that in payment for their occupation of Honey Lake Valley he wished to "learn to till the soil and live like a white man."[15] This may well have been true prior to the silver strike in the Comstock Lode, and prior to the daily destruction of the Indian food supply, but the record of the time shows that Chief Numaga and the other Paiutes were nearing the end of their tolerance for abuse.

Captain Weatherlow and Thomas Harvey had tried. They had done the best that they were capable of doing, but they had failed in their mission. Nobody knew this any more than they did. As they rode away from Chief Numaga's camp, they were fully aware of one thing: Indian trouble, even an all-out war, was being fashioned in the gathering of Paiute bands at Pyramid Lake.

Considering the possibility of danger for any white man caught alone near Pyramid Lake, the Honey Lakers felt it was their duty, on their homeward journey, to stop at the various camps of cattlemen and warn them of the impending crisis. Yet even though the cattlemen appreciated the advice to get out while they could, "they said the snow was so deep they could not get away, and they might as well remain and take the chance of losing their cattle by the Indians as to attempt driving them through the snow."[16]

The only request the cattlemen made was that any proposed attack against the Paiutes be held off until warmer weather had melted the snow enough so that they could drive their cattle out of the area. In their order of priorities, the dollar value of live beef came first. Their personal safety was treated as a luxury, a necessary risk for the proper operation of their business.

Weatherlow and Harvey had put their own lives on the line, but the only luck they had had with the dice of chance was to ride away from Pyramid Lake alive. All the rest had been a loser's game, and they knew it as they headed their weary horses in the direction of Honey Lake Valley.

3

When the two men arrived at Honey Lake, they gave a full report of their Pyramid Lake adventure to Governor Roop and the other citizens of the valley. In a matter-of-fact way, Weatherlow explained he believed an all-out war with the Paiutes was inevitable.

But many of the Honey Lakers thought he was stretching events out of proportion. Now they conveniently doubted that the Paiutes had committed many of the depredations upon the settlers. It was easier to attribute most of this trouble to the Pit River Indians. Oh yes, there was the murder of Dexter Demming, and that was a definite incident that could be blamed on Smoke Creek Sam's band. Yet that wasn't truly a sign of a coming all-out war. After all, they argued, Smoke Creek Sam always had been a troublemaker. Furthermore, Jack Demming always had hated Indians, and he had a long record of killing any lone Indian he happened to come upon. The odds were pretty good that the Paiutes had killed Dexter because they mistook him for Jack.

To make matters worse, there were some Honey Lakers who considered their warning in the same way they would have considered the shouts of excited boys. These settlers refused to recognize any Indian as a potentially dangerous foe. As far as they were concerned, the Paiutes "were cowardly and would be afraid to attack the settlements."[17]

Governor Isaac Roop, however, did not treat the news of events at Pyramid Lake in a cavalier manner. Deeply concerned about the shape of things to come, he wrote a letter on February 12, 1860, to Brevet Brigadier General Newman S. Clarke, who was commander of the Department of the Pacific. Within the context of his letter from Susanville, Governor Roop included the reports of Lieutenant Tutt's pursuit of the killers of Dexter Demming and of Captain Weatherlow's experiences at Pyramid Lake. There could be no misunderstanding of what Governor Roop meant. In the very first sentence of his letter, he stated that the settlers of Honey Lake Valley were "about to be plunged into a bloody and protracted war . . ."[18] with the Paiutes.

In the final paragraph of this call for help, Governor Roop asked for specific aid. He asked the army to send a company of dragoons, arms and ammunition, and "a fieldpiece"[19] to drive the Paiutes out of their strongholds. But nothing was done to help prevent the outbreak of warfare.

The chances of peace were vanishing almost as quickly as the first melting snows in the high country. Brave talk in both white and Indian settlements was rapidly spreading fear and hate. The time for talk between the races was passing into the dark memories of too many hurts for too many years. The scar tissue of emotional blows shut out the memories of good talk and good times. Militant shouts and cries for bloody violence were fast becoming deadly companions who would be ready to lash out as the warmth of spring brought forth the first signs of life renewal.

CHAPTER 7

The Deadly Spring

All during March and April the tribes gathered at
Pyramid Lake and made their camps. From near and
far they came to meet in council. There was Chief Wahe—
Winnemucca's brother—and his band from Walker Lake.
From far to the east came the Shoshoni Chief Qudazoboeat, who was married to a Paiute woman. Chief Sawadabebo, half Bannock and half Paiute, came all the
way from Powder River with his warriors. Chief Saaba,
called Smoke Creek Sam by whites, had been at the lake
and waiting for war since his February run-in with
Captain Weatherlow and Thomas Harvey. Chiefs Hozia
and Nojomud of Honey Lake Valley had brought in their
people. From the Big Bend of the Carson River to the
southeast came Chief Yurdy and his people. Antelope
Valley was represented by Chief Hazabok, and from the
north came Chief Sequinata and his tough band of Black
Rock Desert warriors. To the northeast, from Humboldt
Meadows, came Chief Moguannoga and his men. Added
to these chiefs and their fighting men were Chief Winnemucca and War Chief Numaga. Even a cold spring was

a time for growing, a time for life renewal, and the smokes from the many camps near Pyramid Lake were the first shoots of a season of strange contrast, a season when death replaced life, and tossed the natural cycle into a whirling frenzy.

But even talk of war cannot take place without food to make a man and his pony strong. Yet though warmer weather was slow in coming, the last snow patches began to melt in shady draws and canyons, migrating flocks of waterfowl darkened the sky as they returned from their warmer winter feeding grounds far to the south, to settle at Pyramid Lake and at the many shallow marshes of the Great Basin.

Black and gray Canada geese, the great white snow geese, and ducks of every conceivable color, shape, and size—canvasbacks, goldeneyes, mallards, and pintails—settled down among the tules for their season of breeding. Along with them there was a vast multitude of shore birds ". . . the stilts and the avocets who were 'the same birds in different clothes,' the phalaropes, the curlews and the killdeer that, the Indians said, could whip up a dust storm by flying in circles while crying their plaintive songs. And there were the great white pelicans that glided endlessly like strings of pearls high in the sky until it was time for nesting on the sand dune island in the Carson Sink and on Anahoe Island in Pyramid Lake."[1] All was motion, endless, easy motion in the air and on the water, and it marked the thousands and thousands of waterfowl with their cries, calls, honks, shrill note songs, harsh squawks, and lightly trilled whistles.

Water and air, air and water carried the normal cycle of the seasons, and repeated the imprinted behavior patterns from another time, another age. Talk of war, talk of rash deeds by the white invaders was a steady undercurrent. But it needed the daily gifts of the earth to keep it alive, for even the power of hate and the desire for revenge must be nourished. If not, they, too, will wither and blow across the earth like dry and brittle tumbleweeds caught in the hot air of a whirling zephyr and sent skipping and bouncing across the parched land in full glare of the bright sun.

The men could talk and plan, but food had to be gathered. Women and girls waded, waist deep, into the icy waters. They reached clear to their armpits to the squishy, muddy bottoms of the marshes. Here they found the new shoots of cattails, shoots covered with brown, soggy leaves. For bodies yearning for green food, the cattails were the first green plants to ease the hungry craving that had increased with each day as the People endured the long, hard winter. In the marshes they stole the first eggs of the nesting birds, and carried them in green tule baskets that they had quickly made. Then when they waded ashore, they gathered "small flat plants called carved-seed,"[2] roots to be boiled and eaten, and "the first leaves of the squaw cabbage, which had to be boiled twice to remove the bitterness."[3]

But women and girls were not the only ones who had to take time out to replenish the almost empty food baskets. Men made tule boats, and they paddled toward the nesting ducks and geese. Close to the nesting areas, the men set their nets about three feet above the water by attaching them to supporting forked sticks which were held steady by driving the sharpened ends into the muddy bottom. Then the hunters frightened the feeding waterfowl. As the birds began to flap their wings and make their takeoff run across the surface of the water, their extended necks became entangled in the nets.

Ducks, geese, cattails, seeds, and roots were only part of the spring harvest. Grass began to poke upward through the wet and thawing land, and grass meant feed for ponies, and feed for game animals that men and boys hunted: white-rumped antelope, mule deer, big-eared jackrabbits, squirrels, sage hens, quail, doves, robins, and many other kinds of small birds. But most of all, by the first part of May, the spring season saw the first spawning run of cui-ui suckerfish, and the large spring trout, called tamaagaih, head out of Pyramid Lake to make their spawning run up the Truckee River.

In normal years this would have been the season to gorge oneself after the lean months. Men and boys would have kicked fish ashore, grabbed and speared them. All day long—day after day—the cui-ui and the large cut-throat trout would have been caught and handed to the women and girls standing on the riverbanks beside hot fires of burning driftwood. The fish would have been baked on the glowing coals, and when they had been cooked, the Indians would have had an orgy of eating. Then when they had satiated themselves, the work of filleting, smoking, and drying fish for times of hunger would have begun as the women worked and gossiped.

But this spring was not a happy time. Food was gathered, but an all-out effort did not take place. The many bands had not come for a harvest of food, and the purpose of their visit ate at their spirits like the taste of a massive bitterroot that had never been boiled and made edible. The season still had too much winter. Dis-content was in the air, and bitterness cut short the hunt-ing and gathering, stopped the gossip and laughter, and each man moved around as though he lived with pain and hate in a karnee of fear.

2

The chiefs and their best warriors met around the council fire. There was much to talk about. If there was to be war with the whites, plans had to be made.

Each council meeting followed an established ritual. Chief Winnemucca, his face deeply wrinkled with scars of age, called upon the Buhagant,[4] or spiritual leader, to offer a prayer to the Great Spirit. Following this prayer, Chief Winnemucca slowly filled his pipe, tamped the tobacco with his forefinger, then lit it with a burning stick from the fire pit. When the pipe was going well, Winnemucca drew deeply and let the smoke drift from his mouth. Then he turned and passed the pipe to his right. In this manner the pipe was passed around the circle of seated men. Five times the pipe went around the circle, five times from right to right as each man silently filled his mouth with smoke before passing it on. When the smoking ceremony was over, five songs were sung while the wind carried their voices out across the shifting colors of the lake.[5]

Each chief, in his turn, spoke his feelings. In this manner, all the accumulated wrongs done to the Indians by the whites were given to the winds. The sorrows, the lasting emotional wounds left little doubt as to the course of the council conversations. Talk had been tried once too often. There was no longer time for talk. There was only time for action, time for vengeance, time to run the white coyote back across the tall, western mountains.

Chief Winnemucca sat and listened to the others. While it was known that he favored war, he "declared neither for peace or war."[6] Shrewdly, he sat back and waited as the other chiefs assumed "the responsibility of acting."[7] One after another the chiefs made known how they felt.

The Shoshoni, Chief Qudazoboeat, was for war. Chief Sawadabebo of the Bannocks was for war. Chief Saaba from the Smoke Creek band was for war. The Honey Lake Valley chiefs—Nojomud and Hozia—were for war. Chief Yurdy from the Big Bend of the Carson River was for war. Chief Sequinata of the Black Rock Desert was for war; and Chief Hazabok from Antelope Valley was all-out for war. Hazabok told the council of chiefs and warriors that he would "supply the warriors with bullets, by changing their tobacco into lead; to cause the ground to open and swallow the whites; and to kill them with fierce storms of hail."[8] Yet all the while, Chief Winnemucca remained silent, and so, too, did War Chief Numaga. But when the time came for him to speak, Numaga—the Giver of Food—voted against war. He spoke slowly, as though he wished the men to consider each word. But the words all added up to one thing: Numaga believed it was not wise, in fact even foolish, to go to war against the whites.

All the men in the circle listened to Numaga's arguments. When he had finished, they were silent. Chief Winnemucca stared coldly at Numaga, and the disgust in the old chief's face was easy to see. Winnemucca had never liked Numaga. There was too much about him that bothered Winnemucca, too much he did not understand. Numaga was too friendly with the whites. He had crossed the mountains and worked for them. He spoke their language, and now all the whites in the land looked upon him as the great chief of the Paiutes. There were many reasons, good reasons, for Winnemucca to feel uneasy around Numaga and to dislike this proud man who spoke as though he were one of the white coyotes.[9]

Because the men at the council preferred to have a unanimous decision, Numaga's position forced them to postpone their plan for war. They were puzzled by what they had heard. After all, many of them must have thought, War Chief Numaga was the man to lead them into battle. Yet he spoke against war. He spoke for peace. There was reason to think, to talk things over in their individual camps. For it was one thing to go to war, but it was quite another to ride into battle without the best war chief of the Paiutes.

3

In the days that followed the first polling of the chiefs and their warriors, Numaga "rode from camp to camp, from family to family, friend to friend."[10] He reasoned with them, counseled and pleaded with them. War with the whites was not the way. War with the whites would only bring destruction upon the People. At each camp, he was listened to with respect, and treated with dignity. Yet his arguments fell on silent ground. Without words the answers of the other chiefs were made plain, and all the silent faces, the faces of friends who did not speak of what he had said but only of the weather, the ponies, and the hunting gave Numaga their answers. Silence added to silence became noiseless words, and the quiet faces made it all too clear. Numaga's words were no more than an evening breeze that caused no waves on the great desert lake.

Discouraged and disheartened by the reception he had received from old friends, Numaga returned to the main camp near the mouth of the Truckee River. Even here among families he had known since he had been a young boy, since he had run through the tall sagebrush and caught and killed his first jackrabbit, he was met with coolness. People either stared at him with scorn openly etched in their faces, or they turned away when he approached so that they would not have to meet the searching and probing gaze of his eyes.

Numaga walked all around the camp. Dogs followed in his footsteps, and children smiled and greeted him. But man after man, woman after woman turned away as he drew near. Only in his own karnee did he find love and warmth. Yet his eyes told him that his woman worried, that she, too, was concerned about his standing alone against the wishes of his People.

He sat for a long time inside his karnee before he made up his mind. Then he got up, stretched, walked outside, and stood alone in the open. He knew what had to be done, and that he alone could do what was necessary. But he stood silently for a long while, and looked at the full sweep of the land that he loved: the tall desert mountains—barren except for sagebrush, piñon pines—and pockets of willows and quaking aspens that marked areas where there were springs; the island of pelicans; the bloated tufa rocks carved into strange shapes by years of wind and sand; the tall pyramid-shaped rock that was like an arrow maker's tool; the sharp sticklike rocks at the southwestern end of the lake; the camps of basket-shaped karnees with thin streamers of smoke curling upward; the herds of ponies feeding on the newly sprouted grass; the flights of great-winged pelicans slowly drifting along just above the water, heads swinging from side to side watching for some sign of movement, some flash of fin; and most of all, the vast surface of Pyramid Lake stretching out from the narrow channel of the Truckee River at the south and gradually spreading out as it filled the basin far to the north and caught the reflection of the sky and the ancient terraced beach lines left over from long before the Paiutes had chosen this place as their home.

One thing was very clear to Numaga. It would be better for one man to die, one man to give his life than to have his People suffer and perish in a long, bloody war. Knowing this, seeing it as clearly as the waters of a mountain spring, he realized that he alone had to hold the attention of his People. And he knew he would do so by fasting. If need be, if it would prevent the coming storm of violence, he would fast until his body returned to the sage-covered earth, until his spirit vanished into the Great Camp of the southern sky where Coyote would lead him to his brother Wolf.[11]

Once again, Numaga glanced around the camp. He saw children playing games and dogs running after them. He saw women working: filleting strips of fish and hanging them from brush windbreaks, grinding the first seeds and berries into a paste for eating, weaving baskets, sewing rabbit skin blankets, nursing babies and then putting them back into cradleboards lined with the down of snow geese and the softest rabbit fur. He saw the men watch him, momentarily, then go back to work chipping arrowheads, straightening arrow shafts by putting them through a hole in a coarse stone and gently rubbing back and forth to remove the excess material from the shaft sides; and he saw other men raising and aiming the new rifles—trying to get the feel of the weapons, trying to use these weapons like a natural extension of one's hands and arms. All of this he viewed as though he might never see any of it again. Here, while friends and relatives watched, Numaga knelt on the sandy ground. He paused momentarily for another look at the lake and all the country around it. Then he relaxed, let his body stretch out on the ground with his arms in front of him like the spread wings of a great bird, turned his head to one side, and lay there as though he were dead.

During that first day, time slowly drifted by like the passing thunderheads. His stomach growled and churned from hunger, and his mouth became dry and parched. Muscles cramped from time to time, but he shut the pain out of his mind, let a warm drowsy feeling overcome the strain, and the cramps passed. As they did, the need to urinate overcame his control, and he felt and smelled the warm liquid as it puddled and was absorbed by the ground. All that first day and into the night, women of the camp came to him with food and water, but he refused their offerings. As the sky became dark with night, he felt his body shiver. He tried to hold it still, but he could not stop it from reacting to the cold. Not even the warmth of nearby campfires reached him; no heat escaped the circle of seated families to come his way. His world was the taste of dust, the low murmur of voices around the fires; and once before the camp became quiet for the night, his woman came to him with a rabbit skin robe, but he refused to accept it. Finally, the only sounds left were the movements of feeding ponies, the snoring of old people in their karnees, the final cracking and sputtering of the fires, and then the distant and lonely barking of the coyotes.

On the morning of the second day he was awake at dawn. His body was stiff and cold as he turned his head toward the east and watched the rising sun. Far out on the lake he heard the flapping wings and the first cries of the hunting pelicans. While all around him, he heard the early stirrings of old women as they crawled out the low openings of their karnees and started the morning fires. The old women gossiped as they worked, and some of their talk and laughter was about him. Then their conversations were drowned by the voices and movements of men and women and boys and girls as they began another day of hunting, fishing, and gathering. Again, women brought food and water to Numaga, and once again he refused to eat or drink.

All that second day, he felt light-headed and weak. Sounds became much louder than he remembered them, and he was sure that he heard men talking at the far end of the lake in the camp of the Smoke Creek band. His other senses also became more acute, and he smelled all the odors of his own body as though each one were separated and presented to his nostrils in individual eating baskets. The odors of the camp dogs, the old men and women, the babies in their cradleboards, a bleeding woman in her separate brush dwelling, and various kinds of food all came to his nose individually.

But what was strangest of all were the visions that ran in and out of his thoughts like scampering prairie dogs. He was in a world of feet: feet that appeared by his head to stand and offer food and water, feet that ran by kicking dust and laughing with fun, dog feet that stopped and licked his face with a wet tongue. He was in a world of crawling and flying insects that lit on him or walked across his head and face and the rest of his body as they traveled on their way. He was in a world of glaring colors, of water that seemed to move out of the lake and reappear in the shadow of the mountains, of light reflecting off tiny crystals and coming toward him like grounded stars. He was in a world where all his life became mixed with the earth, the sun, the brightness, the darkness, the shifting winds, the blue-gray sagebrush, and the coolness of new blades of green grass.

Still, he remained in his position. He held the earth

with his outstretched arms and the palms of his hands as he prayed to the spirits for the safety of his People, holding onto himself, drifting in and out of consciousness for all that day and through the cold and darkness of the second night.

On the dawn of the third day Numaga heard a ringing in his ears. It seemed at first to come from far away, as though he were once again across the tall western mountains at the place of the Black Robes in San Jose, California. The ringing was the bells at dawn, the great bells in the towers of the Mission that always awakened him to the song of the white man's God; the ringing that called him to come forth to pick the ripe crops of the warm season, the crops that sent the aroma of their pungent fruit on the warm breezes of morning.

But the third day of his fasting was a dream in the daylight. Reality was limited to the sharpened sounds, to the grains of earth that now punctured his skin, to the early rays of the sun that were like sticks from a hot fire, to the smell of cooking food that made his stomach churn and ache, and to the faraway talk of familiar voices —voices that came to him in whispers, then in what sounded like across-the-canyon shouts.

"He will die, die, die!" the voices said.

"Yes," they whispered, "help him. Stop him from doing this to us."

Numaga listened, and he wondered: "To us, to us, why to us?"

One after another, friend after friend, man after man, woman after woman, the People spoke to Chief Winnemucca. And the request was always the same.

"Stop him," they said. "Do not let him die before our faces, in front of our karnees!"

Then there was silence followed by the crunch of sand

and bits of wind-ground stones, and Numaga knew that someone walked toward him. He listened as the sounds of footsteps drew closer and closer. Then he saw the broad moccasins decorated with horseshoe-shaped rows of brightly colored trade beads. He turned and tried to look upward, but the sun was far too bright for his eyes. He fell downward into the ground, and it was then that he heard Chief Winnemucca's gruff voice[12]:

"Your skin is colored by the glance of the sun," he said. "But your heart is white like the underfeathers of a pelican. Go! Go away and live with your white friends!"[13]

Numaga did not move, nor did he say anything. He waited for Winnemucca to say more, but the old chief was through. He turned and walked away, and Numaga heard his steps on the ground.

More talk went on in the camp. More voices asked for someone to stop what was bound to happen. All the while the sun moved across the sky, grew warmer, then began to lose its heat. Late in that day, other men came and stood around him.

"Get up or we will kill you,"[14] they said.

War Chief Numaga waited for the killing blow, but none came. He waited for more talk, but none came. When there was only the sound of breathing, he twisted his head and stared upward at the men. "Do it if you wish," he said, "for I don't care to live."[15]

But the death blow did not fall, and Numaga heard the men speak of another council. As they moved away from him, as he heard their moccasined feet crunch the grains of sand, he realized that another council was forming, that sometime during the late afternoon or in the morning of the next day the war-minded chiefs would meet again to vote for or against war.

4

While Numaga continued to fast, and the other chiefs talked of another council, the event which would set their final course had begun to assume shape. Two young girls had not returned to camp from a day of looking for roots. Their parents had searched way beyond Pyramid Lake, ". . . found trails which led up to the . . . traders named Williams."[16] They talked to these white men, who ran a combination grog shop and trading station on a knoll above the Carson River about sixty miles northeast of Virginia City,[17] but the three brothers from Maine said that they had not seen the girls. They even invited the parents into their log house to look around, but there was no trace of the missing girls.[18]

The parents returned to Pyramid Lake, and spoke of the sadness in their hearts. Friends listened and grieved, then said that they would help to look for the girls again on the next day.

But early on the following morning a transaction at Williams Station resulted in the elimination of a search party and the formation of a war party. On his way home to Pyramid Lake, a Paiute hunter stopped at Williams Station. The men who were there fancied his pony, and spoke to him of a trade. For his fine pony, they were willing to give "a gun, five cans of powder, five boxes of caps, and five bars of lead."[19] The hunter considered this a fair exchange, and let the men take his pony into their barn. Then they handed him the caps and powder, but refused to give him the five bars of lead.

Not wishing to make this kind of trade, the Paiute handed back the caps and powder and walked to the barn to get his pony. At once, the station keepers set their dog after him. Before the hunter could stop the animal, the dog sunk its teeth into his leg. He yelled from the pain, and the traders laughed. But more than pain and laughter greeted him. For as he kicked the dog away, he heard the muffled voices of Paiute children coming from beneath the barn floor. The warrior quickly mounted his pony, dashed by the whites, who tried to stop him, and rode rapidly to Pyramid Lake.

When he galloped his pony into camp, he met the search party. He told the father of the missing girls what he had heard, and Chief Natchez and Chief Moguannoga, the leader of the Humboldt Meadows band, stood by and listened to his story.

Chief Moguannoga, the man called Captain Soo by the whites, quickly formed a raiding party. He selected a mixture of Bannock and Paiute warriors, including the father of the missing girls and Chief Natchez. Altogether, there were nine men in the party. Each man was a well-trained warrior, and each man had lost all hope that differences between the races could be settled by peaceful means.

The sun was already moving past its midday peak when they rode away from Pyramid Lake and headed for Williams Station. By the white man's calendar it was May 7, 1860. By any method of recording seasons and days, it was a day and a year that would end the time for talk. The mounted warriors had seen too many seasons of hurt, too many broken promises. The time had come to strike back, and they knew that this was the force that drove them on a fast ride toward the white trading post.

The sun was dropping low in the western sky when the warriors reached the eastern end of the Carson River, "a few miles west of The Narrows, where the river flowed through a narrow, and steep-walled canyon."[20] Near the river bottomland, about a half mile from the station, they picketed their ponies in a grove of cottonwoods. Then, on foot, they quietly climbed the high knoll overlooking the river. It was almost sundown as they approached the log station on the California Trail, and they could see the thin column of smoke drifting lazily into the air from the cabin's chimney.

But just before they reached the log cabin, four white men stepped outside and stood waiting. As one warrior said years later, "They look mighty scared, and talk heep to Captain Soo. . . ."[21] But the talking was in vain, for the Pyramid Lake raiders were convinced that these men were guilty of kidnapping the two girls for their own pleasure. Yet the whites kept talking and talking, and they moved about, looking this way and that, as they talked.

Then, all at once, one of the station keepers stopped talking, stared wildly, ducked away from the surrounding circle of Indians, and began running in the direction of Samuel Buckland's[22] Station. Two warriors ran after him, and caught him before he got very far away, and dragged the man back to stand with the other terrified whites.

Panic was in the air. All the men at the station had turned in color. They were like the bloodless bellies of dead fish. But they made noises. Their mouths kept moving and moving, talking and talking. Words came like flights of frightened ducks running across the waters of tule marshes and flapping into the air.

"No, no! They had not seen any girls! Yes, they were certain of this; they were absolutely sure. No girls, none, none at all!"

"The man who tried to run? Why? Why did he run?

He ran for his life. Yes, that was it. He ran for his life. He thought he was going to be killed!"

"No! They had not seen any girls! My God! They had even let the mother and father look around their house. Surely, they knew that. Hadn't the mother and father told them? There were no girls! None, none at all!"

"Yes, yes, they remembered the Paiute with the good pony. They had seen him early that morning. Yes, they had offered to trade, but fairly, they always traded fairly."

"No! They had not said anything about lead. The man had misunderstood. Maybe it was their poor use of the language. Maybe they thought he knew more English. That was all there was to it. Then he took his pony and rode away."

"Their dog? Oh, the dog, yes of course, the dog bit him; but that was an accident. No more than that, just an accident."

"Girls? The man said he had heard girls? He was wrong! He had kicked their dog, and the dog had yelped. There were no girls in the barn!"

"Underneath the ground? How could that be? There was no cellar in the barn. The man was wrong. He had made a mistake. He only thought he had heard girls. Yes, that was what it was all about. He had thought he had heard girls. The dog had yelped when he kicked it, and he thought he had heard girls!"[23]

The men became more and more excited, and the warriors stood and watched them. Then another of the whites broke away. He ran toward the bluff, jumped, and tumbled downward until he reached the river. Warriors running right behind him saw him hesitate momentarily; then they watched as he jumped into the icy, swift current of the river. The man flailed away with his arms, frantically trying to swim; but he could not keep his head above the water. On shore, the Indians watched him go under, come up again and gasp for air, then go under for the final time. They watched his body as the swift water carried it downstream; and when it drifted into an eddy, they pulled it ashore, carried it up the bluff, and threw it into the log station.

On seeing his dead companion tossed like the carcass of a gutted deer, one of the three remaining men shouted at his captors, drew his long-bladed hunting knife, and tried to fight his way into the open. But his try for freedom was quickly halted when some of the Indians managed to grab his knife-wielding arm. In a swift movement they yanked his arm upward behind his back, and pulled hard on it until the bones snapped; and the man screamed and fell to his knees, where he sobbed and began to retch. Yet even then, he pleaded for his life in between sobbing and heaving, but all hope came to a quick end when the warriors choked him until his eyes bulged, his face turned blue, and his body sagged and fell to the ground.

With two men dead, the war party did not hesitate to kill the other men. How they killed them remained uncertain in the memories of the Paiutes who had been there on that bloody day. What is certain is that the final victims of vengeance were slaughtered in a hurry.[24]

After killing all the men at the post, the Indians went into the barn to look for the lost girls. They found the trapdoor leading to the cellar, pulled it open, and were sorry that they had killed the whites so quickly. Both girls were "lying on a little bed with their mouths tied up with rags."[25] Shocked and horrified at their condition, the men gently removed the crying girls from their cell of torture. Their father took them into his arms, and comforted them. The other warriors hated the easy fate of the dead whites. Their deaths had come much too quickly for what they had done. But there was no living body to strike out at in rage and fury. There were only the dead. But there were the dead! They ran back to the log cabin, picked up the dead outside, carried them into the cabin and quickly scooped the burning logs and glowing coals from the fireplace onto the floor.

When Williams Station was fully on fire, they walked back to the river bottom, where their horses were picketed. Here where they could watch the final fire and smoke from the burning building, they made camp until two or three hours before dawn broke in the east. Yet even as they watched their own anger become fire and smoke, they sent a warrior on his way to Pyramid Lake with news of what had taken place at Williams Station.

5

After three days and nights of lying spread-eagle on the ground, after three days and nights of going without water and food, Numaga felt the first warmth of the rising sun of the fourth day as though it were a campfire on a distant mountain peak. The sounds of people beginning the new day were strangely mixed with a steady ringing in his ears. He was colder than he had ever been in his whole life. He shivered and shivered, and though he tried to control his body, he could not stop. As he shook from the cold, he also felt numb and cramped. His body was so stiff that he wondered if he could even move it at all.

As the morning sun rose higher, he began to feel warmer, and his shivering stopped. His woman came to him. She knelt beside his head and offered food and water. Again, he refused. But this time even the odor of

food nauseated him. His woman begged him to drink
some water. He slowly shook his head against the dry,
sandy soil. Again she tried. She held the pitch-covered
water bottle close to his mouth. With great effort, he
forced himself to speak, to move his tongue against the
dry surfaces of his mouth, to send words between his
swollen and cracked lips, to tell her that he would not
drink, and would not eat until his people realized what
a terrible thing they were planning. He heard her sob,
and he twisted his head to watch her as she got up.
Then he listened to her light steps as she walked back to
their karnee.

When his woman was gone, Numaga tried to sleep beneath the warmth of the morning sun. But he was awakened by voices that drifted in and out of his thoughts,
voices that spoke harshly and were filled with hate for
the whites.

"They have cut our pine nut trees."

"They have driven their animals to the land where
there is grass for our ponies. Then they have told us that
we must pay for lost animals. But it is they who steal *our*
grass and *our* ponies!"

"An old man hunting rabbits, an old man all by himself
was roped and dragged until there was no skin left on
his bones. A boy hiding in the sagebrush saw it all. And
when the old man was dead, they cut his scalp and
yanked at his hair until the skin pulled free. Then they
laughed. They passed around a bottle, and the boy
watched them drink and laugh!"

"Yes, and that was not the first of our People they
killed. They have killed others who were traveling alone."

"And the women, what of the women? They have taken
women, used them, and sent them back when they were
sick and not safe to touch!"[26]

Man after man spoke out, and then Numaga heard Chief Winnemucca's gruff voice. He heard him ask each man what he thought should be done, and as each one replied, the answers became a chant of sameness: "War! War! War! War! War! War!"

One thing rang clear in Numaga's mind. The council was already meeting, and the vote was for war. All the days and nights of heat and cold, of thirst and hunger had not made any difference to the chiefs. He would have to struggle to his feet and make one last effort, one last try to stop this insane move, this unleashing of fury that would see the desert soaked in blood, and drive his People into flight like an enraged, wounded bear.

All the days and nights of remaining in one position, of going without food and water had taken their toll. War Chief Numaga strained against his arms, and he was like a child making his first attempt to crawl. He pushed against the ground with his hands to lift his body upward, and he felt sharp pains shoot through his cramped muscles. For a moment, he was able to hold himself up. Then his arms quivered like those of a young boy pulling back the string of his first bow, and he fell face forward into the gritty soil.

He felt his heart pounding against his chest, and he gasped for air as dirt entered his mouth. Then with a cry of anguish and pain he used all his strength and pushed his heavy shoulders into the air. He shifted his stiff knees against the gritty sand, and felt the sharp grains cut into his flesh as his knees slid underneath his heavy torso. For the first time in three days and nights his world became what it had been before he had learned to live with the surface of the earth. He stared at the vastness of Pyramid Lake, and his eyes quickly filled with tears as he squinted to shut out the glare of sun against water.

Behind him, Numaga heard the men of the council stop talking. He heard all talking in the camp come to a halt. All that was left was the crying of a baby here and there, the occasional barking of a dog, the soft neighing of nearby ponies, and the hunting calls of pelicans and sea gulls far out on the lake.

He rested until he was sure he could move his legs. Then, slowly, moving one leg at a time, he staggered to his feet. He stood there feeling the numbness leaving his legs, giving way to sharp, needle-like pains. Again, he waited until this passed. When most of it was gone, when all he worried about was his own weakness, he turned and faced the camp. One step at a time, holding his gaze on the karnees and the distance between him and the men seated around the council—the men who had quickly shifted their eyes to appear as though they had not heard or seen him—Numaga moved forward as though he had risen from the dead and had to be led by Coyote in his first attempt to walk.

Painful step after painful step, Numaga slowly walked toward the council circle. The distance was not far—no more than the length of five bows placed end to end—yet it was a walk across the longest desert, a climb up the steepest mountain.

After what seemed like weeks of wandering in the desert, Numaga reached the rim of the council circle. He waited as two chiefs made room for him, and as he stood, he felt his heart pounding, and he could hear his own heavy breathing as though it were the movement of waves against the shore of the lake during a great storm. He stood at the opening the chiefs had made for him, and across the circle he heard one man whisper:

"He comes from the ground like the uncovered dead, and his face is that of a ghost."[27]

Numaga stared at the man who whispered, and the warrior stopped talking and looked downward. Then Numaga looked all around the circle. Seeking out each face, he tried to capture each man's eyes. All the while, the ringing in Numaga's ears continued, and he feared he might not have the strength to speak of what he knew, to tell the angry chiefs that what they planned was the death of the People.

Slowly, making sure of his footing, holding himself erect, Numaga walked into the center of the council circle. Again he stood and caught his breath. All the chiefs remained silent; and when Numaga looked beyond the circle to the fire pits and karnees of the camp, he saw that even the women were not talking, and that the older children stood and silently watched.

At first, Numaga was not sure he could speak. His mouth felt as though it were caked with dried sand, and his lips were swollen and cracked. When he opened them, the first sounds he heard were dry and raspy—sounds of an ancient man, a man trying to speak to the living one more time before Coyote barked inside the karnee.

One of the chiefs moved around, stood up, and Numaga saw that he had a pitch-covered water basket. The man moved toward him, and without saying a word, handed the red-colored basket jug to him.

Numaga nodded to him. He held the opening against his lips, and the first flow of cool water flooded his mouth with pain. His teeth ached, and the cracks in his lips and inside his mouth stung. Quickly, he rinsed out his mouth, and spit a mixture of blood, phlegm, and water onto the dry earth. Then he brought the water bottle back to his mouth, and very cautiously—almost drop by drop—he drank. But he was very careful. He did not want to drink too much, become sick and have to throw up.

After his first taste of water in three days, Numaga rinsed out his mouth once again. When he finished, he walked over to the man who had brought him the water, thanked him, and placed the basket jug alongside his crossed legs. Then he turned and walked back to the center of the circle.

"While I belonged to the ground," Numaga said, "I heard angry voices, voices that called for war. I heard no man speak out for peace. I heard no man say, 'Let us try one more time to talk to our white brothers about the wrongs we have felt.' "[28]

Numaga paused and waited for anyone who wished to speak. But the circle of men remained silent. They sat and waited for him to continue.

"I have heard all of you, my brothers," Numaga said, "and you speak as young boys at play. You say you would make war on the whites, that you would drive them from our meadows, that you would send them running back across the tall, western mountains. Have you thought of what this war would mean? Do you know how many of our People would die in such a war?"[29]

Again Numaga paused, and this time he walked across the circle to the chief with the water jug. Before he got there, the man stood up, handed him the jug, and waited as he took another drink. When Numaga finished drinking, he again nodded to the chief. Then he turned and slowly walked back to the center of the council circle.

Before he spoke, Numaga glanced at the camp, and he saw that the women still were not working, that they were watching and waiting. Again he looked at the chiefs. They, too, were silently waiting; and except for Chief Winnemucca, their faces were relaxed and calm. But Numaga saw the frown on Winnemucca's face, and he knew that his old adversary was having trouble holding back his inner rage.

"My brothers," Numaga said, "you would make war upon the whites. I ask you to pause and think of what this war would mean to our People. The white men are like the stars over your heads. You have wrongs, great wrongs, that rise up like those mountains before you; but can you, from the mountaintops, reach and blot out those stars? Your enemies are like the sands in the bed of your rivers; when taken away they only give place for more to come and settle there. Could you defeat the whites in our own home, from over the mountains in California would come to help them an army of white men that would cover your country like a blanket. What hope is there for the Paiute? From where is to come your guns, your powder, your lead, your dried meats to live upon, and grass to feed your ponies while you carry on this war? Your enemies have all of these things, more than they can use. They will come like the sand in a whirlwind and drive you from your homes. You will be forced among the barren rocks of the north, where your ponies will die; where you will see the women and old men starve, and listen to the cries of your children for food. I love my People; let them live; and when their spirits shall be called to the Great Camp in the southern sky, let their bones rest where their fathers were buried."[30]

Numaga stopped. His heart was pounding, and he inhaled deeply as he tried to get enough air into his burning lungs. While he remained standing in the center of the circle, the chief with the water jug got up and came to him. He waited as Numaga drank, then returned to his position. The silence was broken, and the chiefs began to talk. As Numaga listened, he heard one after another come to his side. And though his legs trembled with weakness, and he felt light-headed, he knew that his final effort had stopped the useless shedding of blood.

Yet even as he listened to the chiefs talk of waiting, of going to the white leaders to state their troubles, Numaga saw a lone rider approaching the camp from the southeast, and the man was riding his pony at a full gallop. He wondered why the man rode in such haste. Then as the rider neared the edge of camp without slowing down to cut the flow of dust, Numaga could only think that the warrior who was now dismounted and walking toward the council carried news of trouble. And when the warrior stepped into the circle of chiefs, Numaga saw that the young man was nervous and excited.

Pointing to the southeast, the warrior quickly said: "Moguannoga, last night, with nine braves, burned Williams Station on the Carson River, and killed four whites!"[31]

With the young man's words running in his thoughts like the echo of a boy's shout to the winds, Numaga looked at the karnees. He stared at the old people whose hair was like the first snows of winter. He watched the mothers with their young babies in cradleboards on their backs, and the laughing children playing with the barking dogs. Then he gazed at the blue water of the great desert lake until the glare of the sunlight off its surface made his eyes water. Finally, he looked toward the southeast, and his expression was of great sadness as he said: "There is no longer any use for counsel; we must prepare for war, for the soldiers will now come here to fight us."[32]

PART III

THE COST OF VIOLENCE

1860

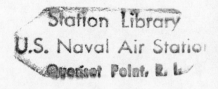

CHAPTER 8

An Indian for Breakfast

April was a cruel month. The snow fell and melted, then repeated its pattern until the ground was hard with ice in the morning, slippery with mud at noon, and hard with ice, once again, at day's end. The bone-chilling wind, the wind the whites called a Washoe zephyr, whipped across the barren landscape in a steady scream, and turned Virginia City, Gold Hill, and Silver City into camps of raw, freezing punishment that spared no man—least of all, the man without a large grubstake.

But though the men endured and dreamed of fortunes to be made on the Comstock during the warm months, even their dreams were to be no more than another cruel joke for most miners. The easy pickings were already tied up in claims, and the big strikes were going to require more than a strong back and a willingness to burrow into the hard ground from dawn to dark. Few miners had the financial backing to hire others to hack into the earth for them, and most of the fortune seekers were so low on funds that they could not afford the high price of a regular shelter. For these men their habitat was of the rudest kind:

> Tents of dirty, ragged canvas pieced out with tattered clothes coated with grime—hovels of pine boards roughly nailed together and pierced by bent and rusty stove-pipes —heaps of broken rocks with shapeless crevices into which men crawled like lizards—shallow pits partly covered over with boards and earth—and embryo adits, dark slimy holes into which the melting snow dripped with a monotonous plash—these were the winter homes of the citizens.[1]

If the freezing temperatures became more than they could stand, the men were "forced to wait till a late hour for the privilege of spreading their blankets, at a dollar a head, on the floor of bar rooms and saloons."[2] For in this sagebrush land of very little timber, in this territory isolated from California during the winter by snow-covered passes, building supplies were at a premium, and sometimes almost impossible to purchase even if a man had a steady jingle in his pockets.

Trapped in this raw, unhospitable land, subjected to its unrelenting winds and snows, the miners awaited the warmth of spring and summer. They were citizens of despair imprisoned by the land they had come to plunder. They were filled with pent-up rage, but they could do no more than curse the elements and know that even their shouts of hate were doomed to be silenced by the icy, howling winds.

So April passed, and May arrived. And while the days were not yet completely free of winter, the men spoke of warmer days, of the coming months that would make all the suffering and waiting worthwhile.

2

Massacre. The dreaded word of the American frontier reached Virginia City on May 7, 1860. Pony Express riders—J. B. Bartoles and J. H. Smith—carried the terrible news.[3] Massacre! Massacre at Williams Station on the Big Bend of the Carson River.

All during the freezing months of winter the men of the Comstock country had struggled to stay alive. But survival had meant enduring the bitter cold of the winds and snows of winter. It had meant finding enough to eat in camps and shack towns that were running out of food and were low on whiskey. It had meant holding on to enough money to get a start in the diggin's come spring. Now the one curse they had never even considered focused all their rage, all their suffering of having endured the long, cold winter. Massacre! Indians on the warpath! Goddamn the savage, redskin bastards!

The news traveled across the Sierra Nevada via telegraph lines. In the May 9 issue of the Sacramento *Union*, the story of what had happened at Williams Station was date lined Virginia City, May 8:

> Last night a most horrid massacre was perpetrated by the Indians below the Great Bend of the Carson. J. Williams arrived at Buckland's near the bend, and gave information of the murder of his two brothers and five other men, at the same hour, and the burning of the house after or during the perpetration of this shocking butchery. On his way up, Williams called at the two other houses on the opposite side of the river, and the doors were open, but loud calling at a short distance failed to induce any signs of life about the premises. He supposes all are murdered;

they number some twelve or thirteen others. The Indians are about five hundred strong, and all mounted. They pursued him to within six miles of Buckland's and gave up the chase.[4]

Here was terror dancing wildly in the streets. Here was the nightmare carried overland from that early heritage of the first European settlers on the Atlantic seaboard, from the first frontiersmen who dared to cross the mountains and move westward. Here was the inherited memory of a silent night turned into a last scream before death, a night of quick death, slow death, mutilated death, but in the dawn of a new day the dried blood, the distorted face, and the final rigid pose of death.

The men met in the streets, the saloons, the rough cabins, the tents, and the rude dugouts. They gathered together, and they talked excitedly, loudly, even patriotically.

And it is not difficult to imagine what their talk was like. Yet in the end, after the men had run out of arguments that ranged from pure hatred of the Indians to saner voices that cried out for restraint, one thing was certain: there was a large blank space between what they knew and what they didn't know.

And nobody was very sure about anything. The Pony Express riders had not carried detailed information. They had brought news of disaster, but the extent of the disaster was not truly known. There had been a raid on Williams Station, and the trail-side grog shop had been burned. Some men had been killed by some Indians. How many men were dead, and how many Indians were on the warpath varied from man to man, saloon to saloon, and town to town. Conjecture was married to fear, and the child was half excitement, half panic.

At Virginia City the general belief was that five hundred Indians had killed every person in the vicinity of Williams Station, or if the mass murder had not yet happened, homes of the other traders and ranchers, and camps of prospectors were doomed if armed help didn't ride to their rescue. And while hard news was sparse, the newspapers filled in the blank spots with stories of an "eyewitness" account by James Williams, though the reporters failed to mention that they had not interviewed the lone survivor. In this manner the news of the massacre spread from town to town, and was telegraphed from Carson City across the Sierra Nevada.

One reporter even went so far as to place James Williams in a hiding place in the willows and then to send him to the scene of disaster. Here, the writer said, Williams "found one of his brothers murdered, and another one able to tell him that the Pah-Utes had done it. The other five men were murdered."[5]

Not completely satisfied with just a "first-hand" description of the carnage, the creative reporter then wrote a vivid account of how the Indians chased James Williams on his way to Buckland's. Performing like a true hero the surviving Williams brother "rode down one horse and then jumped upon the other, and reached Buckland's, exhausted."[6]

Within the first hours of the vague reports about the raid on Williams Station, the few grains of truth gave way to a landslide of myth. Truth was dead in the ashes at the Big Bend of the Carson River. The time had come for action. If Indians were allowed to get away with one massacre, no man, woman, or child would be safe. Strike back! Hit them hard and fast! Take two eyes for one! *Ride for vengeance!* became the rallying shout, and it rang throughout the towns and camps of western Utah

Territory. All the way from Chinatown (present Dayton, Nevada) to Virginia City, from Carson City in Eagle Valley to Genoa at the foot of the Sierra Nevada, men picked up their rifles, shotguns, pistols, and pepperboxes. They met at cabins, in tents, on streets, and inside saloons. They drank whiskey for strength, shouted for courage, and became great military men and Indian fighters as bottles and kegs filled their minds with visions of glory, for the protection of American lives, and by God, for the preservation of civilization against the attacking savage hordes.

3

All during the night of May 8, the men of Virginia City met and talked of what they had to do. Self-proclaimed leaders with dubious military experience took it upon themselves to call for volunteers. Some of these immediate "captains" even "issued their orders to press into service horses wherever to be found."[7] But other citizens who were not so inflicted with excitement, not so ready to rush off to battle, did not fancy the idea of giving up their horses to a wild-eyed mob. They saw no reason for this mad dash into the desert to avenge the honor of the Williams brothers, or any other merchant of misery who specialized in cheating trail-weary pioneers and peaceful Indians.[8] Such owners of impressed mounts did not hesitate to dismount roughly the glory riders who had taken their horses.

All through the night the men of Virginia City met in small and large groups. They heard speakers such as popular young Henry Meredith—law partner of William Stewart, who tried to talk Meredith out of this adventure.[9] But Meredith was too excited to listen, and he cast his lot with this democratic army that found it had enough men for three companies. Certainly, they would need an over-all captain, and they elected Archie McDonald to this post of leadership for the campaign. And when the long night of forming the Virginia City army ended, one news-paper reporter looked at the whole group with a jaun-diced eye and wrote:

There has been a vast deal of talk, noise, and confusion, collection of rifles, muskets, revolvers, and knives, and an immense punishment of whiskey. Could the Indians be as effectually consumed, peace would soon be restored.[10]

But Virginia City's volunteers were only one part of the force that was forming in a passionate fury. Down the grade from Virginia City, the Silver City Guards gathered together and called upon one-legged R. G. Watkins to lead them into battle as their captain.

At first, Watkins declined the honor. Quite realisti-cally, he pointed out that he was crippled. Yet the men would not listen. To them, he was a man of great military experience, a man who had lost his leg while a member of William Walker's filibustering expedition in Nicaragua. Furthermore, some of the men claimed that Watkins had been their leader in Nicaragua. What these same cham-pions did not know was that Watkins was a former naval officer during the Mexican War, and that he had lost his leg in a San Diego street brawl in 1851. However, he had had the courage to send the amputated leg to his op-ponent as a trophy of war.[11] And Watkins had not lost his courage or his flair for the dramatic. He agreed to be the leader of his "former comrades" who had fought un-der his direction in "Nicaragua." Then, to be certain that he would not fall off his powerful horse during any encounter, Captain Watkins "was strapped to the saddle."[12]

In Eagle Valley the guiding hand in the formation of the Carson City Rangers was none other than Major William Ormsby, who truly had been "one of Walker's fillibusters."[13] A man of very excitable nature, a man quick to make a judgment, Major Ormsby was Carson City's man for a bad season. His own personality convinced others who should have known better that the time had come to teach the Indians a lesson. But Ormsby never bothered to point out the danger of such a hasty attack. Instead, he gathered about him a party of men who followed him "apparently more with the idea that they would have a lark and a prospecting trip than anything else."[14]

However, Judge John Cradlebaugh was one member of the Carson City force who did not let rumors and momentary excitement blind him. While he agreed to ride out with the others, he made it quite clear that his first duty was to check the reliability of the various reports. If the Paiutes were truly on the warpath, he would join the rangers in fighting them. But if the killings at the grog shop were justified, if the Paiutes were not getting ready for an all-out war, Judge Cradlebaugh stated that he believed the course of action should be decided by vote. He did not think any man should ride off to war without just cause.

With only one leading voice calling out for reason, the quickly assembled and undisciplined Carson City Rangers rode out of Eagle Valley at eight o'clock in the morning on May 10 and headed for the charred remains of Williams Station. By this time, there was yet another rumor that aroused their tempers and sent them forth as defenders of white civilization, for a rider had come in

from the edge of the Forty Mile Desert and reported that
the Indians had fortified themselves at Ragtown—the first
far western trail settlement in the Great Basin.

Meanwhile, the fourth prong of the vengeance fork had
taken shape in the small town of Genoa, next to the steep
timber-covered flanks of the Sierra Nevada. Here in the
pioneer settlement, once known as Mormon Station,
the men gathered under the leadership of Captain Thomas
F. Condon, Jr.,[15] to form the Genoa Rangers. While they
represented a small community and were the smallest
contingent of men, they were not to be dismissed lightly.
Among the tough and hardy members of the rangers
was John "Snowshoe" Thomson, who used skis and
snowshoes in his lonely winter task of carrying the mail
from Placerville, California, across the Sierra Nevada to
Utah Territory. Yet "Snowshoe" Thomson was only representative of the Genoa Rangers. In their own way, all
the others were men of the frontier, men to be counted on
by friends and to be reckoned with by foes.

Thus, formed in excitement, all four detachments—
Virginia City, Silver City, Carson City, and Genoa—were
the men and boys of a hasty army. And each group of
riders left its respective town with a feeling of pride, a
sense of martial glory. Yet to the eyes of dispassionate
observers the four units of this volunteer army constituted
no more than an undisciplined, leaderless mob of more
than one hundred poorly armed riders.

But the brave and patriotic soldiers believed that they
were a stout fighting force, that they were heroic defenders of a just cause. It never entered their minds that
the Paiutes would actually put up a fight. Instead, these
raw recruits truly believed that this was going to be an
outing, a way to loosen up the muscles after the long,
hard winter. They would raid the Paiute villages, take

some good-looking women as prisoners, shoot anybody who tried to stop them, bring home any good horses they found, and give the Indians a lesson they'd never forget.

All of this military adventure would be a kind of spring tonic, no more than that. Then, fully believing their own bravado, the loosely knit band of armed miners took yet another drink of whiskey, and gave vent to their hatred and their feelings of superiority in a shout that summed up the true nature of their expedition: "An Indian for breakfast and a pony to ride. . . ."[16]

CHAPTER 9

The Big Bend of the Carson River

When the first force of the avenging army neared the Big Bend of the Carson River on May 10, 1860, even the weather had taken a turn for the worse. Seeing that his men were cold and tired, Major William Ormsby must have considered that a momentary stop at Buckland's Station would be a good break. For he could see that they were hunched over in their saddles as they tried to expose as little as possible of their bodies to the cold wind that blew across patches of snow that were shaded by willows or overhanging bluffs above the river. What Major Ormsby did not know, however, was that a furious wind storm would lash Virginia City during the night almost as an omen of bad luck. As one journal keeper wrote:

Wind blew a hurricane in night. Blew down Rassett's two story frame house. Broke down two tents. Broke rafters of our store tent badly. Many tents & houses blown down. Wonder people are not hurt or killed. 12 at night went to Saloon & staid till day light.[1]

All the signs pointed toward disaster. The news of the killings at Williams Station, the cold ride across the open flats of sagebrush, the need to follow the course of the Carson River and be exposed to any hidden riflemen in the willows or positioned behind boulders on top of the canyon walls, and the damned winter weather in the second week of May—all these factors were enough to make any man leary of his volunteer tour of duty.

Yet, onward the army rode until they made their first real halt at Buckland's Station—about ten miles west of Williams Station. Here across the river from the future site of Fort Churchill was the log cabin store and saloon established by Samuel S. Buckland—a rawboned man whose deep-set eyes seemed to glow with a hidden madness. Samuel Buckland had come to California in 1850 via the Isthmus of Panama. Here the man from Kirkesville, Licking County, Ohio, had joined the other gold seekers in the Mother Lode country. And it was here that Buckland and James O. Williams struck up a friendship and finally traveled to Utah Territory together in 1857.[2]

But Samuel Buckland had not gone into business on the California Trail with the Williams brothers. Instead, he selected his own site where the river widened out, where there was abundant building timber "in a most beautiful grove of cottonwood trees growing in an open and smooth lawn-like meadow,"[3] and where excellent well water was easy to come by. Then during the cold winter of 1859–60, Buckland constructed a toll bridge across the Carson River, and he set the following fees for its use: "$2 for heavy wagons, $1.50 for light wagons, $1 for buggies, and 25 cents for pedestrians."[4]

A bridge across the river, supplies for sale, extra livestock to replace trail-weary animals, and a good supply of gut-warming whiskey made Buckland's Station a natural stopping place for men who had crossed the Great Basin, or who were heading into the desert wilderness. The hasty army of self-proclaimed Indian fighters was no exception. Many years later, Samuel Buckland recalled the look of this makeshift army, and he wrote that not only were these men poorly armed and ill disciplined, but also they were "full of whiskey."[5] And, no doubt, some of the whiskey had been sold to the volunteers across the rough bar at Buckland's Station.

2

The Carson City Rangers were the first contingent of volunteers to reach the Big Bend of the Carson River. The sun was already dropping low in the western sky, and the cold wind of the coming desert night chilled the riders as they scanned the countryside in the gray light of afternoon. They rode their tired horses up the point of a sagebrush-covered foothill and topped the ridge. Here on a plateau overlooking The Narrows—that steep-walled canyon where the river made its final rush toward the Carson Sink—the men saw the remains of what had been Williams Station.[6]

While the pride of Carson City waited for the other units of the army to ride into view, Major William Ormsby appointed W. F. Mason to the position of coroner; and the task of searching the rubble of ashes, burnt adobe bricks, and blackened timbers for the bodies of the dead began. The charred corpses of three men were found in the ashes of the building. Two of the dead "were recognized as males,"[7] but the third body was so badly burned it was impossible to make a positive identification. As for the reputed fourth and fifth victims of the raid, the rangers found no actual bodies. Yet the blackened framework of Samuel Sullivan's wagon stood in front of the collapsed trading post like an uncovered fossil of some prehistoric beast. Seeing this, the searchers assumed that Samuel Sullivan had also been among the victims of violence.

While the volunteers stared at the leavings of death, Major Ormsby gave orders for the making of camp and the burial of the dead. For until the forces from the other towns and camps appeared, the open plateau overlooking the Big Bend of the Carson River was going to be their headquarters.

Late in the afternoon, Captain Archie McDonald and the Virginia City companies appeared. The volunteers were tired after their long ride, and they straggled into camp, picketed their mounts, gathered next to the campfires of burning sagebrush and mesquite, and drank whiskey-spiked coffee. The dead were already buried and the men stood around the campfires and discussed what their next move should be as they waited for the volunteers from Silver City and Genoa.

But while the big talkers were in the majority and spoke in loud voices that carried throughout the cold night air, other men had their doubts and misgivings. For more than one of the minority the possibility of just cause gnawed at his reason. All through the long, sleepless night the question of pursuit or return became the major issue; for there was one inescapable fact that made pursuit a dubious proposition. The Indian raiding party had left a very plain trail[8]—too damned plain for comfort.

Charles Forman, who had come to California from Tioga County, New York, in 1853, had hardly arrived in Virginia City when he was called upon to troop off to fight the Paiutes. Twenty-five years old, newly hired for the Virginia City express office of Wells, Fargo and

Company, young Forman saw the makeshift army for what it was, and in later years wrote his account of the long night of decision on the wind-swept plateau overlooking the Big Bend of the Carson River.[9]

The hotheads were all for pursuit and battle, but Forman and others were not so sure. As the New Yorker realistically put it, "we were very poorly armed . . . very poorly mounted, had but few rifles in the whole company, and had but little ammunition and a small amount of provisions."[10] But worst of all, the Indian fighters were without "any organization or discipline in the command."[11]

Like young Forman, the United States District Judge for Carson County, Utah Territory, John Cradlebaugh of Carson City did not like what he saw at the camp of the excited whiskey-drinking defenders of white civilization. Judge Cradlebaugh had gathered men about him to come to the defense of the "threatened" communities of western Utah Territory. He had not volunteered to wage a general campaign against Indians who probably had a very good reason for their raid on Williams Station. After all, the Williams brothers had a reputation for shady dealings with both white emigrants and the neighboring Indians. Taking all this into consideration, along with the obvious fact that a general Indian uprising was not taking place, Judge Cradlebaugh decided that the need to pursue the Indians was totally without foundation. He advised his men of his thoughts, and suggested that each man make his own decision as to whether to continue with the others in what might well be a reckless and unjust war against the Indians.[12]

For most of the men who had traveled this far under Judge Cradlebaugh's leadership, the decision was very easy to make. Come morning, they would saddle their horses and make the long ride back to Carson City.

There were a few, however, who got caught up by the excitement, and they made the decision to join the volunteer army in its adventure in madness.

Far into the night the wrangling continued. The Indian haters held forth at great length. They brought out all the old atrocity stories they had learned as children, embellished the tales to fit the moment, played upon individual fears and prejudices, and replaced logic with a raw blend of terror, excitement, and heroism. The moment of glory was waiting for them come daybreak. Then, at sunrise, they would mount their horses, ride across country to a point where the Truckee River made its northward turn toward Pyramid Lake, follow the river to its mouth, and give the Indians a lesson right in their own backyard.

Men of sober thought argued against such hasty action, pleaded for an investigation of what had really happened, and suggested that it would be wise to talk to the Indians before jumping to any conclusions. Some even brought up the fact that Captain Lance Nightingill—a friend of Chief Numaga—had "offered to join the party if they would go with a flag of truce,"[13] so that he could talk to Chief Numaga about what had happened and have him turn the murderers over for a proper trial. But reason and realistic consideration of any possible facts had no place in the plateau camp. The shouters of hatred, the angry militants who had turned away from Captain Nightingill at Virginia City were not about to listen to this plea. They quickly pointed out that Captain Nightingill was not among the assembled force, then glanced at the blackened outline of the station and freshly turned mound of earth. All were highlighted by the wind-blown campfires. All were there to see. There was the hard and final answer to reason.

At this point in time, the men of violence became quiet, but their very presence cinched the outcome of the vote with the two bonds of fear and hate. The tally of pros and cons was no more than a mere formality. When it was over, it was easily apparent that "the large majority were strongly in favor of pursuit and it was decided to take the trail early next morning."[14]

Even at this late moment, some of the men suggested that if there was a possibility of a battle it would be wise to select a commander of the various companies. For while Major Ormsby had assumed a kind of leadership, the volunteers lacked a definite officer to give them directions. Charles Forman heard men speak of the need for appointing a leader for the whole army. As he later wrote, "nothing of the kind was done, and the command consisting of several independent companies, went into battle in that disorganized condition."[15]

3

Thus the long night passed on the lonely plateau. During the cold hours before dawn, the fires burned out; and in the gray light just before daybreak, only thin wisps of smoke curled skyward from a few last embers beneath the white ashes.

At daybreak the campfires were rekindled to heat some coffee, and it was then noticed that some of the horses were missing. Major Ormsby quickly ordered Forman and another young man to saddle up and try to find them.

The riders scouted down the Carson River without luck. Then they headed upstream again and found the straying animals feeding in one of the meadows alongside the river. But when they came back to camp with them, the only men left were the owners of the horses. Without so much as stopping to thank the young men who had found their mounts, "these men put their saddles on their horses and at once deserted"[16] them.

CHAPTER 10

Death on the Truckee

The trail that led from Williams Station toward the Big
Bend of the Truckee River was much too obvious, and
young Forman and his partner couldn't help but notice
that they were following a well-marked path. In the sagebrush and on the open stretches of sandy soil were scattered articles taken from the grog shop—articles that had
been carried for a distance, then tossed aside like trail
markers. In addition, there were tracks of unshod Indian
ponies, the deeper imprints of shod horses carrying riders
that had been made by the volunteers, and tracks "of a
large number of cattle and horses"[1] which the raiders
had driven off. It was easy to follow the path of the
Paiutes, far easier than it should have been.

Things were not happening in a normal pattern. The
trail was too easy to follow, the darkening sky and the
icy wind belonged to winter, not to spring. Then it began
to snow—lightly at first, but as the hours passed the sky
vanished, and the men hunched their shoulders and looked
for the disappearing trail as they rode into the whirling,
stinging clouds of wind-driven snowflakes.

By midafternoon of this Friday leftover from winter, this strange eleventh day of May, the two riders reached the great curve of the Truckee River where the mountain waters from Lake Tahoe and the run-off streams of the Sierra Nevada stopped an eastward journey and swung north toward Pyramid Lake. Here they caught up to the volunteer army.

The men had made camp in the shelter of the cotton-woods and willows near the river, picketed their horses in the sparse meadow, and built campfires. They huddled close to the flames and talked of their situation.

"My God," a man rubbing his hands would say, "who'd thought the damned weather . . . ?"

"In this crazy country," another would say, "anything might happen. Come sunup, she might be so warm that we'll wish it was snowing."

"That don't change one thing. We're mighty shy of goods."

"Hell, don't worry it too long. Major Ormsby sent men out to the settlers."

"You're figurin' the Paiutes didn't take care of them like they did at Williams?"

"They didn't bother Buckland."

"What the hell does that prove?"

The believer would try to convince himself and the others: "You know the Indians never did like the Williams boys. Hell, I think they just did *them* in. No more than that. The boys will bring back supplies. You just wait and see."

Hunkered down, his rump close to the sputtering fire, his coat pulled up high around his neck, the doubter had the last say: "Hell, friend, I ain't so sure that the boys Major Ormsby sent out will even come back. They just might hightail it right back to Virginia City."

1. Chief Numaga, great leader of the Pyramid Lake Paiutes ca. 1860's. *(Courtesy Nevada State Historical Society)*

2. Chief Numaga as he appeared in 1870, one year before
he died of TB. (*Courtesy Special Collection Department,
University of Nevada Library*)

3. Old Chief Winnemucca (Poito) dressed in a favorite military uniform. *(Courtesy Nevada State Historical Society)*

4. Chief Natchez, son of Chief Winnemucca and brother of Sarah. *(Courtesy Nevada State Historical Society)*

5. Captain Jim, greatest Washo chief, as a very old man.
(Courtesy Nevada State Historical Society)

6. Peter Lassen, pioneer trailblazer and close friend of the Paiutes. (*Courtesy The Bancroft Library, University of California*)

7. Brigadier General Frederick West Lander, engineer, wagon road surveyor, and peacemaker, as he looked at the beginning of the Civil War. (*Courtesy Nevada State Historical Society*)

8. Captain Joseph Stewart, commanding officer of The Carson Valley Expedition of 1860. (*Courtesy Nevada State Historical Society*)

9. Major William M. Ormsby, ill-fated leader of the Carson City Rangers. (*Courtesy Nevada State Historical Society*)

10. Warren Wasson of Genoa, friend of the Paiutes and their best Indian agent. *(Courtesy Nevada State Museum)*

11. The Needles, tufa outcroppings at the northwest end of Pyramid Lake. *(Collection of Philip S. Cowgill, Reno)*

12. Timothy O'Sullivan photo of the Big Bend of the Truckee River. The campers were members of the Clarence King Survey of the Fortieth Parallel. *(Courtesy The Bancroft Library, University of California)*

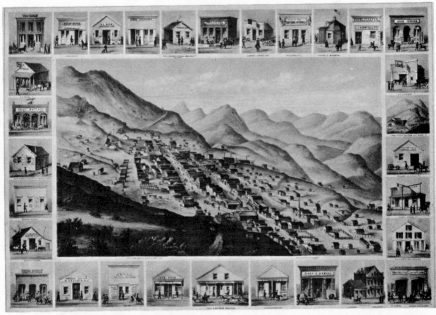

13. Virginia City, Nevada Territory, 1861, showing its tremendous growth since 1860. *(Courtesy The Bancroft Library, University of California)*

But the doubter was wrong. Before nightfall, the riders returned to camp. No, the Indians hadn't bothered any of the other settlers. Yes, they had some supplies in their saddlebags, and come morning, the settlers would bring plenty of provisions into camp.

Feeling relieved, the men tried to make themselves as comfortable as they could. But the wind was blowing harder by the hour, and there wasn't any letup in the storm. If anything, the snow was coming down faster as it turned the campsite into a winter scene. One thing was certain: it was going to be a long, cold night. And if it didn't break clear by morning, all the supplies in the territory wouldn't make a bit of difference. There would be one choice, and only one choice. They'd have to head on home and hope they didn't suffer from frostbite on the journey.

2

After a miserable night, the volunteers rolled out of their bedrolls to a clear, cold Saturday morning. During the night, the storm had covered the ground with three inches of snow. The men crowded close to the campfires, cursed the weather, and passed bottles of whiskey around as they waited for the coffee to get hot. While they ate what rations they did have, they peered beyond their camp, and watched the trail behind them for some sign of the settlers who had promised to bring supplies.

Many of the men grumbled about their situation. A few even suggested it might not be a bad idea to head on home. All the bravado was fast disappearing. It had been one thing to boast of what they were going to do to the Paiutes while they were in the comfort of saloons and other meeting places back at Virginia City and

Carson City. But who in hell had ever thought it would snow in the middle of May? Things were not working out as they had planned, and there simply was no way of getting around that fact. Now, to make matters even worse, there was no sign of the settlers with the provisions. The men grumbled, took another drink of whiskey, and crowded closer to the campfires.

While the command waited, Major Ormsby put William Marley in charge of a scouting party of five men—including Charles Forman. Their orders were to ride toward Pyramid Lake "to find where the Indians were lurking."[2] They mounted their horses, joked with their friends about good-looking Paiute women, then struck the high, open plateau on the eastern side of the Truckee River. Here the light snowfall had barely covered the well-worn Paiute trail leading to Pyramid Lake.

Long after the scouting party had become no more than small, moving shapes that blended into the distant configuration of the landscape, the settlers appeared at the camp with the needed supplies. Shortly after, the volunteers headed north from their last camp. It was almost noon, and the snow had melted. As the riders left the Big Bend of the Truckee River, "three men who were afraid of the Indians, and who were on foot, were left behind."[3]

The path along the narrow bench of the ridge that overlooked the river was muddy and slippery from the melting snow. It was very tough going for the horses as all of them were in poor condition.[4] During the long winter, the hay supply had run so short in town that the animals were given only enough to keep them alive. Then through April and into May the cold weather continued, and it delayed the start of spring grass except for a few sheltered pockets containing small meadows. Now, three days since the start of the journey, the gaunt and tired mounts grunted and groaned, and moved very slowly.

Mile after weary mile, the volunteer army traveled north toward Pyramid Lake. But they moved as though they were caught in a dream where all action was reduced to a minimum speed from a maximum effort. To the west, the riders saw the afternoon sun begin to descend toward the large, billowy thunderheads gathered above the glistening white peaks of the Sierra Nevada. Riding in single file in the deeply-rutted Paiute trail on the high and wide open plateau, the men looked at the meandering Truckee River far below. Then they stared ahead for some sign of their scouts. When they didn't see them, they feared the men had been ambushed somewhere up ahead—maybe in a hidden draw or just beyond the summit of the ridge they were climbing. But just as they were beginning to believe their own imagination, the front-riding scouts came into view.

The men rode directly to Major Ormsby, and he asked if they had seen any Indians ahead of the main command.

"No, there were no Indians."

Not satisfied, Major Ormsby inquired about sign. Were there fresh pony tracks in the damp ground? Had they seen anything at all that might indicate that the Paiutes were watching their advancing column?

"Yes, there were plenty of fresh pony tracks—make no mistake about that."

"Were they near the trail?"

"They were more than near it. Tracks, fresh tracks—on the trail, alongside it, and all over the damned hillside."

"Scouts?"

"We figure they've been watching every move we've made."

"But you saw no riders—not even a glimpse?"

"Nary a peek, Major. But we'll see them before too long. Pyramid Lake's not too far ahead."

The scouts had reported, but it didn't make the men breathe easier. These scattered pieces of information only jarred a man's confidence, and silent faces of worry hardly masked the stomach-churning fear the volunteers felt as they rode deeper and deeper into the country of the Paiutes.

Shortly after the scouts had returned, the plateau trail narrowed, and the volunteers slowly rode up a steep, sagebrush-covered slope that sliced through the plateau, then angled downward toward the river. Here, about ten miles south of the lake, Major Ormsby detailed a few men to serve as a rear guard at the pass if it became at all necessary to retreat.[5] The rest of the army began the downward trek toward the wider part of the river gorge where the sagebrush formed a ragged fringe on the outskirts of the meadowland.

As the volunteers neared the bottomland, they were within three to five miles from Pyramid Lake. The riders could see open meadows on both sides of the river, and "a belt of large cottonwood trees with underbrush among them, skirting the stream for the entire distance."[6]

Once again, Major Ormsby sent the scouting party ahead of the main command. This time, the outriders saw two mounted Paiutes. They quickly rode back and reported this, and Ormsby promptly ordered them to try to capture the Indians. William Marley and his scouts turned their horses and headed back. They picked up the trail of the Paiutes and followed them for two miles in the direction of the lake. But before they managed to overtake them, they quite suddenly came upon a party of warriors, who immediately charged after them. Realizing that they were badly outnumbered, Marley shouted for his men to retreat. Spurring their tired horses into a gallop, they raced back to the main command, which was "then some five hundred feet above the river, with that and the lake both in sight."[7]

As they neared their command, the scouts looked back, but the pursuing warriors were no longer in sight. Marley blurted out what had happened, and Major Ormsby, without the slightest hesitation, gave the signal for the command to prepare for action and to continue their advance toward the lowland.

Watching ahead for some sign of Indians, the volunteers became very quiet. No longer did they complain about the chilling wind of late afternoon, and no longer were saddlesore riders cursing the rough, slippery trail. Other than the moaning of wind and the distant rush of the fast-flowing Truckee River, the only sounds the men heard were made by the movements of their tired horses —the squeaking of shifting saddles, horses grunting and groaning, and passing of air; and horseshoes striking loose rocks as the animals stumbled on the downward trail.

When they reached the flatland of the river valley, there were no Paiutes in sight. The volunteers stared at the country around them. It was easily apparent that the meadow they were now in was a pocket that would be difficult to escape. To the west, they could see the worn, cliff-like bluff bordering the wide curve of the river. To their southeast, they could look back and see the steep trail they had just descended. To the south, they could see that the high water of the river rushed through a narrow canyon. While to the north, the riders saw that the valley widened out where the river entered Pyramid Lake. One thing was certain to everyone. If they were ever going to turn back, now was the time.

But they hadn't come this far to give up the pursuit. Major Ormsby looked at his men and gave the signal to advance north toward Pyramid Lake and the Paiute camp. And though the men felt their stomachs knot up, though their mouths were dry, their armpits cold and clammy, and their anal openings wet and moving, they masked their fears by assuring each other that they were about to give the red devils pure hell. With all their self-righteousness fully intact and untainted the 105 men and boys rode forward like crusaders prepared to teach the heathens a complete and fatal lesson in the ethics of Christian justice.

3

War Chief Numaga—his long hair swinging back and forth across his broad shoulders—watched over the main force of his warriors and kept them mounted but out of sight. The behavior of the whites reminded him of antelopes, and he knew that he was pulling them his way in much the same manner as a Paiute antelope hunt. Curiosity was the bait, and they had not been able to resist it.

The whites had seen two of his men, followed them, fell back when more warriors gave chase; but they had not been able to resist their own feelings. Now he had more than the scouts. The whole force was moving deeper and deeper into the trap he had so carefully planned. And he knew every move they made and where they were from moment to moment by the cries of sea gulls and pelicans —cries made by his carefully placed observers, who were high on the ridge and belly-flat in the sagebrush.

The invaders were now passing through the wide meadow. They were riding by the river bend, where the cottonwoods shimmered in the afternoon breeze, and where the thick underbrush in an ancient riverbed hid Chief Sequinata[8]—that small, wiry man who had the courage and strength of a cornered badger—and his wild and tough band of fighters from the barren country of Black Rocks.

Now the moments were passing like the blurr of a frightened quail's flight. Numaga glanced at the sky, and he saw that the sun was beginning to drop behind the tall western mountains and shadows were already flowing across the land like grounded storm clouds. He could hear the movement of the white army as it rode closer and closer to the final stretch of the river before it flowed across the wide sandbar and became part of the great desert lake. He looked, once more, at his main striking force, and he knew his warriors were ready for what had to be done. They were hunched forward on their ponies, and their arms were outstretched as their hands pinched the nostrils of their mounts to keep them from neighing at the approaching ponies of the whites. Some of his men carried the new rifles they had gotten from trading with the whites or that had been given to them by the Bannocks. Others had their best hunting bows, and they carried a full quiver of arrows. A few of the warriors had both weapons.

The silent warriors gave no sign of feeling the cold. War Chief Numaga lightly grasped his smooth and worn combination pipe and battle-ax to be ready for his signals. He could see the tense muscles of his men as the late afternoon sun highlighted them. Like early morning pelicans slowly flapping over the great lake in search of careless fish, the Paiute warriors were also ready and waiting for the exact moment to enact their role in this dance of life and death.

But the mounted men waiting near Chief Numaga were

only the second part of his well-designed trap. Numaga
had already told them what they were to do: they would
show themselves, act as decoys just out of rifle range, and
pull the white army up from the bottomland. The tired
and weary ponies of the whites would have to climb upward once again. They would have to struggle for footing
against the slippery, loose soil of the long slope—the slope
that began high on the steep ridge and slanted gradually
downward to the head of the big meadow that bordered
the last stretch of the river. Yet Numaga had made it
quite clear to his warriors that they were not to remain
on the ridge, and not to fire at the whites. They were the
bait to draw the whites upward again, to tire out their
ponies that much more. When this had been done, when
the whites had grasped at the bait, the warriors were to
ride their ponies into a draw and stay out of sight until
they heard the sounds of battle.

Another band of mounted warriors was located high
above on the ridge to the south. They formed the third
part of Numaga's trap, and were to remain out of sight
until the whites had started after him. Then they were to
show themselves, and form a wide flanking semicircle to
cut into the line of retreat. When they received his signal,
they were to tighten their curve around the southern end
of the trap.

Finally, there was the fourth part of the trap. To make
sure it was all ready, Numaga stared at the sagebrush on
the ridge that the whites were to be coaxed into coming
up. All was as it should be. He was certain the whites
would not see the warriors he had on the ground. All
along the path up the slope they would have to take if
they followed his decoy, he had placed warriors behind
the sagebrush. Then he looked toward the last stretch of
upraised land that bordered the bottomland and the

Truckee River right up to the point where the land flattened out to form the big meadow and the beginning of the lake. Here was the mouth of his trap, and here behind the sagebrush on the higher ground he had placed more warriors. He looked at where his men were positioned, and he saw that they could not be seen. All four parts of his trap were ready, and he could tell from the sounds of the moving white army and from the bird cries of his scouts that the battle was about to begin.

For an instant Numaga turned and glanced back at the vast desert lake that was almost red in the light of the dying sun. Then he looked at the mounted men crouched over their ponies. He nodded to them, nudged his heels into his pony's flanks, and rode toward the crest of the open slope. His warriors moved in unison with him to form a broad line of riders that would stand out on the skyline and be very easy for the invaders to see. All the waiting was over. The first movement of a deadly plan had started.

4

The army of volunteers was near the opening to the big meadow. Ahead they could see the vast reaches of Pyramid Lake. The island of pelicans stood out, and near it was the great pyramid-shaped rock that gave the lake its name. But far to the north end of the lake the riders saw the fading light of afternoon reflecting off sharp, wind-shaped rocks—rocks that stood like giant-sized needles, or like the petrified horns of some monster that had died in the youth of this endless desert. To the miners and townsmen from the raw settlements of the Comstock Lode and Carson Valley, none of this strange country looked quite real. It gave them a feeling of having suddenly discovered an untouched and alien world.

Yet even as they stared at the desert lake, their horses walked slowly along until they were almost past a low ridge to their right—a long, sandy slope that cut downward from the plateau and terminated at the entrance to the big meadow that reached to the mouth of the Truckee River and the beginning of the lake. At this point, the riders looked upward and to their right.

Lined out across the ridge, almost a half a mile away, the men saw more than a hundred mounted warriors. But there was no sign of immediate attack. The Paiutes were not raising their weapons, and except for one man on a black horse who rode up and down in front of the line as though he were their chief, there was no movement. The Paiutes were simply holding their position and watching every movement of the volunteers.

The men watched the chief on the black horse as he rode back and forth. While they were not certain, some of them said that he carried a large battle-ax in one hand; others said that it was not a battle-ax but a white flag. Whatever, he kept motioning with it as though he were going to signal an attack.

A. K. Elliott, who had come from Clear Lake, California, to seek his fortune in the rich Comstock Lode, had a telescopic rifle that he carried across the pommel of his saddle. As a member of Virginia City Company No. 1, he obeyed Captain Archie McDonald's order to use his telescope to find out what the man on the black horse carried in his hand.

When Elliott had finished looking through his telescopic sight, he lowered his rifle. Captain McDonald immediately asked him what the object in the Paiute's hand looked like, and Elliott replied that as near as he could tell it was more like a battle-ax than a white flag.

This was enough for Captain McDonald. To him, it was obvious the Paiutes were up to no good. Again, he spoke to Elliott. This time, he ordered him "to fire at the chief holding the battle-ax."[9]

As the report of the shot echoed off the desert hills, the chief turned his horse and quickly joined the main body of his warriors. Numaga signaled, and without hesitation they advanced forward until they were right on the brow of the hill. "They jumped off their horses, who stood perfectly still, apparently well trained for an engagement, and instantly after they fired."[10]

All the calmness, all the whiskey bravery that had been with the men from the moment they had decided to ride out and teach the Indians a lesson was quickly disappearing behind faces of fear. Major Ormsby tried to rally the army, and shouted to Captain McDonald.

"Let's charge them!"

Captain McDonald, however, was no longer in any mood for heroic action. He shook his head and told Ormsby it made more sense to retreat to the grove of cottonwoods. There, at least, "they would be protected on one side by the river and an open plain on the other."[11]

The Paiutes on the brow of the hill yelled and kept on shooting. Something had to be done in a hurry. Major Ormsby sat stiffly in his saddle, glanced at the confused army, and shouted the command to charge. Then he spurred his tired horse and started up the slope. No more than thirty or forty men followed after him, and as Charles Forman later wrote: ". . . our horses were poor and many of them could not get up the slope, while many of them became unmanageable and broke back to the timber along the river."[12]

The men who had charged up the slope found the going slow and tough. Their weary horses struggled for footing in the damp, sandy soil. Then as they were almost at the crest of the ridge, the line of horsemen vanished. The volunteers rode forward, and crossed the ridge, but the Paiutes were gone. At this moment, volley after volley of rifle fire came at them from all sides as warriors who were on foot or who were hiding in the sagebrush opened fire.

Terrified and not knowing what to expect next, the white army's frightened horses "became so unmanageable that they bucked the revolvers of their riders' holsters, and forced them to drop their guns."[13] While none of the men were wounded, many of the horses screamed as they were hit. Men were yelling and trying to control the animals, and at the same time they tried to find an enemy to shoot at. But the warriors were well hidden in the sagebrush, and in the light of late afternoon they were all but impossible to see. The brave army of miners had ridden into a deadly ambush, and their only hope was to go back to the bottomland.

To add to their confusion, some of the men looked to the southeast. There they saw another line of Paiutes on horseback, and these warriors were forming a half circle —a half circle that was quickly closing off the plateau trail the men had followed on their journey to Pyramid Lake. There wasn't much doubt about what was taking place, and all the men knew it. Not by choice, but through a clever plan "they had charged through an open gate into an Indian corral."[14]

Seeing the danger of their position, Major Ormsby shouted for his troops to fall back! *Fall back and regroup!* became the only cry of hope. But the terrified volunteers could not maintain any semblance of order. What was to be an orderly retreat back down the slope immediately became chaos. Without concern for anyone else, most of the men forced their tired and frightened horses into a stumbling, downhill gallop. The retreat had become a rout, and the men fled by the gauntlet of Paiute foot soldiers who seemed to spring up from behind each clump of sagebrush, each depression in the contour of the land, and each boulder that was large enough to hide a jack-rabbit.

The uphill charge, and short, furious fight had not taken more than thirty minutes. But the nature of the battle was already determined. What had started out as an offensive thrust was now a wild dash of panic-stricken men who hoped they could find shelter for defense against the enemy. With Major Ormsby yelling for the men to retreat in order, the defeated whites struck out for the grove of cottonwoods bordering the river.

About three hundred yards short of the cottonwoods, the riders came to a deep gulch. This was chosen as the place to make a stand, for the depth of the water-worn slash in the ground offered shelter for both the men and their horses.

Orders were given to dismount and prepare for action. But the men were hardly on the ground before the Paiutes who had followed them down the slope began to attack. The men returned their fire, and for about ten minutes they were able to keep them at a distance. Even so, the odds were not with them, for most of the volunteers had either pistols or shotguns, while the Paiutes kept up a steady and accurate fire from rifles and muskets that reached farther than the weapons of the whites.

Major Ormsby had already been wounded, but he kept on shouting commands and tried to rally his men. Many of them were already looking toward the cottonwoods, where Henry Meredith had left his horse, and they were getting ready to run to the cover of the timber when shots began to come from that direction.

Like all the others, Charles Forman was stunned by this sudden turn of events. For as far as he could tell, the line of cottonwoods and the nearby brush were alive with warriors. These well-hidden men kept up a steady pattern of rifle fire, and some even sent arrows whirring into the gulch that had now become a trap. Then to Forman's horror, he saw Henry Meredith climb out of the gulch and start on a dead run for the timber to get his horse.

Expecting to see Meredith drop at any second, Forman was amazed to see him reach the line of timber without being hit. The young attorney ran directly to where he had left his untied horse, for as he had told Forman: "Don't tie your horse; we may want them again pretty soon."[15] But now his horse was tied to a cottonwood tree, and "before he could get it loose the Indians shot him from behind with a rifle."[16]

By now, there were Paiutes coming from every direction. Some were on foot; some were charging the gulch on horseback, and others were riding to the southeast and the northwest as they closed off all routes of escape. The main command broke again, and they left what protection the gulch offered and headed for the river as hard-riding warriors charged from the front, and the Paiutes in the cottonwoods began to move forward.

Major Ormsby continued to shout at the men as he desperately tried to rally them to make a stand in the shelter of the gulch. Forman ran to him and to others and asked for help to try to rescue Henry Meredith. But most of the volunteers would have no part of it. They had only one thing in mind, and that was to get out of this place alive. Yet Major Ormsby and four or five others agreed to help Forman save the young lawyer from Grass Valley, California. But, at best, their efforts were doomed to be nothing other than a valiant attempt. For warriors were coming out of the grove of cottonwoods, firing as they ran; and they were joined by even more Paiutes, who had been hiding in the thick brush of the old riverbed. There was a steady stream of them, and they were yelling, firing rifles, and using short bows with deadly accuracy.

As Forman and the rescuers tried to run against the charging warriors, a whirring arrow passed close by, and it struck someone with a solid thump. Forman turned, and to his horror he saw that Major Ormsby "was hit in the mouth by an arrow."[17] Ormsby pushed the arrowhead out of his open mouth, and then in a fast move he jerked the shaft through his cheek, and the blood spurted out and sprayed his shoulder and side. Despite his condition, Ormsby tried to make sure that his men had a chance to escape. He turned his command over to another of the volunteers, and told him "to see if they could not cut their way through and get away."[18]

But no man could order the terrified men of the once brave army. Escape was their one and only thought. Yet they were incapable of truly considering what their best chance might be. As the Paiutes closed in from all sides, as the yelling and shouting seemed to be the only sounds left on the earth, and as men and horses cried out in pain as bullets and arrows struck home, the volunteers mounted whatever horse or mule was near and headed out of the gulch for the Truckee River.

5

War Chief Numaga saw all of his plan working perfectly. Still, he did not like the idea of slaughtering the trapped and frightened whites. All of it was too much like clubbing terrified rabbits that had run ahead of brush beaters only to become entangled in the carefully placed curve of the long net, where old men and boys quickly clubbed them to death.

Riding his black pony at a full gallop, Chief Numaga circled around the southeast side of the trapped whites, and headed for the line of cottonwoods and Chief Sequinata's band. Other warriors followed after Numaga, and they joined the Black Rock Paiutes as they moved out of the brush and timber and headed after the fleeing whites. Yelling and shooting as they rode and ran, the warriors closed in on the trapped men, who were desperately trying to make a break for the river.

The whites were defeated, and Numaga knew it. All that could come now would be a senseless slaughter as the trapped men became hated animals who were no longer human to the enraged warriors but only creatures doomed to see their blood run out to soak the land. This was not a good thing, and it would haunt the warriors who did it. There were whites that Numaga knew and liked. Men such as Major Ormsby, who had even taken Chief Winnemucca's daughters into his home so that they might learn the ways of the whites. To kill this man when there was no need would serve no purpose other than blind hatred. Realizing all of this, Numaga urged his pony forward and rode between Sequinata's yelling braves and the whites who were trying to escape.

Waving back his own warriors and shouting for the others to stop, War Chief Numaga attempted to halt the frenzied charge. But Chief Sequinata "refused to obey the order."[19] Followed by his yelling braves, who were riding their ponies and shooting at the trapped men at the same time, the tough little chief galloped right by Numaga and started after the retreating whites, who were now heading northwest toward the river.

The whites rode their ponies and others ran on foot. Numaga heard men scream as they were hit with bullets or arrows, and he saw them head right back into the mouth of his trap. As they neared the river, they had to pass within easy rifle and arrow range of a stretch of high ground where Numaga had placed some of his best marksmen. One of the fleeing whites tumbled to the ground as his horse was shot out from under him, and Numaga saw him jump to his feet and try to make a fight of it. He fired one shot that wounded a warrior's knee. Then as he turned to fire again, he was "riddled with arrows and bullets."[20] Some of the whites got beyond the steady fire of the Paiutes in the higher ground, but directly in front of them were the mounted warriors that Numaga had carefully positioned to hold off any attempt to ride north into the big meadow at the head of the lake.

Now, as the warriors closed in from all three sides, the cornered whites hit and kicked their ponies in the direction of the river. Numaga shook his head as he watched them force their mounts into the icy, swift water. It was not possible, and he knew it. There was no way that they could get across. At this point, at this season the river was much too high and fast.

Kicking their ponies, shouting and cursing, some of the whites got into the deeper water away from shore. Numaga saw the ponies fight the current as they tried to keep their heads above the water, but the swift-moving river was too much for them. Ponies and riders were swept back to shore like fallen trees riding the waves. On the banks of the river, excited warriors waited to strike.

But the frantic whites were not through. Even though

they were surrounded and fired at in a steady hail of bullets and arrows, and it did not seem possible for them to escape, Numaga watched the trapped men follow the orders of a tall white man. Fighting almost hand to hand, they managed to break through the warriors and go up-stream to the shelter of the cottonwoods.

Chief Sequinata followed right after the white man who rode at the rear of the others. But as Sequinata neared him, Numaga saw the tall man turn and face the rugged little chief; and it was then that he saw the white man had no bullets left, that he was holding his pistol by the barrel to use as a club. Then like an enraged and wounded bear the tall man yelled, spurred his pony, and charged after Sequinata. The chief from the country of Black Rocks appeared to be startled by this action, and he turned and rode back toward his men with the other man following close behind as though there were only the two of them left in the land. It was an act of great bravery, but it was a moment of fearful madness. This tall man, this man Numaga would always remember as the White Brave,[21] was riding to his death. And death struck him quickly as he chased Chief Sequinata through the line of warriors and finally fell to the ground as bullet after bullet and arrow after arrow struck his body.

What he had feared the most was happening, and Numaga felt sick as he saw the battle become a slaughter—a rabbit drive in which men, not rabbits, were trapped by a net of warriors and killed.

6

Their backs to the Truckee River, and with Paiutes firing at them from the other three directions, the desper-ate miners tried to make a stand in the cottonwood grove.

But even with some protection from the white-barked trees, there was no real chance to hold out, and Major Ormsby knew it. They were running out of ammunition. They were badly outnumbered, and the warriors were cutting off their path to the steep, narrow trail from the bottomland to the plateau.

Weak as he was from loss of blood, Major Ormsby realized that the opening to the trail heading upward was their only chance for escape, and the Paiutes had to be stopped from cutting it off completely. Above the yelling and wild cries, the snorting and frightened neighing of the horses, the moaning of the wounded, and the roar of the fast-moving river water, Major Ormsby shouted to Thomas F. Condon of the Genoa Rangers and Richard Watkins of the Carson City Rangers to take some men and hold the opening to the trail.

Using the cottonwoods for cover, Condon and Watkins led their small squad to the narrowest point between them and the start of the upland trail across the meadow. Then spurring their horses into a gallop, they broke into the open. At first, the startled warriors did not react, but the men had covered no more than a quarter of the distance when they became the central target for every rifle and bow within shooting range. Yet they managed to reach the beginning of the trail without being hit, but here Condon and Watkins were "deserted by nearly all of their men,"[22] who fled up the steep grade toward the plateau.

Shouting for Watkins to head up the trail and cover the pass for the retreat, Condon then turned his horse and rode back across the open meadow. His luck held once again, and he reached the cottonwoods without being hit. Here he quickly told the weakening Ormsby what had happened to his squad, and made it clear that warriors were rapidly closing in on the trail.

By now, steady firing from Paiute marksmen on the high ground sent bullets whistling into the cottonwoods. Then some of the men yelled that warriors were crawling through the underbrush of the old riverbed!

Terror showed in the faces of the men. All the old stories—the stories they had heard from the time they were children—took shape in their minds. They were going to be killed by Indians! And if they were captured—that was the real horror, the worst fate of all! And the vision of what their last moments would be like, the wild imagination of painful torture for hour after hour until the body could stand no more was reflected in the glazed eyes and the stark white faces suddenly drained of color.

Then for a moment the men got hold of themselves as the warriors bounded out of the underbrush and charged into the grove of trees. Fighting for their lives, the volunteers held together in a short hand-to-hand encounter. But as hundreds of warriors closed in, as they shouted their war cries and raised their weapons, the whites jumped on any horse or mule left alive, or they dropped their guns and began to run wildly across the open meadow in a desperate effort to reach the trail to the plateau.

As they ran for their lives across the bottomland, the fleeing men heard the cries of the pursuing braves, the whirring arrows, the sound of rifle shots echoing and re-echoing in the stillness of the darkening day, and the gasp or choked-off scream of a wounded or slain comrade. As they reached the beginning of the upward trail, both riders and runners found that the narrow and steep path that they had come down in single-file order required the same slow method for their climb away from the meadow of death.

Paiutes fired round after round from their cover in the sagebrush on the slope, and from the rear warriors came yelling as they closed in for the final blow. Some of the retreating army started upward, desperately trying to stay alive. Just behind them, the men jammed up at the foot of the trail fought a brutal battle with pursuing waves of warriors. In this furious struggle death played no favorites.

> One horse, with a fatal wound, dashed away to the west, and carried its rider to his death in the timber by the river bank. Two men passing to the right in climbing the heights by a more gradual ascent, went rolling with their horses fatally shot down the bank among the enemies. Young Snowden, as he reached the summit, fell from his horse and expired. A few rods farther on, just a little way to the south and west of the trail, another man threw up his hands with a despairing look, and laid down with his face to the ground and died.[23]

Trying to get the men out of this terrible trap, already bleeding from two wounds, Major Ormsby was hit by two more shots that sent him reeling. Yet somehow he managed to climb aboard a mule and start up the trail as the well-hidden warriors in the sagebrush continued to send a hissing and withering shower of bullets and arrows.

Riding for their lives, Major Ormsby and many of his men reached the open plateau. Behind them on the battlefield were the bodies of many of their friends. But the routed volunteers were not out of danger. Ahead of them was the long retreat on tired and even wounded horses and mules—a retreat that would be a running battle against the victorious Paiutes, who were riding fresh mounts.

As they rode across the plateau toward the Big Bend of the Truckee River, the fleeing volunteers became easy victims if the warriors caught up to them. Much like a rabbit caught in the open, any man whose tired horse dropped back did not have a chance. The Paiutes would yell wildly when they drew near to a white who had fallen behind. Then when they were almost upon him, there would be a shot or snap of a bowstring, and another volunteer would gasp or cry out one last time as he fell to the trail. But this became too easy for the excited warriors, and they developed a more personal touch of death for the doomed men.

A hard-riding warrior would draw right alongside his terrified victim, reach out and grab him by the neck, give a quick jerk and pull him out of his saddle, and let him tumble to the ground. Then while the man was stunned from his fall, the warrior would slide his pony to a halt, jump off, and quickly kill the man with a rifle shot or a deep thrust of an obsidian knife.

Mile after bloody mile this deadly game continued. At one point, where the trail ran along the brink of a high cliff overlooking the river, an excited warrior jumped off his horse to examine or add yet another blow to a fallen white who appeared to be already dead. But "the corpse suddenly brought a revolver to bear and fired."[24] What followed was a nightmare scene from any struggle in any of mankind's wars throughout history. Accepting his own death as inevitable, smelling its very presence, the fallen soldier tried to take one of the enemy with him. Grabbing the warrior and holding him tightly, the white man pulled him toward the edge of the cliff in a frantic dance of death—a mad moment when the final steps would send both men plunging into space to smack against the boulders, to plunge into the swirling water and drift lifelessly with the current. But the ultimate design was stopped by other warriors, who came to their friend's aid, and after they had killed the frenzied member of the retreating army, they rolled his body across the last few yards of sagebrush and shoved it off the cliff.[25]

The going became more and more difficult for the routed army. Not only were their horses and mules worn out, but also the nature of the trail played its role in slowing up the tired mounts. For while they were on a plateau, the trail was not completely level. It was slashed by draws and deep ravines that were slippery from run-off water flowing toward the Truckee River. As the miles passed, the line of retreat became widely separated, and this prevented any chance of the whites bunching together for a defensive and orderly withdrawal.

But the weakening Major Ormsby had not yet given up. For about eight or nine miles south of Pyramid Lake there was a position where he hoped to make a last stand. Here where the mountain and the east bank of the river are very close, the trail from the lake dropped downward to a half-mile stretch of bottomland, crossed that, then headed upward again to a narrow pass leading to the plateau. At this crucial point, Major Ormsby had thought ahead while the army was on its way to Pyramid Lake. Here he had detailed six men under the command of C. T. Lake. Their instructions had been quite explicit: In the event of a retreat, hold the pass so that men can escape.

The position was very well chosen. From the heights a small group of determined men would be ideally situated to hold back a much larger force. And now, bleeding from his wounds in both arms and one cheek, Major

Ormsby forced himself and his wounded mule across the bottomland and up the trail toward the last place for any kind of defense, and the last hope for survival.

As the light-headed Ormsby and the other men neared the pass, they could hear hoofbeats and war cries close behind. But the narrow passage was in view, and soon the rifles of the men stationed there would bring the Paiute charge to a halt. The fleeing riders strained their eyes to see the men who would be covering their escape, but in the gray light of the passing day they could not see anyone. Then as the first men reached the pass and bunched up to go single file through it, the terrible truth of desertion was all that met their frantic search, while to the rear, they heard the wild yells of the warriors and the dying screams of comrades who had just started their climb toward the protection of the missing rear guard.

7

War Chief Numaga let his black pony go as fast as it could up the steep hill toward the pass. He passed by whites and Paiutes who were locked in a vicious fight for life. When he got to the narrow crossing, a scene of bloody chaos greeted him.

Many of the white men had thrown away their guns. Some were running across the open plateau, crying aloud like lost children; and Numaga saw his warriors gallop alongside them, then quickly fell them with one shot. Other members of the defeated white army stayed on their mounts, and they rode among the warriors.

"Please, please, don't kill me!" they cried.

The warriors laughed at such behavior from men, and in a wild frenzy of killing, they rode among them. The sound of rifle shots and whirring arrows intermingled with screams and cries for mercy, and the laughter of warriors who were too wild with the taste of battle to stop their orgy of slaying.

Sickened by what he saw and heard, Chief Numaga shouted for his warriors to stop this senseless slaughter. But it was too late. There was no chance to halt this violent outbreak of hate—hate that had been held back for year after year, season after season as the whites had taken Paiute land, Paiute women, and Paiute lives.

In the midst of this carnage, Chief Numaga saw the man he sought. Still astride his wounded and dying mule, Major Ormsby was being defended by a one-legged man[26]—a man who was strapped to his horse. Above the noise of the shooting and screaming, Chief Numaga heard this one-legged man shout to other whites as he tried to gather them together for a final fight. But none of the men listened to him. Instead, they turned their mounts and rode away like frightened deer caught in the open by a clever hunter.

Then Chief Numaga saw some of his warriors moving toward Major Ormsby at a rapid pace. Seeing this and not wanting this white man killed—this man he had known, this man he had talked to many times in the seasons before the madness of digging in the earth for money had come to the land—Numaga lashed his black pony and felt the powerful animal lunge forward and break into a full gallop.

Passing by his warriors, he neared Ormsby. As he did, he saw the one-legged man and a younger one talking to him. Both were trying to help him, but the bleeding leader of the whites sent them away.

Then as the two men rode on, Major Ormsby followed behind them for a short distance until he reached a small valley alongside the river. By now, it was almost dark,

and Chief Numaga heard his warriors coming right behind him. Yet it looked as though the wounded white
man would manage to escape without his aid. Ormsby
crossed the valley, started up a short grade leading out
of it, and was "half-way up the trail when his saddle
turned, throwing him upon the ground."[27]

Chief Numaga's warriors yelled with excitement when
they saw Ormsby fall, and their ponies drew closer to
the chief's as they started up the hill. Again, Numaga
lashed his pony as he tried to get to his white friend
first. Then he saw Ormsby get up and walk toward the
top of the grade, and it appeared that he might get
away or manage to hide somewhere on the other side.
But suddenly, he turned around and started back down
the hill, coming right toward him and the charging warriors, who were yelling wildly as they closed in for the
kill.

Stumbling, almost falling, Ormsby walked down the
trail. Numaga watched him wave his hands in the air in a
gesture of greeting as though they were meeting for a
smoke and a friendly talk. But close behind, Numaga
heard his warriors getting ready to fire at the stumbling
man. He had to get to him before they did. He kicked his
pony in the flanks, leaned forward, and felt the animal
lunge ahead in a plunge that carried him almost on top
of the white man.

"Don't kill me!" Major Ormsby said. "Don't kill me!"[28]

The pale, bleeding man was almost dead already, and
Chief Numaga could see it. There was one possible chance,
and only one to save him. Raising his bow, Numaga
notched an arrow and took aim. He saw tears streaming
down Ormsby's face as the man stared in disbelief. Then
Numaga said, "Drop down as if dead when I shoot, and
I will fire over you."[29]

But Major Ormsby did not move. He stood and stared vacantly. In that moment, a warrior dashed by Chief Numaga with his bow ready to shoot. Numaga shouted for him to stop, but the brave never swerved his pony. In a sudden swish of death, he shot Major Ormsby in the stomach and then fired another arrow into his face. The triumphant warrior then jumped off his pony, and Numaga turned away as he saw him shove his white friend's body off the ridge and let it roll down the side-hill and into the bottom of the ravine.

8

Just beyond the unguarded pass, N. A. Chandler[30] ran along the trail. His horse had been shot out from under him during the bloody retreat, and he had seen Major Ormsby head back down the hill toward the Paiutes. Now, as darkness began to cover the land, he tried to find a hiding place before the pursuing warriors caught up to him. But hearing their horses and their wild yells, he knew that they were almost on him. He looked around for some last chance to escape and saw a steep cliff over-looking the Truckee River. Running to the cliff, he threw away his gun belt and pistol; and without a moment's hesitation jumped over the cliff feet first and landed in the water just offshore from a sandy beach. As soon as he surfaced, he swam ashore and hid in a thicket of willows.

Chandler waited until he saw the warriors look over the cliff, turn their mounts and ride away. When he felt it was safe, he continued his escape toward the Big Bend of the Truckee River.

Others were not as lucky as Chandler in those last moments before darkness turned any clump of sagebrush into a hiding place. A teenage boy, a nameless boy to the volunteers, put up a desperate fight at the top of the pass against two warriors. But he was no match for their experience and strength, and he died nameless and unknown almost at the start of the trail to Pyramid Lake.

McCarthy and McCloud were two of the last to fall before nightfall stopped the slaying of the fleeing men. These volunteers fought so hard for their lives that when the warriors killed them, they paid them honor by dancing around their bodies. For when the corpses were found, there was a beaten footpath circling them. But McCloud, who was a tall, rangy man, had received the highest of tributes from the Paiutes for his bravery. After he was dead, the warriors "had cut him along the spine, from his neck down, and taken out the spinal sinews . . . for bowstrings."[31]

Man after man paid the full measure for the attack on War Chief Numaga and the Paiutes. Only the darkness of night prevented the death of all the retreating men. The dropping of the sun behind the sharp and darkening peaks of the Sierra Nevada gave the rest of the panic-stricken and routed volunteers the needed cover to escape.

Men crowded into hiding places among the willows and cottonwoods alongside the Big Bend of the Truckee River. There they waited minute after minute, hour after hour. They listened for all sounds, for anything that might indicate that the Paiutes were still searching for them. They breathed quietly. They heard the pounding of their own hearts, and carried a flashing series of final moments in their minds—moments in which they had a caught a fleeting glimpse of a friend, of a drinking companion, of a man they had met for the first time on this expedition of revenge; but it was a thing of the memory, a horrible nightmare of blood and soundless screams, of the last sound of life, and the look and smell of death. It had been a long day for dying, and there was no certainty that the day had ended. So the men kept to their hiding places. They crouched low like hunted game, listened for all sounds, and shivered with cold and fear as the night and their lives grew older together.

By midnight the men heard no more movements from their deadly searchers. They waited a while longer, then they ventured out of their hiding places. One by one, two by two, or three together, they stretched their sore, weary, and in some cases wounded bodies, and eased their way toward Buckland's Station.

All that night the frightened men wandered through the desert. They were in shock. They were hungry. They were tired and wary, and they hoped they were headed in the right direction. But not all the men moved out of their hiding places that night. Some waited until daybreak, and when they were absolutely certain there were no Paiutes waiting for them, they came into the open and struck out for the Carson River and Buckland's Station behind the men who had left during the night.

The badly beaten and frightened survivors of the army of vengeance straggled homeward. Behind them was the perfect trap that had taken the lives of seventy of their friends and companions. Ahead of them was a place to rest, a place to eat, a place to tell of their terrible ordeal in the desert, and a place to send the first terrifying news by telegraph of their defeat and death along the Truckee River.

CHAPTER 11

The Taste of Fear

The story of defeat and death on the Truckee River
reached Virginia City early in the morning of May 13,
1860–the day after the battle. The horseman who carried
the news of this terrible disaster was none other than
C. T. Lake–the same volunteer who had deserted his
post at the narrow pass that had been selected to serve as
a key position in case of retreat.

While he had never been near the actual battle, C. T.
Lake did not let that interfere with his own report of
what had taken place. As worried citizens gathered around
him, Lake told a vivid tale of valor and death against
fantastic odds. A local newspaper reporter jotted down
this "firsthand" account, quickly got it ready for press,
and by 10:45 A.M. the first news had become public.

How many Indians were there? ". . . judged to be two
thousand strong. . . ."[1]

What happened? "Major Ormsby gave orders to
charge."[2]

And then? "The Indians then filed to the right and left,
surrounding the troops, firing occasionally."[3]

But our troops? What happened to our troops? "The ammunition of the forces soon became exhausted, and the Indians on seeing this closed in and poured volley after volley upon them."[4]

But Lake did not stop here. He had the attention of his audience, and he gave them a full account. That is, he told them everything but the answer to two major questions that nobody seemed to ask: namely, where was he when all the fighting took place, and how did he and his six comrades manage to get back to Virginia City before any other survivors? Still, Lake had been at the scene of the battle, and the excited crowd gasped, then cursed in anger, when he told them that Major Ormsby was shot and that most of the white army was "dead upon the field."[5]

Dead? Most of the men are dead?

To this question, to this worst of all questions, Lake gave but faint hope when he told them that some of the men had crossed the river and escaped. As for the others, no real hope was offered; for neither Lake nor his six companions had seen any of the retreating men come through the narrow pass that they had been detailed to guard.

Later, days later, some of them would learn that there had been no guard at the pass to cover the fleeing and wounded volunteers. More than that, they would learn that the pass was nine miles from the battlefield. Now, though, they knew none of this. Now they only knew that Lake carried the first news of defeat and death, and he brought other news of a most terrifying nature. Somewhere in the vast desert, somewhere behind C. T. Lake and the other six men, there was a great band of mounted warriors who were probably riding hard and fast toward the settlements.

2

In the next few days as the true survivors of the Battle of Truckee River straggled into the camps and towns behind C. T. Lake and his fellow deserters, the Comstock country became a land of panic. And there was very good reason for fear as wives, sweethearts, friends, and drinking companions watched the remnants of a defeated army return home with blank faces of sober reality.

Wounded, shocked, in need of whiskey and many nights of sleep, the broken volunteers rode and walked into the settlements without shouts of victory, without laughter and songs of glory. They did not come home in one unharmed and talkative unit. They came alone—by twos and by threes. They came with the look of near death deep in their eyes. For they wore faces of fear, and their fear was highly contagious.

In Virginia City beneath the barren and rough scenery of Sun Mountain, then down the mountainside and through Gold Canyon to the narrow main street of Silver City, beyond that to the flat, wide meadow of Eagle Valley and the small town of Carson City; and finally, across the Carson Valley to the tiny town of Genoa smack up against the eastern face of the sharp and rugged cliffs of the Sierra Nevada, the settlers waited and watched. They waited for their men to come home. They looked at the faces of the survivors, asked about a missing husband, sweetheart, brother, or friend. They learned the awful and ultimate truth, and the panic grew and spread. First, it was by the hour; then it was by the minute as the nursing of the wounded and the counting of the dead created visions of a massive attack by the Paiutes.

"Where is Bill Ormsby? Did he make it?"

"Dead."

"But are you certain?"

"Dead."

"And Henry Meredith? Is young Henry alive?"

"Dead."

"My God! We had a drink, and joked about Paiute women."

"Dead."

Name after name was called, and the answers were always the same: "Dead, dead, dead."

The shocked and the wounded survivors had endured their time in Hell. They had seen the face of Death. They had heard the dying groans and screams of their fellow volunteers, and all of those last, endless hours were too much with them.

Later they would tell stories of individual heroism, of valor, of treacherous cowardice, and of the deadly trap beside the Truckee River. But now their answers were made of weary sounds—sounds that were limited to the short, harsh words of finality.

To the citizens who had remained in the towns, the citizens who were only prepared for a grand victory celebration, the sight of the defeated army caused a general panic. Then the night after the survivors reached home, a report spread throughout Virginia City and the rest of the Comstock country that a full force of Indians was no more than twenty miles away. Many men suddenly remembered they had business in California, and headed across the mountains in a hurry. "Some were on foot, others mounted, often without saddles, all rushing as if pushed by some unconquerable enemy. Their cry was: 'Turn back with your train. Don't go any further. The Pah Utes are on the warpath killing all the whites they come across. No white people are safe in Washoe.'"[6]

A time of dreadful terror had come to Utah Territory. The old horror of Indian raids, of an attack at an unexpected moment, gave birth and grew with imaginations that had been honed on the sharp edges of the American frontier. And all the terror of the nightmare took shape in the daylight of dreadful defeat.

3

Waiting for the worst of all possible events, going to bed at night and finding sleep difficult as they listened for the frantic cry of alarm, the citizens of the Comstock made all the waking moments count as they prepared to defend themselves.

In Virginia City, Pat Ryle's unfinished stone hotel was taken over and called Fort Riley. Behind the stark stone walls all the women and children who had remained in the major city of the Comstock Lode "were corralled for safety."[7] But women and children were not the only ones concerned about their safety. Rumor after rumor enlarged the size of the force of Indians that would eventually attack the roughhewn towns. Paiutes were one tribe, but the word was out that there were tribes from all over. Only the few failed to expand the size and mixture of the force that was somewhere in the desert, somewhere on its way to strike with a piercing cry, to fire deadly rounds of rifle bullets and dark obsidian arrows at the break of any day. The fear of such an attack, the wild dream of such a bloody day lived with men, women, and children.

One newspaper reporter caught all the fear that lived in Virginia City when he described the state of affairs as he went to sleep—with guards outside the city—only to be awakened at the pitch-black hour, the most lonely time of three o'clock in the morning.

Last evening, as doubtless the telegraph informed you, there were rumors of a threatened attack from the Indians, and this community met in town meeting at night and appointed a patriot to watch the approaches to the town. "Indian" was the topic discussed by everybody, many retiring at a late hour, in various stages of excitement, to spend the night in feverish sleep. Among them was an honest Dutchman who slept in a store with four others and awoke, hearing one of his comrades shout (in his sleep), "Indians! Indians!" bolted for the door, *sans culotte*, rushed through the street, with stentorian lungs repeating the cry, "Indians! Indians! Turn out, everybody!" Everybody did turn out, and such an excited party of about fifty as rushed from the hotel where I am, I have rarely seen.[8]

Yet the wild rush of one frightened man was no more than an example of the mood that prevailed in Virginia City. The terror of the times was telegraphed to California in messages of great and dire urgency. Help! Help! That was the message tapped out on the telegrapher's key and carried by wire across the Sierra Nevada. Short of men! Short of arms and ammunition! Send help, and send it fast!

Prospecting holes and tunnels were deserted; the miners enrolled themselves hastily in companies; rusty arms were furbished up; old scraps of lead and water-pipes were melted and cast in bullet-molds; the camps and valley settlements were scoured for stray flasks of powder;

guards were stationed at different points in the town and patrols watched outposts on the surrounding hills.[9]

But Virginia City was not alone in its fear of what the next dawn might bring. Other towns and camps were just as fearful and just as haphazard in their overnight preparations for defense. Below Virginia City, the residents of Silver City got ready for the foe in first-rate fashion. Uphill from the town, at the narrow pass called Devil's Gate, the citizens worked hard on their defense. High above the pass on the rock outcroppings, the men built a stone fort. But this was not to be the penultimate in military strategy, for one of the men in charge had an idea that struck all his fellows as the latest thing in military cunning. What they needed, by God, was a cannon!

So, they built a cannon. Not quite a real cannon, but they did their very best. They selected the largest pine log they could find and bored it out. This done, they circled it with iron bands to hold their masterpiece together. When they were finished, they carefully placed this novel weapon in their stone fort, sighted it so that it commanded a good view of the grade leading up to Devil's Gate, loaded it with links of chain, scrap iron, broken pieces of whiskey bottles, and anything else that might do a man in, or, at the very least, put him out of the fight. Then they took another look at this ultimate of weapons, and rechecked their aim to be certain that their creation was placed so "that when fired it would sweep the canyon for a great distance, making it very unpleasant for any Indians who might happen to be jogging up that way."[10]

Down from the desert range and away from the shadow of Sun Mountain, the residents of other towns were just as terror-stricken by rumors of thousands of Indians heading their way as were the people of the mining communities. In Eagle Valley the citizens took the news of the tragic defeat of the volunteers very hard. Major William Ormsby had been one of the pioneer settlers, a prominent leader, a generous man who was well liked by all, and now he was gone. Not even his corpse was present for his widow to mourn over. There could be no graveside ceremony for his children to carry in their memories for the rest of their lives. All that remained was what the shocked survivors could tell. And what they had to say made men curse the cowards who had deserted their posts in the face of danger, and made them swear ultimate and complete revenge against the savage killers who had taken the life of Major William Ormsby.

But the shouts of anger and defiance by the men, and the weeping and moaning of the women would have to be put aside for a safer moment—a moment when the luxury of emotion could be allowed. Now it was vital to prepare the defense of Carson City, to get things ready for the coming attack of the massive movement of Indians who were reported to be not too far behind the routed army.

Men were assigned to lookout watch, to patrol duty, and to the task of making sure that arms and ammunition were placed in areas where they were most apt to be needed. When this was accomplished, even as this was taking place, "the women and children were barricaded in the Penrod House, and the country around was picketed."[11] Everything was ready, everything except the hours of waiting as the men settled back and made small talk as they listened for the first cry of alarm.

While Carson City made its moves for self-defense, across the valley to the west and overshadowed by the eastern escarpment of the Sierra Nevada, the small town of Genoa received the news of disaster from returning survivors. As in all the other camps and towns of the Comstock country, the people were stunned by this totally unexpected blow. When they recovered from the initial shock, fear quickly replaced grief. How to defend the living became the paramount problem. Short of arms, short of men, the townsfolk turned to the one man in the whole of western Utah Territory who truly knew the Paiutes, the man whom Indian Agent Frederick Dodge always came to when he needed an interpreter. Handsome, dark-bearded Warren Wasson did not fail them in their time of great need.

Looking over the small settlement, Wasson took very little time to size up the buildings that might serve as temporary forts. Plurality was not in his favor, and he saw this right away. There wasn't any doubt as to which building would be adequate for purposes of defense. The only dwelling in the shade of the Sierra Nevada that would suit the dire needs of the moment was his own stone cabin. Without a second thought, he ushered all the women and children into his home, closed the door, posted a guard, and walked over to the telegraph office for "Bee's Grapevine Line,"[12] and tried to contact Carson City for any news of the latest developments.

Warren Wasson tried many times to get his message through to Carson City, but there was never an answer. It was as though the line had been cut, and this notion could mean that somewhere between Genoa and Carson City there was a war party of Paiutes. Considering this as a possibility, Wasson decided that he had better find out what was happening. Carson City could be under attack, or the Paiutes could have overcome all resistance in the small town. There was only one thing to do. Leaving instructions for the women and children to remain in his stone house, and for the men to prepare for a raid, Wasson saddled his horse and set out across the Carson Valley toward the northeast. Eagle Valley was twelve miles away, but he had the cover of darkness. If his luck held, he would be in Carson City before daybreak.

4

While Warren Wasson rode toward Carson City, the real reason for his not being able to contact the operator on "Bee's Grapevine Line," was very obvious to the citizens of Eagle Valley. Message after frantic message was being tapped out on the key as the news of what had happened to the volunteers and the pleas for help were sent humming on the wire across the Sierra Nevada to California.

As far as California knew, the whole Comstock country was under siege. The men who had so gallantly gone forth to punish the Indians for the "wanton murders" at Williams Station had suffered a terrible defeat. How many men were dead or dying on the field of battle nobody could truly say. That was no longer the major alarm. It was not possible to rescue the wounded who were hiding in the brush, and the dead could wait for burial. But hasty action had to be taken at once to protect the men, women, and children who were still alive.

Telegraph message after telegraph message told a horrifying but incomplete tale:

PLACE: Virginia City, Utah Territory
DATE: May 13, 1860
TIME: 10:40 A.M.
Message from report of C. T. Lake: Deserter

. . . Lake thinks that the greater part of the force were left dead upon the field.[13]

PLACE: Carson City, Utah Territory
DATE: May 13, 1860
TIME: 10½ P.M.
Message signed by Geo. Hurst, W. M. Lent, Geo. Story:
Panic Peddlers

The families are all leaving the valleys. The Indians are driving off the stock and murdering the inhabitants.[14]

PLACE: Virginia City, Utah Territory
DATE: May 13, 1860
TIME: 10 P.M.
Message unsigned

Capt. T. D. Johns of San Francisco, has been appointed to the supreme military command. He has, accordingly, declared martial law. Forces are now being enrolled.[15]

PLACE: Virginia City, Utah Territory
DATE: May 14, 1860
TIME: 3 P.M.
Message unsigned

As soon as we receive arms we shall send out for the dead bodies.[16]

PLACE: Virginia City, Utah Territory
DATE: May 14, 1860
TIME: 10 P.M.
Message unsigned

The baggage, mules, provisions and arms are mostly lost. Stragglers have been coming in ever since the fight.[17]

PLACE: Carson City, Utah Territory
DATE: May 14, 1860
TIME: 10 A.M.
Message unsigned by C. E. Goodrich

The reports of yesterday are confirmed. At least 60 or 70 must have been killed.

Capt. Joe of the Washoe tribe, has come in and surrendered nine guns to Capt. Proctor, which is evidence that he wishes to preserve peace. This will subject the Washoes to the most bitter hatred and warfare from the Pah-Utes and Shoshones.

W. Wasson and others have gone to Long Valley, to warn the inhabitants there. Couriers have been sent in all directions.[18]

C. E. Goodrich set the story straight, or as straight as any man with a calm mind could, given the limited amount of factual information at his disposal. Yes, there were seventy volunteers dead. Yes, Captain Joe—though it was no doubt Captain Jim—of the Washos had brought in all the firearms belonging to his people. And yes, Warren Wasson had started on his way to Long Valley. On his arrival at Carson City he had volunteered to ride northwest through more than a hundred miles of hostile Indian country to warn the inhabitants of Honey Lake and Long Valley of the outbreak of warfare, and to contact a company of cavalry that had come southeast from Fort Crook and was supposed to be camped at Honey Lake Valley.

Riding day and night, remaining in the saddle on the same powerful horse for fourteen hours, Warren Wasson saw no Indians at all as he hurried to catch the cavalry and "deliver a telegraph order from General Clarke of the San Francisco Presidio to ride south to protect the terrified citizens of the Comstock."[19] While behind Wasson, panic prevailed.

PART IV

SAGEBRUSH SOLDIERS

1860

CHAPTER 12

California to the Rescue

News of the disaster at Pyramid Lake hit the population of Northern California with all its hysteria magnified and distorted by blank spaces not filled in by the clicking of a telegrapher's key. From minute to minute, hour to hour, the story of what had happened near the mouth of the Truckee River changed with the nature of the dispatches. All the men were dead, most were dead, some were dead. But men were also missing. My God! What about the missing? What had happened to them? And the women and children? What about the women and children? Blank spaces in between the code of sounds, blank spaces to be filled in by imaginations, by fearful images created by the dreadful unknown, images that pictured only one thing: *Massacre!*

At Placerville, California, in the red clay foothills of the Mother Lode country just above the Sacramento Valley, the townsfolk held a relief meeting on May 13, 1860—just one day after Major William Ormsby had made his fatal and final military decision. At one o'clock in the afternoon, the theater was crowded with excited citizens who could hardly contain themselves as Mayor Swan called the meeting to order. Following a series of impassioned and patriotic speeches, Mayor Swan got his town meeting under control. Various resolutions were made and adopted so that Mayor Swan was authorized "to procure arms and ammunitions and forward them instanter."[1] In addition, a messenger was sent on his way to Coloma, where he was to enlist the help of the Coloma Grays. Then the men at the meeting "promptly and liberally responded to the subscription list, and a large sum was paid in before the meeting adjourned, to defray expenses in sending arms, etc."[2]

2

Governor John G. Downey was visiting San Quentin Prison when the first news of the Paiute victory reached Sacramento. Secretary of State Johnson Price quickly assumed the responsibility for aid. He contacted various units of state militia,[3] and advised them to prepare for action. From Downieville—where the late Henry Meredith had many close friends—word was sent back that the Sierra Guards were ready to begin their march across the mountains to give the killers of the handsome Virginian a taste of pure hell. From San Juan came word that the San Juan Rifles were ready for duty, and from Nevada City the message stated that the Nevada Rifles were ready to go but were in need of percussion caps. This request was fulfilled in a hurry by sending a special messenger northeast from Sacramento with the needed caps.

Next, the Secretary promptly notified other nearby military organizations to prepare for duty and to stand by until they received orders from Governor Downey. Alerted to the situation, the Sutter Rifles and Independent City Guards of Sacramento, the Coloma Grays, and the Marysville Company awaited their marching orders. Then in a move to get immediate aid to the stricken settlers of Carson Valley and the towns and camps of the Comstock, the secretary "ordered that 200 stand of arms and 5,000 cartridges, with an escort of fourteen men, be dispatched as soon as they could be got ready."[4]

Outraged at the very idea of white men being killed by Indians, and running on pure emotion, the citizens of Sacramento held a relief meeting in front of the Orleans Hotel. In the warm May evening, as they swatted mosquitoes, the men waited for the meeting to begin. They waited, and they talked of this terrible event, spoke of the dead whose mutilated bodies were sprawled out somewhere in the sagebrush desert on the eastern side of the Sierra Nevada.

"I hear tell there wasn't more than a handful got back alive," a man would state with grave certainty.

The talk of terrible, unspeakable deeds, the tales of the frontier given all the embellishments of town men, of men who reached deep into the darkness of their minds for ancient rites of evil—this filled the time of waiting for the meeting to begin.

But all these conversations of what might or might not be ceased when the former speaker of the Assembly called the meeting to order. Ever since his arrival in the Southern Mother Lode area of Tuolumne County in 1850, James Wood Coffroth made the right moves at the right times. First, he worked as a newspaperman for the Sonora *Herald*; second, he became a politician and lawyer of note. But, most of all, he was well liked, and known throughout Northern California as a dynamic public speaker.[5] So now the former assemblyman stood in front of the anxious crowd as Senator Coffroth, and he had their full attention.

Noting that the news from Utah Territory was very bad, Senator Coffroth told the gathering that the people of California had "to devise some measures for the relief of their brethren in that Territory."[6] Then in true political form he proceeded to organize the citizens at the meeting. A president, two vice-presidents, and a secretary were duly nominated and elected. For democracy was fully in action in front of the Orleans Hotel.

The chairman of the meeting called for resolutions, and the crowd responded with enthusiasm. It was agreed by all that the citizens of Sacramento would send material aid to their friends across the Sierra Nevada. A committee was appointed to carry out the responsibility for the details. This was followed by the establishment of a committee on finance, and listed among its members were banker Darius Ogden Mills and Leland Stanford, who was well on his way to becoming a merchant prince.

All the machinery of government was established. There had been an election. There were officers, committees, money coming in, a grave moral issue—namely, the massacre of white men by Indians—and patriotic fever was about to enter the picture in a series of emotionally charged speeches. Of all the speakers, the one the crowd awaited was Senator Coffroth, and his speech came as the climax for the evening.

Looking at the crowd, Senator Coffroth waited until he had the attention of each person. When all was quiet, the handsome gentleman from Pennsylvania began:

MR. CHAIRMAN AND FELLOW CITIZENS: It was once said by a most distinguished citizen that there was no Sunday in the Revolutionary times. So it is now. There is no

14. Pyramid Lake, the Pyramid with the snow-covered Virginia mountains in the background. This remnant of prehistoric Lake Lahontan is approximately thirty miles long and eleven miles wide. (*Collection of Philip S. Cowgill, Reno*)

15. The Pyramid: standing five stories high, older and larger than the Egyptian pyramids, this rock formation so impressed John C. Frémont that he named the lake after it. (*Courtesy Reno News Bureau, Reno Chamber of Commerce*)

16. Anaho Island, Pyramid Lake, Nevada — one of the largest white pelican rookeries in North America. *(Courtesy U. S. Department of Interior)*

17. Samuel S. Buckland, founder of Buckland's Station. *(Courtesy Nevada State Historical Society)*

18. Chief Numaga's combination war ax-peace pipe, which he gave to Warren Wasson. *(Courtesy Nevada State Museum)*

19. Black Rock Desert. (*Courtesy Dr. Robert H. Amesbury and Nevada State Historical Society*)

20. Ormsby House, Carson City ca. 1860's. (*Courtesy Nevada State Historical Society*)

21. Street scene, Carson City ca. 1860's. *(Courtesy Nevada State Historical Society)*

22. Winnemucca family portrait. From left to right: Sarah Winnemucca. Chief Winnemucca, Natchez Winnemucca, an unidentified member of the family, and a boy who may have been Sarah's son by either Lieutenant Bartlett, who deserted her after his tour of duty, or by Lieutenant Hopkins, who died of TB at Lovelock, Nevada. *(Courtesy Nevada State Historical Society)*

23. Mable Wright's willow frame, grass-covered karnee was built at Pyramid Lake, near the mouth of the Truckee River, in 1964 to show how the Paiutes once lived. It is located on the site where John C. Frémont and his men camped in 1844. Note the conical burden basket, the beautifully woven winnowing tray, the pitch-covered water jug, a rabbit skin blanket, and on the drying rack fillets of cui-ui and strips of jerky. (*Courtesy Margaret M. Wheat and University of Nevada Press*)

24. Sarah Winnemucca as she appeared during her lecture tours in the East and other parts of the country. (*Courtesy Nevada State Historical Society*)

25. Captain William Weatherlow of the Honey Lake Rangers. *(Courtesy California Section, California State Library)*

26. Colonel John "Jack" Coffee Hays, commander of the Washoe Regiment. *(Courtesy California Section, California State Library)*

27. Genoa, or Mormon Station, the oldest white settlement in Nevada.
(Courtesy Nevada State Historical Society)

Sunday in Sacramento to-day. That tyrant who a short time since was arrayed in traitorous rebellion against our Government, has again united with fifteen hundred Indians to murder our citizens. To-day is the time for energetic action. One man has stated what he will give. He is one of our merchant princes. How many are there, like me, who will give their five dollars? We do not want men, but arms and ammunition. Remember, this is not only a war against savages, but against that despot Brigham Young. I ask, then, that every man here give something, no matter how small; but give us the widow's mite. Contribute something to avenge the blood and murder on the great bend of the Truckee.[7]

Here was more, much more to consider. Indians were bad enough, but if the Mormons were behind them, there was no telling what was happening. In the minds of the audience, the Mountain Meadows Massacre of the Fancher party in the fall of 1857 was obviously committed by the Sons of Dan, the secret avengers of the Mormons. And the street moralists who stood and applauded Senator Coffroth's words of prejudice were only too ready to believe anything bad about the Mormons.

All the men in the crowd felt superior to these strange people with their strange ways and their strange ideas. But one thing was certain. Say what they might about the Mormons, there was no denying that they were a tough bunch to go up against. The regular troops had had more than they could handle with them, and there wasn't any question about the fact that the Mormons and Indians got along just fine. All things considered, maybe Senator Coffroth had a good point. Maybe old Brigham *was* behind the Indian uprising.

The idea of the Mormons backing and encouraging the

Indians to go on the warpath heightened the excitement
for the crowd. Nobody stopped to consider whether or
not there was any validity to Senator Coffroth's statement.
Instead, the assembled men willingly accepted the wild
notion that Brigham Young was somehow involved with
the trouble in the Comstock country. Believing this, the
men clamored for Sacramento to come to the aid of fellow
Americans in distress. They gathered about two thousand
dollars within one night,[8] sent arms and ammunition on
the Sacramento Valley Railroad to its terminal point at
Folsom, twenty-one miles up the American River, and
from there the weapons were carried by wagon to Placerville and the start of the mountain wagon road across
the Sierra Nevada. Zealously the citizens of Sacramento
rallied to the frantic messages from across the mountains
and sent immediate help to the beleaguered people of
the Great Basin.

3

Though the news of the disaster at the Big Bend of the
Truckee River caused excitement in San Francisco, the
sense of alarm was not nearly as great as in Sacramento
and the towns of the Mother Lode. Still, Major General
J. P. Haven of the California Militia considered the situation so grave that he decided to go to San Quentin and
discuss the seriousness of this act of war with the governor. So while Senator Coffroth carried forth in front
of Sacramento's Orleans Hotel, the excited General Haven
"boarded the U.S. steamer *Shubrick*."[9] He notified Captain Boggs of the emergency, and the steamer sailed at
four in the afternoon on May 13 from San Francisco, and
arrived at San Quentin shortly after five o'clock. Here
Governor Downey came aboard, and the *Shubrick* sailed

back to San Francisco so that the Governor could meet with Brevet Brigadier General N. S. Clarke of the 6th Infantry.

Aid was needed, and Governor Downey and General Clarke were in complete accord. Yet the machinery of government and what one reporter called "red-tapeism"[10] presented official roadblocks. To make a military move inside the boundaries of California was one thing, but to cross the state line into Utah Territory without permission from Washington, D.C., was something that could cause a good deal of trouble in high places. Furthermore, the number of soldiers that General Clarke had at his command did not present much in the way of a striking force. At best, he thought he could send two companies from San Francisco and one from Benicia. This would mean a total of less than two hundred men. Certainly, these soldiers would be a good defensive force, but there simply weren't enough available men to form an army that could launch an offensive campaign against a thousand or more mounted and well-armed Indians.

Still, the problem of what was proper and legal in this crucial situation continued to plague the governor and the general. They discussed all the possible ramifications of making a military move into Utah Territory until General Clarke "signified his willingness to break through the trammels of 'red-tapeism' of the strict line of his authority, and agreed to assume a certain responsibility upon a proper representation of the facts by the Governor."[11]

A proper representation of the facts? Here was a question right out of a handbook for the proper training of generals. Get the facts. Know what the battlefield conditions are like. Most of all, make sure that somebody in high political office assumes the responsibility for your actions. Surely, this must have been General Clarke's conditioned reaction. There could be no other explanation, for he knew very well that Governor Downey's grasp of what the situation was in the Comstock country was as vague as the incomplete data from the last telegraph dispatch that had been handed to him.

Accepting the scattered and incomplete information he had as being representative of some portion of the truth, some indication of the scope of one disaster and of an impending tragedy of a grand scale, Governor Downey issued a requisition to General Clarke for arms and ammunition. With the requisition in hand, the general sent the following message to the Benicia Arsenal:

San Francisco, May 13th, 1860.

To Captain Callender, Commanding Benecia Arsenal.

—Deliver to Governor Downey, of California, five hundred stand of arms, one hundred thousand rounds of ammunition, and the accoutrements necessary for each stand.

N. S. CLARKE
Col. Sixth Infantry, Brevet Brigadier General.[12]

The first step in the rescue of the Washoe miners, merchants, ranchers, women, and children had been made. Now Governor Downey moved with great dispatch. In that Adjutant General Kibbe of the California Militia was out of the state, the governor placed Major General J. P. Haven in charge of the arms and ammunition to be picked up at the Benicia Arsenal. In his official message to General Haven, the governor stated what he expected him to do once he had received the arms and ammunition:

> You will use all possible dispatch in transporting the arms, etc., to the scene of Indian outrages in Carson Valley, using all necessary economy on behalf of the State.

> Consult with the regular and authorized command of such military expedition as you may find at the scene of action, and take proper receipts of the property.[13]

It was a very long day for General Haven, but it had not yet ended. By eleven o'clock that night he had boarded a special steamer, and in the dark hours before the dawn of May 14, the elderly officer was sailing northeast up San Francisco Bay to the Sacramento River and the Benicia Arsenal beyond the Carquinez Strait, while behind him, General Clarke assumed his responsibility of ordering what troops he could spare for duty in Utah Territory. For it was quite clear to the general that it was the problem of the Federal Government to punish the Indians and find out if they were being influenced by "the alleged collusion of the treacherous Mormons."[14] On that same day, General Clarke sent a letter to Acting Adjutant General Lorenzo Thomas, Army Headquarters, Washington, D.C., in which he reported he was sending a small force—The Carson Valley Expedition—under the command of Captain Joseph Stewart of the 3d United States Artillery to aid the American citizens who were under attack by hostile Indians.

By the time General Clarke had posted his letter, The Carson Valley Expedition was on its way to Sacramento aboard the steamer *Eclipse*. From Fort Alcatraz there were the men of Company H, 3d Artillery, under the command of Captain Joseph Stewart; from the Presidio of San Francisco there was a detachment of eleven men from Companies M and I, 3d Artillery "under the command of 1st Lt. Horatio G. Gibson, and 2d Lt. Edward R. Warner . . . manning two howitzers"[15]; and from Benicia Barracks there was a mixture of Company A, 6th Infantry, under the command of Captain Frederick F. Flint, Company H, 6th Infantry, under the command of Second Lieutenant John McCleary; thirty-seven men from Companies A and F, 1st Dragoons, under the command of First Lieutenant Alfred B. Chapman and Second Lieutenant Richard H. Brewer. Added to this were Captain Tredwell Moore, Quartermaster, and Captain Charles C. Keeney, Surgeon. Altogether, this was The Carson Valley Expedition, and they were on their way to join the various state militia units and the volunteers in the land of Washoe.[16]

4

The steamer *Eclipse* dropped anchor just off the levee in Sacramento in the pre-dawn of Tuesday, May 15. The soldiers from the Presidio at San Francisco, Fort Alcatraz, and Benicia Barracks remained on board until well after sunrise. Then at eight-thirty, with the warm morning sun already making many of them sweat, all the men marched in double file from the steamer to the levee, where they stood at ease for roll call.

When the men were all accounted for, they marched through the city toward the train awaiting them at the depot of the Sacramento Valley Railroad. Reporters for the local newspapers wrote that the soldiers were well armed with Minié rifles, and that Captain Stewart's Company H, 3d Artillery, was well disciplined and very professional in manner. The same was not said about some of the other men, who "were seen strolling in all directions about the city . . . under the command of captain whisky."[17]

The soldiers of The Carson Valley Expedition were colorful in dress as well as manner. One observer who watched the men board the train for Folsom was so taken by their uniforms that he wrote a full description of how the men looked as they started off for war.

> The Artillery men wore blue frock coats, dark mixed pants, (officers with red stripe down the outside of the pants), the regular army military hat, with letter II, in gilt, on front, without pompoon, cartridge box, water cup and sack. The Infantry company wore short blue frock coats, light blue pants, black Kossuth hats, with left brim turned up and fastened with a gilt *attache*, gilt bugle in front, and surrounded with blue cord and tassels, water cup and sack, and cartridge box.[18]

Then in a strange and wondrous way, the reporter for the Sacramento *Union* closed his description of these colorful uniforms by stressing their practicality. "The dress," he wrote, "was stout, plain and new, adopted with a view to service rather than show."[19]

When all the men had taken their seats in the passenger cars, the engineer pulled the line, and the steam whistle echoed throughout Sacramento. Soldiers and spectators cheered, and the train slowly moved away from the depot and began the journey alongside the American River to the end of track at Folsom.

The train made a fast trip upriver and pulled into

Folsom at ten minutes past nine. Here The Carson Valley
Expedition came under the efficient care of Mr. C. T. H.
Palmer of Wells, Fargo and Company. Mr. Palmer had
arranged everything so carefully that only one hour and
ten minutes passed before baggage, stores, and men were
in stagecoaches and wagons and on their way to Placerville, where they were scheduled to transfer to muleback
for their upward climb to the crest of the Sierra Nevada
and the steep descent to the Carson Valley.

Yet all was not completely in accord. Two men from
Company H, 3d Artillery, deserted before the troops were
loaded into the stagecoaches and wagons. Lieutenant
Robinson headed a detail in search of the deserters, but
all they found was where the men had exchanged their
military uniforms for civilian clothes. Though the young
officer was thoroughly disgusted and wanted to pursue
the trail while it was fresh, the army was ready to move
on. There simply wasn't time to waste in chasing two
renegades when the citizens of the Great Basin were in
dire need of help.

Still, for some Californians desertion was a small sin.
This minority complained that the hasty action of Governor Downey and General Clarke would plunge California
into financial disaster. To them, too much money was
being spent on what might very well turn out to be nothing
more than a minor skirmish between a handful of reckless
Comstock adventurers and a band of Indians they de-
meaningly referred to as "Diggers," and whom they casually dismissed as being totally incapable of carrying
out anything vaguely resembling organized warfare. One
Sacramento writer even took every leader of the military
expedition to task. In caustic prose, he assumed the role
of a budget-minded auditor out to defend the Treasury
of the State of California.

As is usual in hurried military movements under inex-
perienced managers, economy has not been very rigidly
practiced. A large number of mules were engaged in this
city at a high price, to be paid by the State, to transport
the arms and ammunition over the mountains. Upon ar-
riving at Placerville ten of them were appropriated by
order of General Haven for his escort to ride. The General himself must have a Concord wagon for his accom-
modation to Strawberry Flat, instead of taking a horse or
mule as he should have done. A man who needs a car-
riage to ride in is out of place in fighting Indians. . . .
The expense of getting the arms and ammunition over,
was properly authorized by the Executive, but it should
have been kept within reasonable bounds. We presume
His Excellency will be astonished when the bills are
presented.[20]

The minority protested, but it did no good. Throughout
Northern California the cities and towns cheered as local
militia units struck out for Utah Territory to join The
Carson Valley Expedition. It was not a time to count
dollars. It was a time to save lives from the dread threat
of savage butchery, and let there be no doubt about it.
But the trip across the Sierra Nevada proved to be much
harder than the men had anticipated. For these were
flatlanders, soldiers who had done their walking and
marching outside the barracks and on the parade grounds.
They were not in condition for this journey, and they
quickly found this out on their first day's travel beyond the
foothill town of Placerville. The wagon road was muddy
and slippery from late rains and melting snows, and
each mile was a tough upward climb in a country that
seemed to be turned upside down to the weary men; and

when they made camp the first night, they cursed the hard going and hoped they had seen the worst of it.

But the second day was worse than the first. The soldiers climbed higher into the mountains. They passed through tall stands of sugar pine and ponderosa, smelled the acrid odor of mountain misery, and stared far below at the rushing waters of the South Fork of the American River. Then they headed down into the canyon, slipping and sliding—both men and horses—until they reached the river. Here, they paused and rested for a time. Then they crossed the river on the newly erected Brockliss' Bridge—the horses and wagons sending out a thunderous clatter as they hurried across to begin the steep upward grade on the other side. At day's end, they were four miles from Strawberry Valley, and they made camp near what they called the San Francisco Mountain House.[21]

Even as they built campfires and cooked the evening mess, the billowy white thunderheads that had been gathering all day became slate gray, then changed to the color of burned logs. The temperature dropped and as the cold wind rattled the limbs of tall pines, the men crowded near the fires. Then it began to snow. At first, it was a light snow. A few flakes drifted on the wind, struck the ground, and melted so quickly that it was as though they had never existed. But these vanishing flakes were soon followed by great flakes that filled the air, swirled in whirlpools of wind, and quickly covered the ground, bedrolls, backs of picketed horses and mules, the few wagons, the two mountain howitzers, and the clothes of the men standing guard.

All that night it snowed, and on the third morning the snow continued to fall. As one soldier wrote, ". . . We started amid snow and the sharpest wind I ever experienced on our way to Lake Valley. It snowed all day, and late in the afternoon we arrived, wet and weary, and lay that night in a deserted log-house."[22]

The fourth morning broke clear and cold, and The Carson Valley Expedition left their rude quarters at Lake Valley, passed by the southeast end of Lake Tahoe, and then turned east to begin the short, steep downward road on Kingsbury Grade that passed through Haines Canyon[23] as it descended to Genoa and the Carson Valley. On this new road, the soldiers rapidly left the tall pine country of the western slope of the Sierra Nevada. As they worked their way down the canyon, they saw short, squatty piñon pines, quaking aspens, and the gray-blue clumps of tall sagebrush. Ahead of them was the sudden rounding of a turn and the first view of the Carson Valley far below and the distant desert mountains to the east of the Carson River—mountains that hid their true size because there were no tall trees to reach skyward and no glistening granite bluffs and domes to make a distinctive form. Instead, there was an endless view of sagebrush that appeared to blend into the sky at horizon's end.

To the men of The Carson Valley Expedition their first view of the Great Basin was more than astounding, for to them it meant the end of a tough trip. Ahead was what they had come all this way for, and they had already seen fear and terror in the faces of men, women, and children they had passed—families who were fleeing westward to escape the ravages of an Indian war. But the soldiers were in high spirits. The mountain trip was all they had needed to get them into fighting trim. All the boys in Washoe had to do was hang on a little longer. California was coming to the rescue.

CHAPTER 13

The Washoe Regiment

Help was on the way. Messages from California made
that quite clear. But help was, at very best, only leaving
Sacramento to begin the long journey across the Sierra
Nevada. This did not mean that salvation would arrive
in the Great Basin to be anything more than a burial
party, a gathering of uniformed gravediggers. Salvation
couldn't wait for marching soldiers. Salvation had to be
in the Carson Valley and in the barren mountains of the
Comstock Lode right now. Salvation had to be formed
out of whatever raw material was available, and not
dependent upon what might or might not arrive in time.
At this crucial moment of fear, the citizens of the Comstock country looked to themselves, and they saw salvation
in the form of two highly experienced military men who
had arrived in Virginia City shortly after the disaster
beside the banks of the Truckee River.

One of these men of arms was none other than Colonel
John Coffee Hays—frontiersman, Texas Ranger, ex-sheriff
of San Francisco, and—most of all—a noted Indian fighter.
The other military man was Major Daniel E. Hungerford
of Downieville's Sierra Guards. But Major Hungerford was

a good deal more than a local militia officer. He had been a colonel during the Mexican War, and had landed with General Scott's invasion army when they established a beachhead at the port of Vera Cruz. After this major battle, Hungerford had been in the forefront of one hard fight after another as he and his men worked their way up and across the Sierra Madre Oriental and on to Mexico City for the final, bloody engagements of the war. Here then were two men for Virginia City at a desperate moment: a seasoned Indian fighter and a professional soldier.

2

A committee of Virginia City's citizens was appointed to ask Major Hungerford if he would help them in their hour of need. For along with his well-known military experience, they pointed out to him that Downieville was much closer to the Great Basin than Sacramento.

Would Major Hungerford send a telegram to the Sierra Guards and tell them to come on the double? That was the essence of their request.

Major Hungerford explained that he fully recognized the gravity of the situation, but there was one hitch to their request. The arms and ammunition belonged to the State of California, and the Sierra Guards were part of the California Militia. For him to order them to march across the boundary line of California into Utah Territory would constitute an act of invasion.

But the members of the citizens' committee were not willing to give up in the face of rules and regulations. They persisted in their request, and one after another voiced their need of military help.

Major Hungerford listened to the men. He heard them out, one by one. As he did, he thought of the dreadful situation. This was not a time for rules and regulations. This *was* a time to act, and to hell with all the formalities. The people of the Comstock country needed help, and by God, that's just what he'd give them.

Without further discussion, Major Hungerford told the committee he would do as they wished. While men tried to thank him, he walked away from the gathering and headed for the telegraph office. He quickly drafted a message and had it sent to Dr. E. G. Bryant of the Sierra Guards:

Virginia City, May 13, 1860

To E. G. Bryant, *Downieville:*

Send me immediately all the arms and ammunition of the National Guard. Telegraph Lieut. Hall at Forest City to send all the rifles in his posession. Send to Goodyear's Bar, to Captain Kinniff, to send me all his rifles. Forward as soon as possible. Big fight with the Indians. The whites defeated. Send me your heavy saber. Spear, Meredith, and Baldwin killed.

Signed, MAJOR D. E. HUNGERFORD[1]

Any reservations that still nagged Major Hungerford about his stepping across the line of his authority lasted for no more than an hour. At the end of that time, a telegram from Governor John Downey placed an official seal on his actions.

San Francisco, May 13, 1860

TO MAJOR HUNGERFORD:

Sir, You will please collect such arms and ammunition as you can find in Downieville, and forward them, by express or otherwise, to the scene of action in Carson Valley.

Respectfully, your obedient servant,

JOHN G. DOWNEY[2]

All the experience of a seasoned military officer made Major Hungerford a man of decisive action. With the political obstacles out of his way, he moved with rapidity as he prepared to defend and avenge the citizens of the Comstock country. He sent another message to Downieville, in which he instructed the officers of the Sierra Guards to organize the men into four companies. Also, he notified them that he, personally, would leave Virginia City and ride out to meet them en route. So it was that five days later the major entered Virginia City—with his saber in its scabbard—riding at the head of his troops, who rode and marched behind him in fine military fashion to the loud cheers of welcome from the crowds of people lining the street.

One hundred and sixty-five men, all armed and equipped, carrying forty rounds of ammunition per man[3]—it was a grand and welcome sight coming less than a week after the first defeated and wounded survivors of the Battle of Truckee River had stumbled home with news of disaster. Cheer after cheer echoed in the icy air on the eastern slope of Sun Mountain. It was easy to see that here was the beginning of an army that would avenge the dead, and it had a *real* soldier riding in command.

3

Yet even while Major Hungerford rode at the head of the Sierra Guards on Friday, May 18, correspondents of

San Francisco newspapers were sending back stories about
the desire of the populace to have the old Indian fighter
Colonel John Coffee Hays command the fast forming
army of volunteers and the various companies of California Militia as one striking force to be known as the
Washoe Regiment. At first, this idea did not appeal to
Major Hungerford. He pointed out that he had trained
the Sierra Guards, that they were accustomed to his
commands, and that they would be much more effective
under his leadership. This did not mean that he had no
respect for Colonel Hays's ability as an Indian fighter,
but fighting Indians was one thing, commanding a large
military organization was quite another matter.[4]

Still, the need for co-operation was paramount. Rec-
ognizing this, Major Hungerford reluctantly agreed that
his men could serve under the command of Colonel Hays
if that was the desire of the citizens. This left things
wide open, and there was no longer any need to hesitate. This was an Indian war, and what they needed
was an Indian fighter like Colonel Hays, who had spent
years fighting some of the toughest Indians the Southwest
had to offer. The townsfolk were elated and full of re-
newed courage. With the leadership of Hays, they'd drive
the Paiutes right out of the country.

But Colonel Hays made one thing quite clear. He was
not going to accept the command of the Washoe Regiment
unless he were placed in a position of complete control.
All the men were to obey him without questioning his
orders. If they were willing to do so, then he would do
his very best to lead them to victory.

"Yes, Yes!" That was the answer from the people of
Virginia City. Anything that Hays wanted, he could have,
and they were quite willing to follow all his orders.

Satisfied that things would go his way, Colonel Hays

accepted the command of the Washoe Regiment. Later, in a message to Governor Alfred Cummings of Utah Territory, Hays explained why he had agreed to accept this position:

> Having had some experience in the Indian wars of the southwest, I was urged in every direction to take the command of this expedition. As this was tendered me by the unanimous vote of the officers and also privates, I could not, with a sense of duty, decline. Accordingly, on the 24th May, I assumed the command of the regiment, and proceeded to make the necessary appointments.[5]

Appointments was a key word. For in this very democratic army there were three principal field officers—Colonel Hays, Lieutenant Colonel Saunders, Major Hungerford—three surgeons, an acting adjutant of infantry, three officers serving as quartermasters, one commissary officer, fifteen captains, and ten lieutenants. As one San Francisco reporter put it, "There are a great many *military* men here at present. I should think a fair estimate would be, that every other man was a man of *high military* standing. 'Captains' are as thick as blackberries in autumn, while 'Majors,' 'Colonels,' 'Brigadier Generals,' common 'Generals,' and 'Adjutant Generals' are the only titles considered worthy of being borne by this highly respectable crowd."[6]

Altogether, the Washoe Regiment consisted of eight companies of infantry and six of cavalry. The total number of citizen soldiers varied between 544 and 578 men, who strutted the streets of Virginia City like conquering Roman Legions. But their company names made them typically American. For they marched and rode as the Carson Rangers, Carson Rifles, Coloma Grays, Highland

Rangers or Vaqueros, Independent City Guards of Sacramento, Nevada Rifles, San Juan Rifles, Sierra Guards,
Silver City Guards, Spy Company, Sutter Rifles, Truckee
Rangers, and Virginia Rifles. It was an American mix,
a wild conglomerate of various sections of the nation
suddenly transplanted to the wind-blown, muddy streets
of this raw mining town clinging to the side of Sun Mountain. They were patriotic, cocksure, and endowed with
a heritage of hate for any and all Indians.

To show their gratitude for Colonel Hays's leadership,
the citizens decided that it was only fitting and proper
to present a man of his stature with a gift that matched
his personal history for valor in the face of danger. One
of the leaders of this movement of gratitude, described
what took place:

> We made up a purse to purchase for Colonel Jack Hays
> a war charger—bridle with Spanish bit, saddle of Mexican
> adornment, spurs jingling with silver bells. We chose an
> orator to make the presentation speech. It was earnest
> and eloquent. I made it myself. I referred to his heroic
> deeds in Texas and his patriotic achievements in the
> Mexican war; we relied upon his valor to revenge the
> dead and to protect our settlement from the horrors of an
> Indian massacre; closed up with a little poetry and a
> peroration to the American flag, the starry emblem of
> liberty, and handed Colonel Jack the bridle.[7]

When the speaker handed Jack Hays the reins of this
splendid horse, the audience pushed forward. Prospectors,
miners, speculators, and gamblers stood waiting for whatever words of wisdom the Indian fighter might have to
say at this glorious moment. But Hays was a taciturn

man of action. He stared at the anxious faces watching him, cleared his throat, and said: "He's a derned good hoss, and I'm much obleeged."[8]

Expecting more, awaiting a full-blown speech, the crowd remained silent for a moment. Then when they realized that this was it, that the famous Texas Ranger had said all he was going to say, everybody laughed and cheered. When they finished, Colonel Hays mounted his new horse and looked at the Washoe Regiment lined up in marching order and ready to travel. A light snow was falling and melting as fast as it hit the muddy street. This was not a place to train his army, and Jack Hays was well aware of it. There wasn't enough grass or hay for the horses and mules, and there was too much whiskey for the men. Knowing all this, Colonel Hays hesitated no longer. He gave the signal to move out, and to the loud cheers of Virginia City's residents, the Washoe Regiment marched and rode out of town, and headed downgrade toward the lower country and the Carson River.

4

As the Washoe Regiment began its twelve-mile journey to their first night's camp, the regulars of The Carson Valley Expedition were resting in Carson City after their long trip across the Sierra Nevada. Even before leaving Virginia City, Hays had received a message from Captain Joseph Stewart. Like most of the men preparing for this war, Captain Stewart had complete faith in Jack Hays; and he notified him that when the time for attack arrived, his troops would rendezvous with the volunteers and carry out their duties under Hays's command.

In the meantime, the Washoe Regiment worked its way down the mountain, passing through Gold Hill and Silver

City, and they made their first night's camp at Miller's
Ranch below Chinatown. Here Colonel Hays looked over
the men and supplies, and he became well aware of three
facts: the men had to be given some notion of military
discipline; the supplies were not nearly as much as they
should have for the campaign, and the arms and ammunition of the California Militia were sorely needed.

There was no trouble in getting the militia armaments.
All that required was a requisition upon General Haven.
But supplies were another matter. Indians and the possibility of a raid did not help to lower the prices of
provisions and horses and mules. Merchants and ranchers
in the Comstock country were not about to offer any bar-
gains—not even for an army that was coming to their
defense. Before the soldiers had departed from Virginia
City the price for horse feed had been "raised to $7 per
night, and three prices were charged the little army for
everything they needed."[9] The cost of flour ran from
seventy-five dollars per one hundred pounds to whatever
the traffic could bear. Even the cost of freight hit at the
limited resources of the Washoe Regiment, for it ran as
high as "a dollar a pound on some articles."[10] As in all
wars, the profiteers were more than willing to convert
military action into monetary addition.

In an attempt to get around the money-makers, one
company of volunteers from Sacramento indulged in their
own form of robbery. Unknown to Colonel Hays, these
men decided that impressment was the answer for getting
supplies and mounts. But their reasoning was not based
on need alone. For they, too, saw a chance to make some
money out of this adventure. Before the Washoe Regiment
had reached its first camp below Chinatown, the impressment company had done a fair job of taking rifles, pistols,

food, blankets, horses, and mules from citizens all along the way from Virginia City on down the grade to the lowland.

Yet what had seemed to be a good venture turned against the impressment men at the camp outside Chinatown. Outraged townsmen and ranchers stormed into camp, and wasted no time in voicing their fury to Colonel Hays.

"What the hell is going on?" a man would say. "I thought this was an army, not a goddamned bunch of horse thieves!"

"He's right, damned right, Colonel! And a cottonwood limb is where a son-of-a-bitch of a horse thief belongs!"

Still another would complain about the theft of his rifle and pistol; another about food from his cabin and blankets from his bunk. Impressment had never been popular with Yankees, and none of these men looked upon any threat of an Indian raid as being a good enough excuse for robbery, especially if the theft went under the British name of *impressment*.

Hays wasted no time in setting things straight. He had disgruntled owners point out their confiscated horses and mules, and he quickly separated the champions of impressment from their stolen mounts. Next, he made the men step forward and return all rifles, pistols, and other supplies that they had seen fit to take from their owners. Then in a fury that let the whole regiment know that he would not tolerate such acts, Colonel Hays unceremoniously dismissed the one Sacramento company that had initiated this practice of theft in the name of emergency.

With this serious problem solved and with the errant Sacramento men expelled, Colonel Hays and the regiment settled down for the first night. At daybreak, with a mixture of rain and sleet pelting their faces, the volunteers rode and walked to a temporary desert camp near Reed's Station, some twenty miles east of Carson City. Here, Hays sent his scout, Michael Bushy, toward Williams Station to look over the country for any sign of a Paiute war party. As the former mountain man rode away from camp, the Washoe Regiment began its very short training period in a sagebrush flat near the Carson River —a flat they named Camp Hays.

The volunteers worked hard and tried their best under miserable conditions on the wet, soggy sagebrush flat. But training time was running very short, and Colonel Hays was not too certain about some of his troops. Most of all, there were a few officers whose conduct did not convince him that they would react in the right way in the face of danger. These men were too nervous and too willing to talk a good battle, and Hays felt that they might panic and run the first time the Paiutes yelled and charged toward them. To find out who would make the right move and who would let fear take charge, Jack Hays decided to test these officers who strutted around the campfire.

On the wet, rainy night before the Washoe Regiment left Camp Hays, the colonel worked out a trick to test the officers he was worried about. After evening mess, he joined the talkative fellows as they sat around the campfire and spoke of the battle they would be riding into in the next few days. While they carried on at length about what they would do to the Indians, Hays placed an unopened can of fruit into the fire. Then as the men continued to talk, he moved back from the fire, sat down on the tarp covering his blankets, pulled his hat forward to shield his face from rain, and leaned back against his saddle. All at once, the can of fruit exploded like a mountain howitzer, shattering the stillness of the night, and showering coals, ashes, and fruit in all directions.

"Injins!" Hays shouted; then he gave the Delaware war cry.[11]

The stunned officers jumped to their feet. Some of them stood—outlined against the campfire—and stared into the darkness. Others ran wildly away from the camp and into the muddy sagebrush flat, leaving their guns behind. And a few cool-headed men jumped away from the firelight, grabbed their guns, and got ready for action.

Satisfied that a thorough lesson had been taught, perhaps one that these green soldiers would remember in the next few days, Colonel Hays called to the running men. He assured them that everything was all right, that there were no Paiutes charging the camp, and he laughed as they came back to the fireside. Their clothes were torn, wet, and muddy from running, stumbling, and falling into the sagebrush and onto the ground. But most of all, their self-satisfaction, high esteem, and inordinate pride were badly bruised.[12]

There was no need to lecture the officers about what had taken place. Every man in camp was well aware of what had happened, and every man knew that if the attack had been real that many of them would now be dead or wounded. So as the bugler played taps and the first night watch stood its guard duty, the men of the Washoe Regiment bedded down. Come dawn, they would break up camp and continue their journey toward the Big Bend of the Carson and the ashes of Williams Station. Yet one thing bothered Jack Hays, and he kept thinking about it as he stared at the glow of the dying campfire: Michael Bushy was a good scout, a man who had spent his life on the frontier, and he was long overdue from his journey to Williams Station.

5

On the morning of May 27, the Washoe Regiment departed from Camp Hays. While the rain had stopped
sometime during the night, the ground was muddy and
slippery; and the cold wind made a man's eyes water and
his nose run. Dark clouds sailed overhead, driven by the
steadily blowing wind currents. For once, the foot soldiers
had the advantage over the cavalry. The mere act of
movement kept them halfway warm. But the men on
horses and mules shivered all the way from the training
camp to their next stop. No longer were volunteers concerned about avenging the dead. The campaign had
hardly started, but gripes were being voiced by many of
these big talkers who had seen themselves as immediate
heroes back in the comfort of Virginia City saloons. But
the cold, wet weather had dampened a good deal more
than the earth; and as the men made camp once more
alongside the Carson River, all the glory they had hoped
for had almost vanished as they ate half-cold food, drank
coffee that tasted more like dirty water and was tolerable
only because it was hot, and huddled in damp bedrolls
around the fires for warmth.

To Colonel Hays, though, his volunteer army was beginning to look better. He had been in too many tough
battles during his life to put much reliance on soft town
men filled with talk and whiskey. Bringing the regiment
into the desert to train had done just what he had hoped
it would do. Now his soldiers were rid of their illusions
of an easy victory. What Jack Hays saw in this last camp
before they made the next day's move to Williams Station
was a griping, hardened force that was angry and fully
ready for a tough fight.

Then, to complete Colonel Hays's satisfaction, he had a new scout to replace the missing Michael Bushy, and his scout was not another mountain man down on his luck and trying to scratch out a living now that the great times of the fur trade were long past. The man who had volunteered for this duty was none other than long-bearded Warren Wasson,[13] and Jack Hays couldn't have asked for a better replacement. Not only did dark-haired Wasson know the country, he also knew the Paiutes. Nor was his knowledge of these Indians slight. To the contrary, Wasson knew their country, their customs, and he spoke their language fluently. More than that, he got along with most of the Paiutes, and was a friend of War Chief Numaga.

Hays and Wasson talked about Bushy's failure to return from his scouting trip, and both men agreed that something out of the ordinary must have taken place. And in this case, out of the ordinary probably meant one of three things. The Paiutes had seen him, and Bushy had decided to go into hiding until the regiment appeared. The Paiutes had captured him and were holding him as a hostage. Or the warriors had caught him off guard and killed him. Of these three possibilities, it struck Hays and Wasson that the most logical thing was that somewhere ahead of them they would find Michael Bushy's corpse.

The next morning the Washoe Regiment broke camp even before the first light of dawn. The weather remained cold and damp, and the sky still belonged to winter. Slowly, the volunteers worked their way through the Carson River Canyon, passing by the overhanging bluffs and the stands of cottonwoods, quaking aspens, and willows that shimmered like green waves as they were whipped back and forth by the steadily blowing wind. After they came out of the canyon, they passed by Samuel Buckland's Station and looked with longing at his rude log trading post, for they knew that Buckland's raw whiskey was better than no whiskey at all and that it would warm a man's blood if it didn't do anything else. But Colonel Hays was not about to call a halt. Instead, he headed west from Buckland's to the open sagebrush country. Ten miles ahead was Williams Station, and Hays planned to reach it before nightfall.

CHAPTER 14

Skirmish at Big Meadows

It was already twilight when the Washoe Regiment crossed Big Meadows, forded the Carson River at the Big Bend, and climbed upward to the plateau where the remains of Williams Station stood. The charred buildings, scorched tools, and blackened rubbish stood out on the bluff as a grim reminder of the true nature of warfare.

Not far from the burned-out buildings, there was a mound of earth that had been turned over by Major Ormsby's men as they had passed this way on their fatal march to Pyramid Lake. At the head of this grave, there was a rough pine board, and the following was carved on it:

Sacred to the remains of the persons murdered on the night of May 7th, 1860, at Williams' Station, on the Carson River. It being the partial remains of three bodies.[1]

The rude gravemarker was a sobering sight for the men, and they were unusually quiet as they made camp for the night. But Colonel Hays had no intention of even risking the possibility of being caught off guard. While most of the volunteers were busy with their assigned duties in setting up camp, Jack Hays called to Captain W. B. Fleeson of Spy Company. He told Fleeson that he wanted him to select ten of his best men and to ride two or three miles in advance of the regiment and establish another camp to serve as a warning base. Next, Hays spoke to Captain J. L. Blackburn of the Carson Rifles, and sent the Deputy U. S. Marshal of Utah Territory out with two dependable men to locate the Paiutes and try to lure them toward the regiment's main camp in the morning.[2]

Now Jack Hays could relax for the night. Everything was set up just as he wanted it. His advance camp would prevent any surprise attack, and come morning the scouting party would locate and decoy any Paiutes who might be in the vicinity. By then, Hays figured to have his men positioned in such a fashion that any band of Indians in pursuit of the scouts would be certain to ride into a trap on the open meadowland across from the Big Bend of the Carson River. And Hays was certain that the Paiutes would chase Blackburn and his two companions, for he had instructed them to give the impression that they had been caught alone and off guard, and to ride for their lives. It was a very old trick, but it was a good one that Hays had learned from the Indians during his many campaigns against them.

2

The men of the Washoe Regiment stood close to the fire as they drank their morning coffee. For once it wasn't raining, but to the west great thunderheads were gathering over the Sierra Nevada, and the westerly wind chilled the men and made them shiver.

"She's a cold son-of-a-bitch," a volunteer would say. "I ain't worried about the Indians any more. It's freezing to death that bothers me."

"Hell, friend, if it wasn't cold, you'd be crying about the heat."

Back and forth the talk went, and weather was the main topic. The Paiutes were almost out of their minds. Some of the men even said that they figured the Indians had hightailed out of the country. But others said that the Indians were around all right. They were just staying out of sight, waiting for the right moment. Yet there wasn't much doubt about the miserable weather. So the soldiers crowded the fire and wondered what Colonel Hays was watching in the distance.

Somewhere just out of sight, Hays knew that Captain Blackburn was trying to lure the Paiutes into Big Meadows. Scanning the distance, Hays watched for some sign of movement, something that would give him the signal to position his troops for a surprise attack.

Yet even while Hays watched for his men, Captain Blackburn and his two companions had found a Paiute camp, and were riding for their lives. Following behind them, at a full gallop, were more than a hundred hardriding and well-armed warriors, yelling and shooting as they tried to catch them.

The three volunteers spurred their horses and rode as fast as they could toward Big Meadows and the Big Bend of the Carson River. As they neared the river, they galloped by Captain Fleeson's advance camp. When the soldiers saw Blackburn and his two companions gallop past, they knew they had made contact with the Paiutes. Now Captain Fleeson got ready to carry out his phase of

Colonel Hays's plan. The men of Spy Company quickly saddled and mounted their horses. Each soldier had two rounds of cartridges, so at very best they might delay the warriors for ten or fifteen minutes. Everything had to work just right. One mistake, and that would be the end of the gamble, and the end of their lives.

At first sight of the warriors yelling and charging through the sand hills in their direction, Spy Company struck out and headed into Big Meadows and rode for the cover of the cottonwoods and quaking aspens alongside the Carson River.

When Hays heard the first sound of rifle fire, he rode at the head of thirty mounted soldiers in a charge toward the Paiutes. But as he neared them, and the besieged men of Spy Company, the warriors quickly divided their force and sent a fast-riding group of men who threatened to outflank the whites.

Seeing what was taking place, Major Hungerford sent a force of men to halt the movement of the warriors along the sand ridges beside the river. In the short fight that followed, one of the white soldiers was wounded, and a few of the Paiutes were hit. But nothing was decisive, and both sides retreated.

After this first test of strength, Hays and Hungerford pulled back closer to the Big Bend of the Carson River. Here the two officers considered their position. Somewhere, out of sight among the sand dunes, was the Paiute force. But how large it might be was no more than a guessing game. Some of the men who had been pursued by them estimated that there were between fifty and one hundred warriors; others said that there were at least three hundred well-mounted and well-armed fighting men. Colonel Hays persisted in his belief that he had caught the Paiutes off balance and that now was the time to strike them hard.

Yet Hays had learned a lot from this brief encounter with the Paiutes. While he was not sure that this was anything more than a raiding party or a group of warriors sent out to test his strength, he had already learned that War Chief Numaga had a keen sense of military strategy. To ride into the sand hills after the Paiutes might very well be just what Chief Numaga wanted him to do. Realizing this, Hays sent men out with orders to get just close enough to try to draw the Paiutes back into the open. In this way he hoped to maneuver them into a position where they would have to fight a full-scale battle in the open.

When the small groups of men from the regiment neared the sand hills, the Paiutes appeared well out of rifle range; and both sides fired ineffectual long-range shots at each other. Then in an obvious attempt to lure the Washoe Regiment into their own trap, the warriors rode back and forth on the ridges of the sand hills, but just out of range. Colonel Hays estimated that between fifty and one hundred mounted warriors came into view, and one thing was quite certain, these horsemen were among the finest riders he had ever seen.[3]

As Colonel Hays watched and admired the exhibition of horsemanship, he saw the Paiutes begin to retreat into the sand hills again. Figuring that he might have one more chance to draw them into the open meadow, he followed with part of his regiment. But he lined his infantry in between and behind the cavalry. Their orders were to remain as concealed as possible and to come out at the very last moment if the warriors should attack. In this way, Hays hoped to decoy the Paiutes into a position where they would be highly vulnerable to the fire power of his foot soldiers.

In addition to this scheme, the ex-Texas Ranger protected his men from any flank movement the Paiutes might make by ordering Major Hungerford to place his men in a position where they could easily move to the left or the right. When all was ready, Hays gave the order to move forward.

Slowly the volunteers worked their way toward the sand hills. It was a deadly game of sparring, of trying to catch the other side off guard, of waiting for the right moment to make a quick and bloody move. Then just as it appeared that the scheme was really working, as the Washoe Regiment got within rifle range of some of Chief Numaga's warriors, the sound of shooting and the sudden cries of wounded men made it all too clear that the Paiutes had also been waiting for men to come within range of their weapons.

The exchange of shots was short between the two forces, and it hardly added up to success or failure for either the Paiutes or the whites. Yet two things were quite evident as the warriors moved away from Big Meadows—they had been sizing up the potential power of the white force, and they possessed good rifles and even better horses than any of the volunteers.

But even though the skirmish was short, it had taken its toll. The shaky and battle-tested men counted seven dead Paiutes left on the first sand hill overlooking Big Meadows, and they saw that three men of Captain Fleeson's Spy Company were wounded, and that two of Captain Blackburn's horses had been wounded and one killed. Still, the men had come through in their first taste of action, and they were supremely confident that they had easily chased the Paiutes back into the desert.[4]

But while his men talked of an easy victory, Colonel Hays thought otherwise. To him, the Paiutes had tested the strength of his army, and that was all it came to at the end of the shooting. He still had no way of knowing how many warriors would be waiting for him as his regiment moved toward Pyramid Lake. The only thing he was truly certain about was that War Chief Numaga and his warriors might not prove to be as easy foes as his green men wished to believe. And he was more than happy when he heard one of his men shout: "Here comes the regular army! By God, we'll give it to them now, boys!"

3

Captain Joseph Stewart and the regulars arrived in the afternoon, and the captain rode at the head of the column. He was a man who had the look of a professional soldier about him. His hairline was already receding, and when he removed his hat and greeted Colonel Hays, his broad forehead and the front portion of his skull looked much like one of the granite domes in the high Sierra Nevada, complete with a fringe of brush covering at the rear and on the sides. Thin neck, thin body, that was Captain Joseph—sometimes called "Jasper"—Stewart. But he was all military, and make no mistake about it. Colonel Hays took one look, and he immediately liked the cut of the man. For he saw a hardness in this soldier that could be counted on if the going got rough. There was nothing about this man that even suggested panic. But there was a great deal about him that left no doubt as to how he would react in time of danger.

After Colonel Hays and Captain Stewart exchanged greetings, they got right down to the business at hand. Stewart's questions were short and to the point. He wanted to know how large the Paiute band might be, how they were armed and mounted, and whether or not they would put up a stiff defense.

Jack Hays answered as best he could, but his own knowledge of the extent of the Paiute force was limited to what he had seen in the day's skirmish. As to arms and horses, he was able to tell the captain that the Paiutes possessed rifles as good as their own and that their horses appeared to be in better shape and a lot faster.

Captain Stewart listened intently to all that Hays had to say. Then he asked once again about the possibility of the Paiutes putting up a strong defensive battle.

Hays shook his head. No, he did not think they would stand and defend their position. Their movements during the brief battle at the edge of Big Meadows simply didn't indicate that they wanted an all-out fight. Hit and run was what Hays figured they'd do. Catch a man off guard here, another there, strike fast, then retreat. Hit and run, that's what the army would be up against.

For the moment that was all Captain Stewart wanted to know. The afternoon was getting late, and it was necessary for his men to make camp for the night. When that was done, then it would be time to decide on an operational plan. But one thing was clear to Hays as Stewart and the regulars moved past and established their camp some two miles away—the Paiutes were going to be up against a larger, stronger, and much more disciplined army than Major Ormsby's frightened volunteers. Including the thirty teamsters and the camp followers, Colonel Hays tallied the Washoe Regiment's contingent as a force of 590, and out of this number, 300 soldiers were mounted as volunteer cavalry. Added to this, there was Captain Stewart's army of 212 regulars. Altogether, the volunteers and the regulars presented a formidable show of strength,[5] and Colonel Hays was confident that its size, its arms and ammunition would be so impressive to War Chief Numaga that he would avoid any direct clash between his warriors and the army of the whites.

As Hays thought of the show of power that the Paiute scouts were now observing, he believed that this temporary outbreak of Indian hostility was almost over. Still, even as he watched his men establish a new camp in Big Meadows, he wanted to leave nothing to chance. For some of his soldiers had found the missing fourth victim of the raid on Williams Station—a man identified as "James S. Henning of Virginia City."[6]

To avoid being caught off guard by the Paiutes, Colonel Hays moved the camp of the Washoe Regiment into the center of the meadowland. Guards took their regular tour of duty around the perimeter of the camp. Beyond the guards, there was another group of men, who encircled the meadow up to a distance of three miles from the main camp. In addition, a company of men was stationed on the other side of the Carson River to protect the regiment from any surprise attack that might come from that direction.

All the next day, the Washoe Regiment and The Carson Valley Expedition rested in their respective camps. The men cleaned their weapons, checked their gear, and got ready for the desert march from the Big Bend of the Carson River to the Big Bend of the Truckee River. Colonel Hays and Captain Stewart met and talked of how the campaign might be carried out to the best possible advantage. Both men agreed that to avoid confusion, the command of both regulars and volunteers should be given to one man. Captain Stewart willingly stepped aside, and Colonel Hays assumed the role of commander. With this out of the way, the two officers outlined their plan of movement for the journey to the Truckee River.

Colonel Hays and the fifteen men of Spy Company Number 2 would lead the way, and they would proceed at a distance of one or two miles in front of the cavalry. Behind the horse soldiers would be the infantry; then the drovers and the fifty head of cattle that served as a walking commissary; following the cattle herd would be the thirty supply wagons; behind the wagons would be the main body of the regular army, the remainder of the volunteers, and a rear guard of fifty men.[7]

With their plan of movement worked out to the last detail, Colonel Hays and Captain Stewart parted company for the night. At daybreak, their combined forces would begin the desert trek to the Big Bend of the Truckee River.

4

There was a slate-colored sky as the men broke camp and moved into formation on the morning of May 31. They shivered with cold as they looked toward the west. Hanging over the dark, brooding Sierra Nevada were dark thunderheads bunched together. But as the men watched, they saw these wind-driven clouds move toward them— pushed by air currents that came across California from somewhere out in the Pacific.

When all the army was on the move and stretched out in single file according to the nature of the terrain, the line of this combined force was at least three miles long. To protect the marching and riding soldiers, there were outriders on both sides to guard against a sudden hit-and-run raid, and the rear guard. Even so, a few Paiutes did appear in the distance from time to time, but they remained well out of rifle range.

But Indians did not worry the men as much as the weather. They kept looking upward and to the west, and they talked of what bothered them most of all—the coming of another storm, another wet camp.

"Well, she's cool, anyway," a man would say.

"Cool? What do you mean, cool? The way I see it, we'll be damned lucky if it doesn't snow come nightfall."

Yet another man, a man who had done some prospecting in the summer of 1859, would add his own special knowledge to the comments on the weather. "Be glad, boys, that she's cool. Last year at this time, if you was to pick up a rock to kill a rattler, you'd burn your hand just as bad as if you'd put it and not your bacon into the frying pan. I'll tell you, boys, it's a sight better to shiver a little than wonder if your skin's on fire."

The man of the hot summer memory did have his point, for the march to the Big Bend of the Truckee was fairly easy. By four o'clock that afternoon, with the sky turning an obsidian color, the army completed its desert march. The camp was established, and the men had not even started their campfires before lightning lit up the desert mountains and the rolling boom of thunder followed like some ancient surf pounding back onto shores of its youth. Then the rain began to fall, lightly for a few minutes, then harder and harder until it was a full-scale rainstorm of icy drops that felt as though they had just melted before striking the earth.

All that night the storm filled the camp with water. The early campfires went out, and it was impossible to start another. The men had to eat cold, wet food as they stood and talked about the coming battle and tried to forget that they were soaking wet and miserable. Some men finally got so tired that they pulled their wet blankets around themselves, rolled on the muddy ground, and managed to go to sleep. Other soldiers sought out shelter beneath large clumps of sagebrush, under the groves of cottonwoods, and beneath the supply wagons, while a few of the men constructed "temporary shelters, with boughs and blankets"[8] to protect themselves from the constant wind and driving rain.

The next day the army would begin the final march to Pyramid Lake, and for some of the soldiers, the storm was a bad sign. For among the volunteers were some survivors of Major Ormsby's army. From them, the men learned that Ormsby and his men had pitched their camp at this same location on their last night before riding into disaster. And no matter how easy it was to say that this was a different army under a different leader, one fact remained to gnaw at a man's stomach: somewhere beyond this camp, somewhere downstream from the Big Bend of the Truckee River, the Paiutes would be waiting for them either tomorrow or the day after. The day might change, but one thing remained constant: Chief Numaga and his warriors would still be waiting.

CHAPTER 15

The Battle of Pinnacle Mount

All during the night there was no letup in the storm, and the Big Bend of the Truckee River became a muddy bog. Even when the gray light of day broke, the rain continued to fall, and the day did not belong to the first day of June. Its color blended into the dull silver of the endless sagebrush hills that reached the horizon and became part of the gray and cloudy sky. The cycle of the seasons had lost all meaning for the men of Colonel Hays's command. There had been no sign of spring, and now even summer was hiding in the wind and rain of winter.

While the men ate cold, wet food and drank icy water, they wished that someone had thought to bring along a few bottles of whiskey—not enough so that Colonel Jack would raise hell, but enough, just enough to warm a man's insides and stop the shivering. Huddled together for warmth in the shelter of anything that would keep some of the rain from rolling off their hat brims and dropping on to their sopping wet clothes, they thought about whiskey, warm food, hot baths, and sunny days with only a light afternoon breeze. And they talked about

Warren Wasson and the few volunteers who had headed for the southwest pass leading to Pyramid Lake to make sure the warriors didn't circle around and come at the army from the rear.

The talk went back and forth all that morning and past midday. Everyone agreed that Wasson and the boys with him were freezing their asses. But the men looked at each other, then at the gray sky. One thing was certain: they weren't all that much better off than Wasson. The rain, the endless, cold rain continued to fall. The talk shifted away from weather, away from Wasson, away from pursuit of the Indians. They spoke of how much time it would take to get back to Virginia City. Why, if they headed out now, if they gave up chasing the Indians, they could be at Buckland's Station just after it turned dark. By God, that would be the thing to do. At Buckland's Station there would be whiskey to drink, warm food, and a chance to get dry. The day after that they could reach Chinatown, or if they moved smartly, they might even make it all the way to Virginia City. By Christ! That would be worth dog-trotting all the way up Sun Mountain for. That would be the end of all this sleeping in wet clothes, of shivering until a man's bones like to slip free at the joints. Yet even as they talked, even as they thought of turning back, of heading homeward, the rain stopped.

At first, the men didn't even realize it. Then they saw that drops of water were no longer splashing in the mud puddles, and it was then that they saw Colonel Hays and Captain Stewart talking and pointing north toward the trail to Pyramid Lake.

Colonel Hays passed the word to the Washoe Regiment. They were going to move out and hit the Paiute trail to Pyramid Lake. But the men under Captain Stewart's command would remain at the Big Bend of the Truckee River, and follow behind them on the next day. This way, the reasoning went, the Paiutes just might think that they were going to get a crack at a smaller force and come out into the open for a full-scale battle. This maneuver would give Captain Stewart's men a chance to come in with a surprise attack.

At three o'clock on that Friday afternoon, the Washoe Regiment began to move north toward Pyramid Lake. They followed the same general path that Major Ormsby and his men had taken, but it was almost impossible for them to stay on the Paiute trail. The past days and nights of steady rain had made most of the land into a muddy, slippery, trackless region where the going for horses and men was only halfway normal on the crest of the ridge where the gravelly soil was thin enough so that the run-off had not created a sodden mass of mud. But when they moved down from the ridge and onto the flats beside the roaring high water of the river, the horses bogged every few steps. The traveling became so difficult for the horses that many of the men had to dismount and lead the tired animals across the slippery ground.

The progress of the regiment became a slow and miserable task. Moving from one bog to another, the men cursed the weather as they began to slip and fall more often. To add to their misery, a cold wind began to whip down through the canyon of the Truckee River, and the light of late afternoon began to give way to dark shadows that marked the wind-driven passage of more storm clouds. They had traveled no more than seven or eight miles from their last camp, and now as they began to look for another spot to set up camp for another night, the rain began to fall once more.

Colonel Hays selected a campsite in the meadow alongside the river so that there would be some grass for the horses and cattle. But for the men, it was another wet camp, and everyone agreed it was even worse than the camp at the Big Bend of the Truckee. "The spot was half overflowed by rains, and surrounded by high bleak and desolate hills."[1]

As the men picketed the horses and set up camp in the boggy meadow, the foot scouts who had been looking over the country ahead returned. They reported to Colonel Hays that they had only seen a scattering of Indian scouts, and all of them were retreating. But they had seen more than a few Paiutes heading toward Pyramid Lake. Not too far from the camp, they had found the bodies of three more men who had been part of Major Ormsby's expedition.

Colonel Hays asked if they knew who the men were, but the scouts said that they didn't know enough men from Virginia City to be at all sure. Others who were standing near heard their report, and they called to Captain Edward Farris Storey of the Virginia Rifles.

Captain Storey listened, nodded his head, and agreed to ride out and identify the dead. Silas C. Fletcher, a Missouri man and one of Captain Storey's command, volunteered to go along. But as he unstacked the arms to get to his own rifle, he lost his grip on the wet and slippery stock of his gun. Before he could catch it, the weapon struck a rock. There was a loud report that echoed off the hills, and to Storey's horror, the rifle ball plowed through Fletcher's throat, and he fell backward onto the muddy ground.

Storey knelt beside his friend. One look at Fletcher's face told him more than he wished to know. The glazed and fixed eyes, the muscles frozen into a final mask of surprise meant only one thing, and Storey knew that he would never laugh and joke with Fletcher any more.

Even the pursuit of the dead had caused yet another death. And as Captain Storey and a volunteer rode the upward trail out of the meadow, the irony of their journey must have run through his thoughts like the ever shifting thunderheads drifting through the sky.

No more than a mile from the watery camp, the two riders found the dead men. One body was lying on its face, and Storey saw that it was tall, thin Charles McCloud, and he stared with disbelief at the man's back, for it had been cut open from the neck to the hips along the spine. Near McCloud's corpse was the shorter body of red-bearded James McCarthy, who had been shot through the chest. "By his side was a body recognized as that of A. Elliott, the man who looked through his telescope rifle and fired the first shot . . . the body had two shots in the chest and one in the left arm."[2]

Everywhere around the dead men of Major Ormsby's army there were marks of a desperate struggle—marks that even steady days of rainfall had failed to erase. Sagebrush was trampled and broken, and in one spot where the soil was almost pure sand, it appeared to Captain Storey that one man had burrowed into the sand to try to hide, but had been pulled out and killed on the spot. "The throats of all were cut, and the privates mutilated. None was scalped. All the bodies were naked."[3] Around the dead was a circular path beaten into the earth as though the victors in this furious struggle had danced round and round the slain men in a wild moment of celebration.

Storey and the volunteer did not waste time in this place of death. They led the two pack horses up to the bodies. Then, working as quickly as they could they tied McCloud's large corpse on one of the nervous and shying horses, and placed the two smaller bodies on the other animal. Then they mounted their own horses and began the short ride back to the camp beside the roaring Truckee River.

It was almost dark when they reached the ridge above the camp, but down below the men saw the four horses. And the sight of dead men tied to pack horses did nothing for their spirit. It was bad enough to camp in what was fast becoming a meadow of mud, but the sight of bodies slung across pack horses like dead deer made the men wonder what the next day would bring in the way of bad luck.

2

Downriver from the wet camp, War Chief Numaga sat alone in the shelter of his karnee and listened to the wind and rain pelt the thick grass covering. The home of his People seemed strangely silent now that the women and children and the old people were gone. He missed the laughter of the children and the steady chatter of the women as they went about their work. But the information his scouts had brought to him had left no other choice. For their own protection he had sent everyone except his warriors north to the land of Black Rocks, where they would be safe in the lonely canyons that creased the desert mountains like the wrinkles of an ancient man. He had hoped this move could have been avoided, that the large army of whites would have become discouraged by the weather, that they would have given up this madness and returned to their wooden karnees near the holes they had dug in the earth. But they were not halting. Instead, they were slowly following the trail to the home of the People. Not even the omens of dark thunder clouds and steady rain, not even the fighting at Big Meadows had stopped the movement of the white warriors. Each day they crept a little closer to Pyramid Lake. Each day, like a coyote sneaking closer to the drying meat, they worked their way toward the meadow beside the mouth of the river. Soon they would be so near that he would have to fight them once again.

The battle plan was worked out, and the warriors knew what they were to do. It would be like an antelope hunt. Let the whites think we do not know they are here, Numaga had told his men. Let them come forward with their eyes blinded by thoughts of an easy victory. Only a small group of men shall be in sight. All the rest will remain in hiding. The warriors on ponies, all three hundred as marked on the counting sticks, will remain in the small canyon until I signal with my pelican feather. Let the whites ride down the steep side of the mountain. Let them come off the flatland of the ridge. When they are almost into our homes, almost ready to ride up to our karnees, we will close in on them.

All the questions from Natchez and the other chiefs had been listened to and answered. Draw the whites in, Numaga had told them, draw them in with their own curiosity, their own certainty of having caught us off guard. When they are almost across the meadow, almost in our camp, the riders will move toward them in the shape of a giant arrowhead whirring through the air. Behind the pony men will be the warriors on foot. Crouch low, Numaga had told them, crouch low, and belong to the earth until the time is right to strike. The men had nodded their understanding of what he wanted, and Numaga was certain they would wait for his signal before they struck with the swiftness of the diving eagle that whistles out of the sun.

The warriors who use the white man's weapon just as well as the best warriors use a bow, Numaga had told the gathering of chiefs, shall hide like rattlesnakes in the rocks that watch over the ridge. Here these warriors shall become like the rocks, shall join the wind-shaped rocks and wait without moving. When the whites run from the living arrow of our People, they will run like frightened deer. They will ride their ponies back up the steep and slippery sidehill. They will reach the open land of the ridge, and they will think they are safe. Then and only then, my brothers, Numaga had told them, these warriors with weapons of the whites shall look toward the high, sharp ridge north of our home. When I wave the large feather of the great white bird of the lake, shoot the white man's weapons. But, hear me, my brothers, make each shot find its journey to the target. Aim as though these are the last deer on the mountain, the last chance to keep the People from having hunger eat their bellies.

A sudden gust of wind made the fire in Numaga's karnee flicker and almost go out. He listened to the steady roar of the storm, and he let his mind drift with the shifting currents of wind and the hard patter of wind-driven rain. The season was all wrong. This was not the time of the pogonip, not the time when food became scarce, and when the very old of the tribe began their long and final journey to Spirit-land.

Hunched by his dying fire, his rabbin skin robe pulled around his body, Numaga's thoughts must have been of other seasons, of other times before the coming of the white man. This was the time when men should be netting nesting ducks, when they should be hunting deer and antelope. It was the time of the fish: the strange-looking cui-ui suckerfish, and the tamaagaih—the great spring trout. It was the time to spear and net these fish; the time to eat so much that only sleep kept away the sickness of the belly; the time to listen to the women sing and talk as they filleted the fish and hung them up for drying. It was the time for the women and young girls to steal eggs from the nesting birds, to gather red seeds that had a burning-of-the-tongue taste, to gather red seeds that had a and to pick red berries from the thorn plants—berries that women would travel for two or three days away from the lake to the valley where the red berries lived. And it was a time to see the young babies riding in the cradleboards, laughing and spitting as they were given their first taste of new foods that did not come from the breasts of their mothers.

All of this and more must have been in Numaga's thoughts. For the barren land of the Black Rocks was not where the People belonged at this season. But the season was all bad. Even the storms of winter kept away the sun of summer. And now the whites came to make more war. It was bad and mean, a trick played by angry Coyote. This was a time to live, a time to enjoy life. It was not a time to kill, to end life. Yet Numaga knew that when the night ended and the light of another day began, the war he had never wanted would continue once again; and the smell of death would ride the wind.

3

While the two forces neared the moment of conflict, a small contingent of men under the command of Captain William Weatherlow were suffering through a sleet storm near the mountain pass at the northern end of Pyramid Lake. The short, tough rancher from Honey Lake Valley had taken this position as an independent action in order to cut off any retreat the Paiutes might make to the north after they had run up against the combined armies under the command of Colonel Hays. For though the Honey Laker was Chief Numaga's friend, he truly believed that many lives would be saved and that much suffering would be avoided if the Paiutes were not allowed to retreat but had to endure enough of a defeat to make them come to terms and settle their differences with the whites.

Unknown to Captain Weatherlow and his command of thirty-five men, things were not developing as he had expected. He had arrived at the canyon leading to the northern pass too late to see the old people, the women and children and the guard of warriors, as they passed that way. Weatherlow and his men were reaching the limit of their endurance. In his own mind he had already reached his decision for the next day, and there was no question as to what had to be done. All he had to do was look at his men and their horses, and he realized that come morning, they would have to leave their position and head back to Honey Lake Valley. As he later wrote, they had been "lying in ambush, short of provisions and without fire, for fear of showing our position to the Indians, during a severe sleet storm for over three days, I supposed the fight would not come off and left the position."[4]

What Captain Weatherlow had hoped for simply wasn't going to take place. For the other Honey Lake Company under Captain Bird—the men who had traveled south to join Colonel Hays and the Washoe Regiment—were in no position to ask for a detachment of volunteers to join them and ride around War Chief Numaga's camp to reinforce the freezing Honey Lakers at the northern end Pyramid Lake. So while Captain Weatherlow was forced to give up his plan for preventing any retreat of the Paiutes, what he did not know was that fortune had smiled on him. As things turned out, his small band of rangers would not have to go up against the superior force of Paiute warriors. And though the brave captain cursed the icy weather and the failure of Bird and a group of volunteers to make their appearance, Weatherlow failed to recognize that because no men came to their aid, and because the storm clouds continued to freeze his men with a wild and unrelenting sleet storm, they would be spared an early and violent death.

4

All during the first night of June, the men of the Washoe Regiment suffered through their ordeal at the wet camp. The only thing that offered them any comfort at all was that the wet reeds they had gathered alongside the roaring river made a more comfortable bed for their wet blankets than the muddy ground. But their food supply was another matter. While their cattle herd was still with them, the rain was coming down so hard and fast that it was almost impossible to keep a fire going to cook any beef. Added to this hardship, supplies were running very short. As a reporter wrote, "This is our last day of flour, and we are on half rations."[5] Yet even half rations in this storm became a soggy, tasteless fare that only hunger would overcome.

Just before daybreak the steady downpour turned into a light drizzle. The Truckee River was rising fast and almost ready to overflow its banks and flood the camp. At any moment, it looked as though they would have to drive their animals ahead and take to the higher ground to avoid the water. But as the rainfall became lighter, the river leveled off into a steady roar of churning white-capped water that carried dead timber and great clumps of sagebrush and tumbleweed on a wild voyage toward Pyramid Lake. Then as the gray, overcast morning of June 2 began, the rainfall ceased. The Washoe Regiment crawled out of their soaked blankets, watched the changing of the guards who had encircled the camp during the long, cold night, and stared at the dark clouds drifting across the sky and wondered if the storm had ended, or if it had only paused to rest in its outburst of water-filled fury.

While the men shivered and forced themselves to eat cold food, Colonel Hays conferred with his officers. It was agreed that the dead men in camp should be given a proper burial. After that was done, the extent and location of the Paiute warriors should be determined. This task was assigned to Captain Storey and forty cavalrymen. Hays instructed them to ride with care toward Pyramid Lake, to take every precaution necessary, and to avoid an armed encounter until Captain Stewart and the regulars had marched from their rear guard position.

There was only one flaw in Hays's plan with regard to the regulars. It was going to take most of the day for them to march the eight miles through a country that had turned into an endless quagmire—slippery ground where wagons needed double teams, shoulder help from the soldiers, and where horses bogged to their knees at every step.

Still, while Colonel Hays waited for their arrival, he knew that inaction was no way to keep his discouraged and weary troops in any frame of mind for a battle. Now was the time to shock them into anger in order to keep them going. Knowing this, his first order of this rainless day was the burial of the dead. When the graves were completed and filled, a short prayer was read over the wet mounds of earth covering Silas Fletcher and the three corpses from Major Ormsby's army, and this was followed "with Odd Fellows' honors."[6] At the conclusion of the funeral in the muddy meadow, Hays ordered his troops to empty their guns, give them a thorough cleaning, and wipe them dry. But some of the regiment decided it was far too much trouble to clean their firearms with a rod and cloth. Contrary to orders, they fired their weapons into the air to get the dirt out of the barrels.

Furious at such unprofessional conduct, Colonel Hays's reaction was immediate and to the point. He refused to listen to excuses of any nature, and his orders were stated in clear, precise, short statements. Each man who had fired his weapon to clean it was to stand guard for the rest of the day. One San Francisco reporter, who stated that he was "lying on the ground, under blanket,"[7] and writing on his knees when this took place, wrote, "So soon as a gun is heard, which is contrary to orders, the culprit is marched off to guard duty—consequently, there is a large guard duty to-day. Col. Hays is a good disciplinarian."[8]

While all of this was taking place, Captain Storey waited for Hays to give him the order to lead his small unit of cavalry toward Pyramid Lake. But Jack Hays did not wish to send him out until Captain Stewart and the regulars made their appearance. Yet as the day neared noon, the tough Texan told Storey to begin his mission. Waiting for the regulars might well delay any contact with the Paiutes for another day, and one more day would give them that much more time to prepare an ambush or to ride north into a country where it would be impossible to follow them until the army had gathered additional supplies to back up such a move.

But the key factor in Hays's decision to send Storey ahead was the background of this rugged captain from Georgia. This was not an ordinary soldier that he had selected to send on a tough mission. This was a man who was already accustomed to desert travel and to fighting Indians. For as a young man, Edward Farris Storey had been a lieutenant of the Texas Rangers. In the Mexican War he had fought in the tough northern campaigns which culminated with the Battle of Buena Vista. After the war ended, Storey remained in Texas until his wife's death in 1852. He then traveled on horseback with a group of friends all the way across the arid lands of southern Texas, drifted across the border into northern Mexico to Durango, and crossed the Sierra Madre Occidental to Mazatlán. Here he purchased passage on a vessel sailing to California, and made a stormy—and for some fatal—voyage to Monterey.[9] In short, Captain Storey was a good man to have along if there was any chance of hard going or unexpected trouble.

5

It was nearing two o'clock in the afternoon when Captain Storey and his detachment of cavalry first saw Pyramid Lake. They were riding on the sagebrush plateau beneath the craggy pinnacles overlooking the tableland. From this vantage point, they looked ahead at the incredible lake surrounded by desert mountains. They saw Anaho Island, and just beyond it, close to the eastern shoreline, the great triangular rock that had been John C. Frémont's inspiration when he named this great body of water. Then far to the northwest, where a point of land jutted out to form a cove, the men saw the wind-shaped needle-like rocks standing upright like giant bone awls. The color of the water was gray-blue as it mirrored the sky, and there were great flights of snow-colored pelicans, inland sea gulls, and many other water birds skimming the surface of the lake in a search for food. Astounded by what they saw, the men slowly guided their horses downward on the wet, slippery trail to the long meadow beside the Truckee River.

Now the volunteers were not far from the mouth of the river. Ahead, they could see the Paiute camp, but it was strangely silent, and there was nobody in sight. To the men, the Indian village appeared deserted. Then as they moved along the widening meadow toward the Paiute karnees, their horses were spooked by the sudden noise of large buzzards taking off, and flapping their broad wings in the first stages of flight. The men stared at what the buzzards had been eating, and their stomachs churned with revulsion.

Scattered along the ground in various postures of final death throes were twenty-three of Major Ormsby's men who had been killed in the first moments of battle. While the men of Captain Storey's cavalry felt sick at what they saw, there was very little time for grief or anger. For as they stared at the rigid, grotesque bodies, they suddenly saw over a dozen Paiutes sitting on the ground in the "deserted" camp ahead. But the small group of warriors became an attack force even as they watched. The first puffs of rifle fire hung in the air like small clouds, and the sound of shots echoed and re-echoed from mountain to mountain in a repetitive series of sharp cracks. To the whites, warriors seemed to materialize out of the earth. Then from the rear of the camp a large group of mounted

warriors charged out of a deep ravine, and yelling battle
cries, they galloped toward the stunned men.

Realizing that he was almost caught in the middle of
a very clever trap, Captain Storey shouted for his men
to retreat. Turning their frightened horses in the boggy,
slippery ground, the cavalry headed back toward the
upward trail. Yet as they neared the steep and narrow
path leading to the high ground, the Paiutes began to close
in on them. Storey and part of his force turned to face
the oncoming charge, and kept up a steady rifle fire
to cover the withdrawal of the first horsemen heading
up the hillside.

During the next fifteen minutes, everything became
a nightmare scene. Men yelled and cursed their horses
as they tried to get the frightened and tired animals to
move faster on the slippery sidehill. Shot after shot rang
out as Captain Storey and the men at the foot of the
trail tried to hold off the advancing Paiutes. But time was
running out for the cavalry. Even as they took aim and
fired, they also had to calculate how much longer they
could hold off more than three hundred warriors who
were coming toward them "on horseback in the form
of a wedge with the point advanced, while about the
same number on foot came running up the valley in a
'go as you please style.'"[10]

Things were happening much too fast to risk a holding
action any longer, and Storey ordered his men to cease
fire and move up to the plateau. With the sound of yelling and rifle fire behind them, the men rode their horses
up the steep trail and to the tableland. Here they regrouped, and Storey told them to put their mounts into
a steady trot and strike out for the camp of the Washoe
Regiment. But even as he spoke, Chief Numaga's riflemen on the Pinnacle Rock ledge above the plateau opened

fire. Before the men got their horses moving, Andrew Hasey of the Nevada Rifles was hit by a rifle ball that tore through his muscles and shattered his hip joint. Yet the combination of shock and his own fear of the hard-riding warriors who were on their way up the hill-side seemed to have numbed his senses. For though he knew he had been hit, he had no real idea of how badly he was wounded until he began to feel dizzy from loss of blood.

In the wild ride across the gully- and ravine-creased tableland, the retreating whites continued to be moving targets for the Paiute marksmen. Horses fell from under their riders as the riflemen concentrated their fire on the larger targets, and the riders who were sent sprawling on the ground were picked up to ride double behind other cavalrymen.

When the fleeing whites were almost back to their camp beside the Truckee River, they saw Colonel Hays and some two hundred cavalrymen coming to their rescue. This was just the action that Captain Storey had counted on, and he called his troops to a halt. The time had come to stand and put up a fight.

6

Captain Stewart and the regulars had arrived at the camp of the Washoe Regiment just before the first sounds of rifle fire between Captain Storey's troops and Chief Numaga's warriors signaled the start of battle. The march of the regulars from the Big Bend of the Truckee River had been slow and tough going for men and animals on the muddy ground. But the sound of shooting gave all the men a new spurt of energy.

Hays outlined his plan of battle. He would lead a

strong force of horse soldiers to the rescue of Storey and his men. Then when he had joined forces, they would strike at the main body of Indians. Meanwhile, Stewart and the combined infantry of volunteers and regulars would move in a wide line across the plateau and down into the ravines and gulches to drive out any hidden warriors. At the same time, the artillery would be ready to strike out toward the high rocky ridge if there were any Indians firing from that direction. For this detail, Captain Flint would be the commanding officer, and it would be his responsibility to get the pack horses carrying the mountain howitzers into a position where the cannons could be effective. Other units of regulars and volunteers were to protect the flanks of the army as it moved forward, and the rear guard between the army and the camp was to be in command of Major Hungerford, who was to stand and hold or to advance with the major movement if the conditions of battle so demanded.

The orders were given, the battle plan was fixed. Colonel Hays rode his black charger at the head of his cavalry, and when they reached the tableland, he saw Captain Storey's men retreating under heavy fire. Jack Hays turned and looked at his men. He gave a wild yell, spurred his horse into a full gallop, and led his men in a charge across the rough and slippery ground.

As the yelling, charging cavalry neared Captain Storey's men, Colonel Hays shouted for them to halt and dismount. He quickly deployed his soldiers in a formation that was a walking line of riflemen. Soon, they were joined by Captain Stewart's men, and they all walked across the uneven terrain and tried to drive the well-concealed warriors into the open and away from the ravines, gulches, rocks, and clumps of sagebrush.

But two things were not going in favor of the whites, and Hays was well aware of it. There was a steady crack-crack of rifle fire coming from Pinnacle Mount above and to their right, and the well-fortified warriors were much too far away to be reached by Captain Flint's mountain howitzers. If they were going to win the battle, there was only one thing to do. They had to take the position and knock out the protection that Chief Numaga's men were receiving from the hidden marksmen.

Captain Storey of the Virginia Rifles and Captain Van Hagen of the Nevada Rifles volunteered to make a foot charge with part of their command in the direction of Pinnacle Mount to drive the Paiutes from the cover of the high rocks. And while they started toward the deadly riflemen, the right wing of the regulars moved into the position that Storey and his men had been holding. Then to protect the army from any attack that might come from the meadow below the plateau, Colonel Hays sent a portion of his command in that direction.

As Storey and Van Hagen led their men upward toward Pinnacle Mount, the intensity of the battle increased. There was a wild mixture of sounds that could only belong to a battlefield: shot after shot, yelling and cursing, and the neighing of frightened horses. The fighting became a primordial scene, a leftover from some strange moment of primitive conflict, a vision of brutal madness played out against the bleak and barren background of the harsh desert landscape.

Some of the greener men lost their nerve in their first test of facing enemy fire, and they wasted bullet after bullet in frenzied and unaimed shots at the unseen Paiutes hiding in the craggy rocks. When some of these first-time soldiers did manage to hit one of the warriors who had suddenly jumped up from behind a nearby rock or clump of sagebrush, a barbaric scene would take place. For the victorious man from Virginia City would rush forward, seize the dying or dead man's hair, draw a knife, and cut and pull the man's scalp loose to tie to his belt as a war souvenir to show the boys at the saloon.

The line of regulars and volunteers extended for a mile, and it covered the area from the meadow to just below Pinnacle Mount, but the whites were met by a force as large, if not larger, than their own. Slowly, step after cautious step, the men worked their way closer to the high rocks hiding the sharpshooting Paiute riflemen. But they were taking the ground foot by foot, and the fighting became a close and violent struggle for survival. The late afternoon breeze was filled with the whirring and whistling of singing rifle balls that came as deadly hail. Yet that was only part of the terror. For warriors who had been driven out of ravines and gulches, warriors who blended into ground cover suddenly appeared like newly grown plants and fired point-blank at the advancing whites.

Now the sounds of battle picked up new notes—the last screams and groans of whites and Indians who were hit in vital spots, and the moans and cries for help of the very badly wounded who were unable to help themselves. Yet, in this wild struggle for victory, neither side was willing to give up easily. Captain Storey and his men marched against an invisible but firmly determined foe, and as they drew closer and closer to the high rocks, the rapid rifle fire increased in intensity.

At this moment of the battle, Private A. H. Phelps of Storey's command was killed by a rifle ball that smashed into his forehead, and plowed through his skull. As he fell to the ground, one of the survivors later wrote,

Phelps's "brains stuck out the size of a hen's egg."[11] Before the men close to Phelps truly understood that he was dead and that there was nothing to be done for him, Private James Cameron was also shot through the head. Like Phelps, he hit the ground without screaming out, and when a physician with the command turned him over, he saw at once that Cameron had died instantly, for the rifle ball had struck the top of his head, cut through his brain, and come out at his neck.

Still, the shooting continued, and the soldiers moved forward as Chief Numaga's warriors grudgingly gave up each foot of ground. Then as the drifting clouds blew toward the east, the late afternoon sun broke clear in a burst of brilliant light. The sudden glare blinded the troops, and as they shaded their eyes with their hands and continued their advance, Captain Storey dropped his rifle, clutched his chest, stumbled, and fell backward into a nearby ravine. A physician who had seen the death of Private Phelps was quickly summoned to go to Storey's aid. When he reached the stricken man, he found that another physician—Dr. Bell—had already dressed the wound. But one look at what the rifle ball had done to Storey was all that was needed to tell any medical man that there was very little hope for the wounded man's recovery. "The ball had entered the cavity of the chest, on the left side, as he was in the act of firing, perforating the lungs and paralyzing the lower extremities."[12]

Captain Storey was surrounded by anxious and loyal Virginia City friends, who wanted to know what they could do to help. One of these men walked all the way to the Truckee River to bring back a hatful of water; another wiped the blood as it ran from Storey's mouth with each gasp for air, and a third comrade tried his best to protect the wounded captain from the warmth and glare of the late afternoon sun.

But all the attention was not so well directed. One of the men held a bloody scalp in front of Storey's face and said: "Look! captain, look! Here's the Injun that shot you; three of us killed him."[13]

Storey glanced upward, his face drained of color, and said, "Take it away . . . why should I want to see it!"[14]

Colonel Hays and two officers rode into the ravine to see how badly wounded Captain Storey might be, and when Hays saw the scalper, he wasted no time in telling him just what he thought of him in language that the man would understand. Then he ordered the soldiers to put together a litter and carry Storey down the hill and back to the camp of the Washoe Regiment. With this taken care of, Hays next gave his attention to other wounded men on the battlefield. He made sure that they were helped back to camp, and as the sun passed overhead and began its westward drop behind the Sierra Nevada, Jack Hays ordered troopers to fashion blanket slings and carry the dead down from the plateau.

The power of the Paiutes had been broken for this day, and there were only scattered echoes of rifle fire as the warriors covered their own men who ran into the open to pick up their wounded and dead before they moved across the rocky divide to leave the high crags that they had fought so hard to hold. The Battle of Pinnacle Mount had lasted no more than three hours, but during these hours of hell both sides fought with desperation. And now as the shadows of night began to cover the land with darkness, Colonel Hays knew that the battle was a draw, and that the next day or the day after would see both sides killing and maiming each other once again for control of another stretch of desert.

7

That night after the fierce struggle for Pinnacle Mount, the men gathered around campfires and ate their ration of beef, drank some hot coffee, and looked up at the clear desert sky, where the stars seemed to be almost within reach. This should have been a time of celebration for their survival, a time of animated talk of the day's events. Yet, with guards on patrol duty, with worries about the next move by War Chief Numaga, there was no certainty that a full-scale victory had been won. To Colonel Hays and his army, the only thing that could be considered was that the next day they would bury the dead if they were not attacked at the first light of dawn. The men were quiet, and when they spoke, it was as though they had grown many years older in the course of the bloody afternoon.

Now, as the numb and weary soldiers tried to get some rest for whatever the morning might bring, Colonel Hays counted his casualties and tried to estimate the Paiute losses. A San Francisco correspondent traveling with the army reported that Hays was very pleased with the conduct of his troops, and that the casualties for the battle were in favor of the whites. In a summation of the wounded and the dead, the journalist wrote the following:

> About 20 to 25 Indians were killed, and as many more wounded. About 50 Indian ponies were secured and brought into camp. The Indians were admirably posted, while our own men were without cover. We have to mourn the loss of privates Cameron and Phelps, of the Virginia Rifles. Capt. Storey of the same company was shot through the lungs—we fear mortally. He is a gal-

lant gentleman, and proved himself a true soldier, who fell cheering on his men to the charge. His loss will be felt severely, and be universally mourned. Private Hasey of the Nevada Rifles is severely wounded in the thigh. Four U.S. privates, whose names I have not ascertained, were also wounded—one seriously.[15]

Whether the estimate for the dead and wounded among Chief Numaga's warriors was correct or wrong was hard to tell after the hard-fought battle. In later years—long after this day of suffering and death—various figures for Paiute losses were offered as fact. At one end of the scale, there was a high of 160 killed and an even larger number wounded. At the other end of the scale, there was a low of four killed and seven wounded.[16] But to the dead and wounded of that dreadful day numbers were without meaning.

As for the survivors of the battle, the number of dead and wounded was already lost in fatigue and deep sleep. Only the fearful struggle remained deep within their memories to come into their dreams that night, and for many other nights, with all the vivid terror of that day and to echo and re-echo the terrible reality from thought to thought. So passed the night of the violent day, and at daybreak the dark and bloody nightmares had vanished, and the men awoke to a drying camp beneath a cloudless sky.

On this warm Sunday morning of June 3, 1860, Colonel Hays sent out scouts to see if the Paiutes were getting prepared for another battle. While these riders were away, Hays and the other officers discussed their next move, and talked of the severe fight they expected once they got to the Paiute camp near Pyramid Lake. As they talked of how they should maneuver the army in order to defeat War Chief Numaga's strong force, a detail of soldiers dug a small square entrenchment for defense of the wounded and the supplies, and they called this Fort Storey. All the wounded, both from the regular army and the volunteers, were brought into the camp of the Washoe Regiment, and were placed under a guard of ten men. Forty other soldiers were detailed to guard the cattle and the supply wagons which would remain at Fort Storey. By the time this work was completed, the scouts returned and reported they had made a wide circuit that took them up to Pinnacle Mount, down the other side for a distance, and put them in view of the Paiute camp at Pyramid Lake, but nowhere did they see any sign of Indians.

With the morning sun riding across the sky, heading toward the middle of the day, it was too late to begin the march to Pyramid Lake. Instead, Colonel Hays decided that now was the time to gather the dead—the rotting bodies of Major Ormsby's command and the men who had died in the Battle of Pinnacle Mount—and give them a fitting burial. Accordingly, a detachment was sent out to pick up what was left of Ormsby's army and bring them to the camp. When the putrid remains were placed on the ground, one of the bodies was identified by Dr. W. S. Ormsby as that of his brother. Then in a letter to the widow Ormsby, he wrote:

One of the greatest things for you, my dear sister, is the discovery of the Major's remains, they are badly mutilated, I will give you particulars when we meet. This day we are burying his remains with military honors. The Carson City Guards and others, together with two com-

panies of regulars, Capt. Stewart conducted the cere-
monies to do honor to his remains . . . neighbors and
many others are anxious to render me all the assistance
possible in the solemn performance. Services will be read
at the grave.[17]

And services were read at the graves of all the dead
on that Sunday afternoon "with a concourse of nearly
seven hundred persons in attendance. The beautiful and
sublime service of the Protestant Episcopal Church was
read by Capt. Stewart of the Army."[18]

After the burial, the men prepared for the next day's
march to Pyramid Lake. Weapons were cleaned and
checked, and each man made sure that he had a full supply of ammunition for the coming battle. Assignments for
guard duty were issued, and as the afternoon sun began to
lose its warmth, men gathered sagebrush and driftwood
and laid it in the fire pits so that fires could be made to
roast beef and boil coffee. While all this took place, the
journalists traveling with the army got their accounts of
the Battle of Pinnacle Mount and all the other events in
order, and "Wandering Ned" of *The Mountain Democrat*
closed his story with a complaint to his editor: "Paper is
very scarce—postage stamps scarcely to be had at all;
had I some of both, I would willingly give you a correct
account of the expedition as it progresses."[19]

The spirit of the army and the men who traveled with
it was returning to normal, and all the gripes of any army
on the move were a good sign. For whatever the next
day might hold in store, all the officers had to do was
listen to the men joking and complaining to know that
the troops would be ready for hard traveling and hard
fighting, and it was very likely that they would be in for a
lot of both.

8

Monday morning of the fourth of June was clear and beautiful. Here and there, far to the west, a few billowy white clouds floated in a leisurely fashion just above the highest peaks of the Sierra Nevada. At Fort Storey, the command began to move out on their eight-mile journey to Pyramid Lake and the camp of the Paiutes. As the men moved upward and away from the Truckee River toward the sage-covered tableland, there were cheers from the rear guard who remained behind to guard the wounded, the cattle, and the supply wagons.

Three hours after the army's departure, the soldiers had their first view of Pyramid Lake. They saw it from the last bluff of the plateau, just before they began their downward trek to the long meadow leading to the green floodplain where the Truckee River vanished into the southern end of the lake. Their first view of the lake was almost hard to accept as reality, and like explorers who were in search of a myth, the men could not hold back their joy at seeing what they had almost come to regard as an illusion of desert wanderers, and certainly not something that they would ever see without a touch of madness.

This first view of Pyramid Lake was, as one reporter stated, "the Jerusalem of our crusade and was hailed with delight, for here we hoped to witness the last act of the tragedy."[20] The men rode slowly along, almost as though thoughts of warfare were no longer haunting their minds. To them the sunlight was hitting the lake in such a manner that the water took on a sheen that made it appear "like a sea of molten silver, within its amphitheatre of blue mountains."[21]

To add to the beauty of the scene, directly to the left and down from the plateau was the canyon of the Truckee River. The high waters from the storms and the melting snow of the Sierra Nevada rolled through the narrow opening in angry swirls and waves of white water, broke into the open meadow, lost their rapids, and formed a dark line that grew wider and wider as it crossed the meadow and floodplain on its final journey to the lake.

The army cautiously worked its way down from the tableland to the open meadow. As they did, scouts fanned out in all directions to make sure that they were not riding into an ambush. And while the men waited for them to return, more bodies of Major Ormsby's command were found, including the remains of Henry Meredith. But when the scouts returned from their hazardous duty, they reported that they had not seen any Paiutes in the area, and all signs indicated the Indians had moved out. Still, Colonel Hays was not certain that Chief Numaga had not set a clever trap, and he ordered his soldiers to ride ahead but with due caution.

Yet, when they got within view of the Paiute camp, it was easy to see it was deserted, and that there were no warriors in sight. A campsite was selected about a mile south of the lake; and while the men made preparations for the night, Hays and a small detail of men rode into the Paiute camp and beyond to try to get some indication of what direction the Indians might have taken in their retreat. Following the tracks of the ponies all the way to the Little Truckee, Hays and his men swam their horses across this feeder stream that ran into Mud Lake (now the dry bed of Winnemucca Lake), and cut sign on the other side of the water, and rode back to their own camp knowing that Numaga and his warriors had headed northeast into the rough mountains between Pyramid Lake and Mud Lake.

When he reached camp again, Hays ordered two hundred cavalrymen to be ready to ride in the morning. In the meantime, he made it clear that he wanted the camp to be guarded very closely against any possibility of a night raid or an attack at dawn.

9

The cold air of the desert night still lingered and hugged the earth as the first light of dawn began to shorten the shadows on the rocky and barren northeastern mountains of the Lake Range. Colonel Hays and his cavalrymen rode past the Paiute camp as the steam was rising from the cold water of Pyramid Lake. The riders shivered in their saddles, their coat collars pulled high around their necks. They looked to the north and saw the first flights of feeding pelicans, sea gulls, and other waterfowl skimming the deep blue lake. Then they rode their horses across the Little Truckee River, and headed northeast toward Mud Lake.

The going became very tough for the horses as Hays led his troops upward into the rocky and weatherworn mountains until they had their first glimpse of Mud Lake, which ran along the eastern base of the Lake Range like a shallow, smaller reflection of Pyramid Lake. Here they halted while the tracks of the retreating Paiutes were checked to make sure that there was no variation in their route, no sign that might indicate a break off of men from Chief Numaga's main body of warriors to wait as an ambush party. Seeing no tracks, the troopers continued their northern course along the western shoreline of Mud Lake.

By noon, the cavalry had traveled about twelve miles. It was then that the scouts noticed that the Paiute tracks veered away from the shoreline of the lake and headed west into a deep canyon. Colonel Hays called for the command to halt. He told his scouts to ride into the canyon and make sure the warriors were not waiting for them in a well-fortified position. But the men refused to take this risk. Yet, Hays did not force them to do as he commanded. For these were green soldiers, and there was no way he could be certain that they would not go up the canyon just far enough to be out of view, wait for a time, and return with some yarn about losing the trail. Rather than risk the possibility of receiving this kind of misinformation, Hays called for volunteers to take over their duty.

Five men rode forward as volunteers. Colonel Hays put Lieutenant Robert Lyon of the Highland Rangers in command. With him rode William S. Allen and Ben Webster of Virginia City; S. C. Springer of Silver City, and Samuel Buckland, who had joined the expedition at the Big Bend of the Truckee River.

The instructions from Hays were short and precise. The men were to ride into the canyon, check for Indian sign, avoid a fight, and get back with some intelligence about Chief Numaga's movements. The main column would ride with them as far as the mouth of the canyon. Here they would wait until they returned, or until they heard shooting in the canyon.

The scouts rode cautiously into the canyon, and began to follow its uphill course toward the mountains. Bob Lyon and Will Allen took the lead, and they kept looking up at the high crags on both sides of the trail as they watched for some flash of sunlight against metal that would give away the positions of hidden riflemen. The other men followed behind, and Samuel Buckland looked at the ground and noticed fresh tracks of Indian ponies.

Buckland called to Bob Lyon and Will Allen, "Fresh sign, boys. Let's go tell Jack Hays and have the army back us up."[22]

"I don't give a damn," Will Allen said. "I'm going on up the hill."[23]

That was the end of any discussion. Bob Lyon and Will Allen rode on ahead, slowly working their way up the narrow and rocky trail. The other men followed them up the steep pitch until they all reached the top of the hill. Here there was a massive boulder directly ahead of them, and there were upper and lower paths leading around it.

At this point, Lyon and Allen started around the lower side of the rock, and the other men took the upper path. They proceeded very slowly, stopped every few yards to look around and to listen for any movements out of the ordinary. But everything appeared to be all clear to Buckland. "Webster and myself took out our pipes with a view of taking a smoke, as I was about to light my pipe, I looked down over the bluff and saw two Indians, at the same time calling my companions attention to it."[24]

But even as Buckland called out a warning, there was a loud report of a rifle, and the sound echoed back and forth from ridge to ridge. Bob Lyon saw Will Allen's hat fly into the air, followed by a spurt of blood, brains and bone splinters that sprayed into the air as the scout tumbled from his saddle. Acting quickly, Lyon moved his horse next to the stricken man. "I reached," he said, "from my saddle and tried to raise Will's body on my horse. I did not think of danger; I only saw the bleeding mouth and fast glazing eyes of my friend; but in less than a minute I was surrounded. I believe they intended to capture me alive and secure my horse without injuring him by a chance shot."[25]

Without time to use his rifle, Bob Lyon drew his revolver, got off a blind shot at the warriors closing in on him, gave his horse its head, and began a wild ride down the rough trail. As bullets whizzed near him and the warriors yelled to other Paiutes who were in hiding farther down the trail, Lyon's horse picked up speed and bounded "over the rocks like a frightened deer."[26] Riding by the other scouts, who were just coming down from the upper path around the large boulder, Lyon yelled, "Come on boys, Will Allen is killed!"[27]

Farther down the trail, the fleeing scouts encountered more warriors, who were coming down from their rock perches on the canyon walls. But the men rode by them so fast that none of the shots fired by the Paiutes found its mark. In fact, the only scout to get hit in this frantic downhill ride was Samuel Buckland, and the bullet that struck one of his legs was already spent and didn't even break his skin.

Near the bottom of the canyon, the scouts met Colonel Hays and Captain Lance Nightingill of the Truckee Rangers, who were leading a force of men to come to their rescue. Bob Lyon told Hays what had happened, and asked if he could take the Highland Rangers back up the hill with him and recover Will Allen's body. Hays was furious that another of his men had been killed, and he said, "We will all go!"[28]

Turning to his men, Colonel Hays told them to dismount, and ordered every tenth man to remain behind to hold and guard the horses. With all his cavalry on foot, Hays took the lead as they began the steep hike up the canyon trail.

There were no shots at the advancing army as it worked its way up the trail to where Will Allen had been killed. All the Paiutes were gone, and they had taken the dead scout's clothes and horse with them. The once confident Highland Ranger lay in the hot sun, and a mass of flies had already found his open and bloody mouth and the gaping wound in the back of his head. Colonel Hays sent a group of men back down the trail to get a pack horse for Will Allen's body. Then he gave orders to the rest of the men to watch every move, for they were going to climb the mountain and flush the Paiutes out of their hiding places.

The upward climb was the hardest the men had endured. Each step was in loose shale or on large, sharp rocks. The men slipped, stumbled, fell to their knees, and cursed this land of shale and stone. When they finally reached the first ridge, they rested and stared upward. Nowhere was there any sign of an Indian. But far above them was an even steeper ridge, with a perfect, natural fortress of tall, rocky crags marking its crest. Here was a hiding place for thousands of warriors, and the men watched Colonel Hays as he cupped his eyes with his hands to keep out the glare and looked ahead for some sign of movement. When he finished, he told his troops that it would be foolhardy to continue their climb. By this time the main force of the Paiutes was well on its way into the northeastern desert.

The relieved men said nothing. They sat back against rocks, and looked out at Mud Lake and the endless desert beyond. When they were rested, Colonel Hays gave orders to move out and head back to the horses.

By the time the men got off the mountain and had walked back down the narrow canyon, the sun had already set, a cool breeze was coming up, and the temperature was beginning to drop. Weary and stiff, the troopers mounted their horses, stared momentarily at the stiff body of Will Allen lashed to a pack horse, and began their long ride back to Pyramid Lake.

10

The moon was still hanging high when Colonel Hays and his cavalry were challenged by the guard at the Pyramid Lake camp. They had been gone for all of one day. Now it was two o'clock in the morning of June 6 as Colonel Hays walked to the campfire to drink hot coffee and tell Captain Stewart of what had taken place. When he finished his account, the weary Texan turned in for a few hours of sleep.

By daybreak Jack Hays was on his feet again, and told Captain Stewart that there was no point in chasing after Chief Numaga. By now, the chief and his warriors were far away in a country that no white man truly knew. The best that they could hope for was that the Paiutes would try to return to their Pyramid Lake home.

The two officers talked it over, point by point. When they had finished, they had arrived at certain conclusions which, for them, were obvious truths for this moment in time. These were:

—Wait for the Paiutes. Don't look for them.

—All volunteers should return to Virginia City to ease the drain on supplies.

—Captain Stewart's troops would remain, and construct an earthwork barrier near the Truckee River but one mile from Pyramid Lake to serve as a defense.

—The earthwork would be named Fort Haven in honor of elderly Major General J. P. Haven, California Militia, who had served as a volunteer aide for Colonel Hays's Washoe Regiment during the campaign.

—Captain Storey, now dead of his wound, should be taken by wagon to Virginia City for a proper funeral and burial on Cemetery Ridge.

—The remains of Major William Ormsby and Henry Meredith should be taken back to the settlements for final burial.

—The combined forces of The Carson Valley Expedition and the Washoe Regiment had won *some* kind of victory at the Battle of Pinnacle Mount.

But all the conclusions in the world, all the talk of glory and victory would not bring back the dead. And in the minds of Captain Stewart and Colonel Hays was the nagging fact that War Chief Numaga and his warriors were somewhere in the desert, somewhere just out of vision. But they were there, and they were waiting for the right moment to strike back.

The troopers could laugh and joke, because they were alive, and their taste of war was over for now. But Captain Stewart and Colonel Hays were only certain of one thing: they had forced the Paiutes to retreat, but they had not defeated them.

11

But after the Washoe Regiment had departed, The Carson Valley Expedition waited at Pyramid Lake all through June and into the beginning of July without seeing any more Paiutes. Then as the desert heat began to bother the men, Captain Stewart received new orders from General N. S. Clarke at the San Francisco Presidio. Stewart and his troops were to leave Pyramid Lake and go to the Big Bend of the Carson River. Here they were to select a proper site, and build a fort that would serve as a military outpost for the protection of the Overland Road.

Requests for such a military establishment had come from the Pony Express owners, who claimed a loss of $75,000 during May and June because of Paiute raids, from local ranchers, from the operators of stagecoach and freighting lines as traffic on the Overland Road was stopped, and from all the other settlers of western Utah Territory.

Following orders, Captain Stewart and his troops started construction of an adobe post at the Big Bend of the Carson River, and even before it was finished, Stewart had received permission to call it Fort Churchill in honor of General Sylvester Churchill, an Inspector General and an aged hero of the Battle of Buena Vista in the Mexican War. For though there seemed to be no immediate threat of more Indian trouble, the regular army was not going to take a chance. The Paiutes had not been an easy foe to fight to a draw, and there was no guarantee that they had given up the notion to return and fight on another day of their own choosing.[29]

PART V

AN END TO GLORY

1860

CHAPTER 16

When the Sun Was Low

Angry about having to leave their Pyramid Lake home, Chief Numaga and his People traveled into the southern part of the Black Rock Desert. The vast, arid country, with endless alkali plains that were glaring white in the summer sun, stretched far to the northeast, where it was bordered by dark, rugged mountains that looked like great chunks of obsidian left over from an ancient time of giants.

To take the old, the sick, the women, and children into this barren land must have been a hard decision for Chief Numaga to make. Yet the large army of whites was more than his warriors could handle. The only hope was that once the People had vanished into the desert, the whites would not remain at Pyramid Lake. As a last strike at the soldiers, a reminder of the daily danger they would face from his warriors, Chief Numaga had carefully set a canyon trap beside Mud Lake for the pursuing army. After the trap had been sprung, the warriors retreated north to join the People in the desert.

Hoping that the white soldiers had become discouraged

and would leave, Numaga sent scouts to Pyramid Lake to see if it was safe to return home. But his men came back with bad news. The soldiers were still camped at the mouth of the Truckee River, and they were digging into the earth, throwing up the soil to build a large hiding place.

But for the People the days were made of a fiery sun, and the food was almost gone. Seeing the suffering of the very old and the very young made Numaga's heart heavy. They could not remain on this cracked and parched earth, in this country of barren rocks, much longer. He had to move to a better place until they could return home.

When the cool of evening arrived, they would move farther to the northeast. Here they would make their camp in one of the deep canyons of the dark mountains— one of the canyons where there was water to drink, game to hunt, and grass for the ponies. There they would wait until the scouts brought back word that the white soldiers had left Pyramid Lake.

2

Frederick West Lander had been in Sacramento when the war broke out between the whites and the Paiutes. He had gone across the Sierra Nevada to hire men and pick up supplies for his fourth and final season of work on the Pacific Wagon Road that was designed to be a shorter and easier overland route across the northern part of the Great Basin. All he had left to complete was a little work on sections of the road and improve all springs and water holes to insure safety for the emigrants taking this route.

By the time Lander had armed and supplied his party

of forty men and returned to finish his work on the
Honey Lake-Humboldt trace, the second battle near
Pyramid Lake was over. Lander hoped this was the last
of the conflict between the two races, and that all hostili-
ties were finished. But when he and his workers reached
Honey Lake, they found "the valley nearly depopulated."[1]
To add to the confusion, the residents in the area were
in a state of panic.

There were two very good reasons for this fearful
attitude of the Honey Lake Valley settlers. First, Colonel
Hays and the Washoe Regiment had put away their
military gear, stepped out of uniform, and walked back
into civilian life. Second, Captain Stewart and the regular
army finished their stay at Pyramid Lake, and marched
back to the Carson River to begin the construction of
Fort Churchill, just across the river from Samuel Buckland's station and ranch. These actions by the volunteers
and the regulars left the sparsely settled country northwest of Pyramid Lake wide open to attack by Paiute
raiders who were still smarting from having to leave their
homes and trek into the northern desert country.

From what prospectors on the run and local settlers
had to say, Lander found out that Chief Numaga and
his People were encamped at Wall Springs, just beyond
the Smoke Creek Desert—a long ride to the northeast
from Honey Lake. Yet, from this desert stronghold, where
the canyons served as natural forts and where any approaching horsemen could be seen for miles, raiding parties rode to the southwest to strike the settlements around
the Honey Lake Valley.

In a letter to the Secretary of the Interior, Lander
wrote: "Houses were burnt, stock driven off and several
white men killed. A letter was addressed to me by Major
Isaac Roop, chosen during the last summer as Provisional

Governor, of what is termed here Nevada Territory, being the line of Settlements extending along the eastern slope of Sierra Nevada's and isolated from both California and the Government at Central Utah."[2]

Major Roop's letter was short and to the point. The settlers of Honey Lake Valley needed military protection, and needed it desperately. For Lander there was only one answer to their request. He volunteered his small force of men to come to the aid of the isolated ranchers. However, he made it quite clear that he expected the able-bodied men of the area to co-operate with him in a joint effort to make some kind of peace with the Paiutes. To this end, he was joined by Captain William Weatherlow and his small contingent of Honey Lake Rangers.

With Weatherlow's Honey Lake Rangers and his own men armed and ready to ride, Colonel Lander delayed the commitment of the small army to a direct journey to Wall Springs. Instead, he rode with a scouting expedition to make sure that the Paiutes were not closer to the settlements than Wall Springs. It occurred to him that with raiders hitting local ranchers, there was more than a fair chance that they were camped much closer to Honey Lake than most citizens thought.

And the scouting expedition paid off, for when Colonel Lander returned, he reported that all signs indicated that the Paiutes were two or three days just north and slightly east of Honey Lake. Tired and dusty from his trip, Lander wanted no time wasted. The time to start was right away, and if they did some hard riding, they might even catch up to the Paiutes in a couple of days.

After resting for only a few hours, Lander got a fresh horse; and he rode at the head of the troops as they moved out of the valley in the cool of the evening of June 19, 1860. They did not have a hundred men to

go up against the seasoned warriors, but they knew that
this time Chief Numaga would have to worry about more
than how he deployed his men. For the scouts had informed Lander that the warriors were not traveling alone
—this time the women and children were with them.

3

The first night's ride of Colonel Lander's small force
ended at Antelope Valley, "thirty-five miles from Susanville."[3] Here the weary men camped and slept until the
terrible, sickening heat of the day had passed. Then in
the late afternoon, as the sun began to drop behind the
crest of the Sierra Nevada, they broke camp and started
on their way once more. They rode northeast for two
days until they "struck Madelaine Plains, so-called after
the wife of the celebrated trapper, and ex-chief of the
Snake [Crow] Indians, Jim Beckworth."[4]

At the Madelaine Plains, scouts from the Honey Lake
Rangers found fresh moccasin tracks, and caught sight
of two mounted Paiutes observing their camp from a
distance. That night, the white expedition did not ride
out in search of Indians. Instead, the camp was closely
guarded, and the men spoke in whispers as though they
feared that normal sounds of talk might carry too far
into the darkness and give Chief Numaga's scouts an
exact count of the number of soldiers riding against him.

At dawn, Captain Weatherlow and some of his best
men rode out of camp to try to locate the Paiute stronghold. Before he left, Weatherlow called Lieutenant Tutt
aside and told him that he was to be in command of
the Honey Lake Rangers during his absence. Unfortu-
nately, this caused difficulty in the command. For when
Colonel Lander had all the men packed and ready to

ride into action, Lieutenant Tutt informed him that Weatherlow had given orders to take the Rangers through a nearby canyon, where there were likely hiding places for Indians.

Lander objected to this idea, and pointed out that if they did meet a large force of Paiutes in the canyon their chances of ever getting out alive were not good at all. But Lieutenant Tutt was determined to carry out orders, and so informed Colonel Lander of his intention.

Caught in a situation of having to deal with what amounted to a civilian guard of amateur soldiers, Lander shook his head in disgust, but agreed to go along. For there were not enough men in this expedition to split it up into various fragments. Still, he didn't like the idea of riding into a possible trap, and liked it even less as they entered the canyon mouth, and could see the tall, rocky walls to their left that provided perfect forts for any number of riflemen. Turning to all the horsemen, Colonel Lander said, "Remember, gentlemen, I do not bear the responsibility."[5]

But Lieutenant Tutt was determined to have his way, and it wasn't until later that Colonel Lander learned that the zealous Tutt had misunderstood the orders he had received. Weatherlow actually had told Tutt to avoid the narrow canyon and cross the rocky hills just above it. All of this became much too clear when the rear guard of fifteen men met Weatherlow near the mouth of the canyon.

Upon seeing the men and hearing of Tutt's bullheaded attitude about going straight through the canyon, Weatherlow ordered his troops to ride forward at a gallop in order to catch up to Colonel Lander and the rest of the men. Riding as fast as they could, they caught up to

Lander and the rest of the expedition as they were nearing the end of the narrow canyon.

Yet it was too late to waste time berating Tutt. As
Weatherlow joined Lander at the head of the column,
sharpshooters hidden in the high rocks opened fire on
them. One of the rangers, Alexander Painter, grabbed at
his side, but continued to ride a short distance before
he tumbled from his saddle and fell to the ground.
Painter's brother Ben quickly rode to the stricken man,
got off his own horse as rifle fire seemed to fill the
canyon with crack after sharp crack. Ben examined the
wound and found that the bullet had cut just below the
heart and had lodged near the spine. As he tried to
move his brother, Alexander shook his head and said,
". . . leave me my rifle and shot pouch and go on."[6]

Unable to attack the riflemen in the high rocks to
his left, Lander organized his troops for a drive against
the warriors on the lower hill to the right. Acting as
fast as possible, he sent the supply pack train out of
the canyon to the open plain just ahead. Next, he sent
some of his men to the right with orders to hold the hill
and pin down the sharpshooters while he and ten of his
men made a horse charge against the warriors. In the
minutes that followed, the canyon was filled with the
echoing sounds of shooting and wild yelling. But as
Lander and his men neared the rocky heights of the hill,
the Paiutes retreated "over the rocky hill sides where
neither horse nor foot could follow them."[7]

After this charge, Colonel Lander and his men came
back down the hillside, and he ordered all the remaining troops to ride out of the canyon. When they were
all in the clear on the open plain, Lander regrouped
his force once again and moved toward the open end of

the hill that had been to their left in the canyon. He
handed his rifle to one of his men, held up a white flag
and rode toward the Paiute stronghold. It was his intention "to obtain an interview with the hostile chief,
and if practicable bring the Indians to some sort of terms
by which the war might be closed."[8]

But things did not go as Lander hoped. When he got
within rifle range of the Paiutes, "they shot at him and
although he remained persisting in an interview, they
would not grant it."[9] Instead, they called out that they
wished to fight not talk. Then as they fired another volley
that hit all around him, Lander turned his horse and
rode back to his troops, who were waiting just out of rifle
range.

After Lander had returned to his own lines, he talked
over the situation with Captain Weatherlow. Both men
agreed that any chance for a peaceful meeting with
Chief Numaga was out of the question. If the Paiutes
wanted to fight, then there was no other choice. They
would give them a taste of a cavalry charge and see if
that wouldn't convince them that talking was better than
shooting.

When all the troopers were ready for action, Colonel
Lander gave the order to charge. The men rode at a full
gallop toward the rocky position of the Paiutes, but they
were unable to dislodge them. The rifle fire from the
Paiutes was coming much too close, and Lander ordered
his men to dismount and take cover. During the next five
hours, there were sporadic outbursts of shooting as both
sides tried to gain some kind of advantage. Then as the
afternoon sun began to drop behind the Sierra Nevada,
there was no more firing from the boulder-covered hiding
place of the Paiutes. Colonel Lander sent out scouts to
see what was happening, and when they returned, they

reported the Indians were gone, that they had "retired at all points going still further north."[10]

After the skirmish had ended, Colonel Lander and his men made camp for the night on the open plain. Before nightfall, Painter's brothers and some of his friends climbed into the higher mountains, where they gathered some cedar boughs. Then as the sun began to set, they dug a grave for the dead man, placed cedar boughs beneath and on top of his body, and covered him with earth from the level country that they named Painter Flat.

In the morning the soldiers broke camp and tried to contact the Paiutes again, but they had no luck. For sometime during the night, Chief Numaga and his People had very quietly left the region and had carefully covered their tracks so that there was no sign to follow.

Figuring that Chief Numaga had probably headed east toward the Black Rock Desert, Lander and his men struck the same direction. But when they reached the fortified position around Wall Springs, it was obvious that even this Indian stronghold had been abandoned. With no fresh tracks to follow, Lander had only one choice. He ordered the men to give up the chase and head back to Honey Lake. And by the last of June, the tired horse soldiers rode out of the great alkali flat, passed into taller sagebrush country, and crossed the pass into the Honey Lake country.

The long march in and out of the northeastern desert had exhausted both the men and their horses. And while they had not defeated Chief Numaga and his warriors, they had won one victory. They had managed to survive a long desert trek during the beginning of the deadly summer heat.

But this was not enough for Colonel Lander. He had not come into the Great Basin to fight Indians in the

first place. There was still work to be done on the springs
and water holes between Honey Lake Valley and the
Humboldt River to the east. Knowing this and feeling
anxious about completing his project, the tough engineer
allowed his men and horses to rest for a few days. Then
in the gray dawn light of the Fourth of July they headed
northeast again into the desert to complete their work
on the far western leg of the Pacific Wagon Road.

4

After Colonel Lander and his men left Susanville, they
rode northeast to Mud Springs—the nearest water supply
beyond Honey Lake. Here the work crew lined the bottom
of the water hole with stones to keep the water from
flowing too quickly into the parched earth. When this
task was completed, they continued their eastward
journey to Buffalo Springs, where they sank a fifteen-foot
well. Working in the terrible July heat, the men made
remarkable progress. Not only did they improve existing
sources of water, but also discovered new springs and
cleaned out watering places that were very nearly filled
with silt.[11]

At Hot Springs they constructed a large reservoir, and
diverted the hot water so that it would cool as it ran
from its source to the tank. But their major task was at
Rabbit Hole Springs. Here where the water supply was
so inadequate for livestock that emigrants had to drive
their animals to the Humboldt River for water, Lander's
"labor crew worked for three weeks tapping the water
supply, building a split-stone culvert set in cement to
carry the water to a reservoir of solid masonry. Within
a short time the tank held eighty thousand gallons, and
a train of three hundred emigrants and one thousand

animals, accommodated shortly after its completion, did not materially lower the surface of the water."[12]

Mud Springs, Buffalo Springs, Hot Springs, Rabbit Hole Springs, Antelope Springs, and all the other life-saving water holes were put into shape by Colonel Lander's hard-working men. And the month of July grew shorter, then was gone as the crew worked its way eastward. But even as the work progressed, Lander was not taking any risk of being surprised by a Paiute raiding party. For the protection of his crew, he sent a scouting party to the north with orders to try to locate the position of the Indians.

On August 11, 1860, Lander sent a letter from Rabbit Hole Springs to Captain Hamilton, United States Army, Honey Lake Valley. In his letter, Lander stated that Chief Numaga and his band were in the mountains north of the Humboldt River, and that Smoke Creek Sam and his band were north of the Sink of the Humboldt. He noted that his men had seen fifty Indians "between the Sink and Lassen's Meadow . . . and about one hundred, at different points north of the river."[13]

During the travel of Lander's scouting party, his men took five Paiute prisoners, who were purchasing percussion caps and ammunition from a wagon train. Lander wrote that the emigrants claimed they did not know that an Indian war was taking place; but while this might have been the truth, Lander also learned that there were traders on the wagon road who had come all the way from Carson City with arms and ammunition to sell to the Indians, and none of them could claim that they were ignorant of a war between the Paiutes and the whites. Through his interpreter, he also learned that the Paiutes had an excellent scouting system. In fact, it was so good that the prisoners were able to give Lander a detailed account of his brush with them to the north of Honey Lake, and were fully aware of all the activity along the wagon road—including the number of parties plus a full description of each one that had passed over the wagon road during the past four weeks. Very impressed with the performance of the Paiute scouts, Lander realized that the emigrant parties traveling the Pacific Wagon Road would never be a match for these warriors if conflict should break out between them.

Knowing this and knowing that once he and his men were through with their work, there would be no protection for emigrants on the wagon road, he decided it was imperative for him to have a meeting with Chief Numaga to try to bring hostilities to a halt. In an attempt to accomplish this, he convinced one of the prisoners to take him to see Chief Naana[14] of the Humboldt River Paiutes. For through him, he hoped to arrange a peaceful meeting with Chief Numaga.

But Lander was not naïve about this trip to Chief Naana's camp, for in order to make the journey, he had had to agree to take only his interpreter with him. This was hardly a guarantee that he would return alive, and to make sure that the army was apprised of the situation on the wagon road, Lander wrote to Captain Hamilton about his trip, and told him that if he did not return, that the army should recognize "the necessity of troops on the Humboldt, the presence of the regular Indian agent to enquire into the practices of traders, to enforce the law regarding the sale of ammunition to Indians,"[15] and the fact that if he did not succeed in making arrangements for peace, before long all emigration along the road would come to a halt.

Five days later Colonel Lander was back at Antelope Springs, but he did not come alone. Chief Naana was with him as well as twenty-one unarmed warriors and women and children. In his second letter to Captain Hamilton, Lander pointed out that Chief Naana considered the war to be over so long as the whites committed no more hostilities against the Paiutes. Then to prove his point, he sent runners "along the Humboldt, into the Black Rock country and to the Truckee river to apprise the Indians of a cessation of hostilities."[16]

Still, the meeting with Chief Numaga was yet to be arranged, and Lander was well aware of the fact that he was truly acting on his own in such negotiations. For he had not had time to secure the approval of Indian Agent Major Frederick Dodge. So, using his own common sense, and placing only his own life and that of a volunteer interpreter in jeopardy, he rode out of the Antelope Springs camp with two Paiutes who had been selected by Chief Naana to arrange a meeting for him with Chief Numaga.

Two warriors were selected by Chief Naana to contact Chief Numaga. To aid the progress of their journey, Lander let them ride two of the best government horses. The men said that they were certain that Numaga and a few of his principal men would return with them. Then when Lander asked how long the journey would take, they replied that they would come out of the mountains and meet him and others within ten days at a point on the wagon road known as the Hot Springs.

As the warriors rode away some mountain men who were with a passing wagon train told Lander that he had given away two fine horses. But Lander had complete faith in what the warriors had told him. As he was quick to point out to the doubters, he had already trusted his life to the Paiutes when he rode to see Chief Naana. On that trip the warriors could have killed his interpreter and him and taken the government horses and vanished into the desert. But they kept their word, and Lander said that he believed the Paiutes were men of high honor. If they gave their word, they meant it. No man could ask for more.

5

Colonel Lander, his interpreter, Indian hater Jack Demming, who had avoided both battles near Pyramid Lake, and others from his crew were camped at the Hot Springs on the promised day of Chief Numaga's arrival. They waited underneath canvas and brush shelters to avoid the glare of the fiery summer sun. Before noon, the two warriors to whom Lander had loaned government horses came into view. Riding with them were five other Paiutes. Four of these men were principal warriors; the fifth was Chief Numaga.

Colonel Lander's first impression of this amazing leader was much the same as that of reporter Frank Soulé of the *Daily Alta California,* who saw the chief in the latter part of August at a meeting with the Honey Lake Valley ranchers and Colonel Lander at Captain Neal's ranch. "I was," wrote Soulé, "particularly impressed . . . he is about thirty years old; six feet in height; straight as an arrow, with a depth and breadth of chest which denote great physical strength, and a quiet dignity and self-possession of manner which stamped him as a superior man; his forehead was not high, but broad and expansive, and beneath his prominent brows shone two keen black eyes that met your own with steady and un-flinching gaze . . . his cheek bones were high and prominent, his face rather long and slim, with a strong broad chin, a Roman nose, and a mouth denoting a strong will and decision of character."[17]

As Lander approached Chief Numaga, the leader of the Pyramid Lake Paiutes said, "I will look hard at you first. When the sun is low, we will talk."[18]

For the rest of the hot day, the Paiutes and the whites rested in what little shade the temporary shelters offered. At sunset, as the first shadows began to travel west with the moving sun, Chief Numaga got out his pipe, and told Colonel Lander that he was ready to meet in council.

The pipe traveled the council circle five times, and each man smoked in silence. When the ceremony was over, Colonel Lander spoke to Chief Numaga.

"I have come," Lander said, "to hear all that Chief Numaga has to tell the Great Father of the whites. I shall listen with attention, but I am only a listener. I make no promises. When the Great Father hears from his Children, the Paiutes, he will then know what to do. Perhaps, he might be very angry because his people have been killed. He might send many warriors to fight the Paiutes and kill them. You must talk plain, Chief Numaga. You must hide nothing, for I shall listen with open ears."

"I asked you to wait," Chief Numaga replied, "until night before we talked. It is not because I like the darkness. My heart is very open. It is like the sunshine, but clouds have been before me. Many of my young men have been killed, and there are men here who have killed them. I could not speak at once, for my breath was hot, and it might have burned your ears. But now I have sat upon your blanket, eaten your meat, and have smoked the pipe with you. Now I can speak with a soft breeze in my voice."

Chief Numaga waited, and Colonel Lander pointed to Jack Demming, whose brother had been killed by Paiutes the winter before the war had started. What Numaga and Lander did not know was that the raiders probably had been after Jack Demming and not his brother. And now, unknown to either leader, Demming lied and claimed that he had never killed or harmed any Paiutes.

Numaga remained silent, and Lander continued: "I am glad that some of my men killed Paiutes. For when I came in peace, when I held up the white flag, your warriors shot and killed one of my men, and tried to kill me. That is why I have come with warriors to see you, and not with women. If you wish to speak to women, if it makes your heart bad to see my men, I will go home, and send a woman to speak to you."

Numaga wished to see Jack Demming closer, and Lander had him step forth. Numaga "looked at him steadfastly for some moments but at the time said nothing. He then addressed the Indians who were present very vehemently in his own language."[19]

The interpreter informed Lander that Numaga had blamed Smoke Creek Sam and other bands of Indians from Oregon for the death of Demming's brother. When he finished his denunciation of these other Indians, Chief Numaga turned toward Colonel Lander and said: "Is Numaga a woman that he should *go to council with women?* No!" He struck his broad chest with his fists. "No! Numaga is a man, and the whites know it! They have never heard him cry—no, not once. Ten, twelve snows have fallen since they first came to see Numaga. They were few and they were very poor. They asked the Paiutes for land. They said they would make flour for the Paiutes. They would give them blankets and powder and lead, and that the children and women should be fed. Until last year no trouble had occurred, but the whites had been very mean and had not kept their promises. They had accused Numaga of killing Pete Lassen, one of the best men he ever knew, a man with whom he had slept in the same blanket, a man who was like the Paiutes and had lived among them before the other white people came. During all this time the whites had received more than they had given. It was not their country. But the whites had taken Paiute ponies, Paiute buckskins, and many times they did not pay. White men had been like coyotes—always ready to eat and to bark. They made much talk, and much of their talk was not good."

Chief Numaga paused. Then he said to Lander, "I am glad, at last, to see a white man who comes to talk without promises."

Numaga then turned to the warriors. He spoke of the raid on Williams Station, and he blamed it on a few hotheaded warriors. When he finished, and the interpreter had translated this, Numaga continued.

"Can the Great Father manage all the whites?"

Lander hesitated. "Usually, but there are bad whites as well as bad Indians."

Referring to one of the California tribes that he had heard about, Numaga said, "These poor people were put on reserved land by the Great Father, after the whites had taken their country. The whites promised to feed them, but they did not keep their promise. The People got very hungry, and killed some cattle for food. Then the whites came, and they murdered all—men, women, and children. What of this? Is it not better to fight while the whites are few in our country? Is it not better to die in battle? I am sorry for the women and children who starve in the mountains, but if they all die, why not die before they are shut up by the whites and their arms taken from them?"

Lander had no answer to these questions. He knew that the Paiutes received news from California by runners, and it was obvious that Chief Numaga was completely right. For a band of Indians recently had been massacred by whites in Mendocino County.

Not knowing what else to say, Lander tried to point out that the Paiutes were different, and that much of their land would never be wanted by the whites. Then he said, "You have mountain sheep and antelope ranges that the whites do not want. You have lakes full of fish which the whites do not want. Your men are good riders and herders. Once your people are given cattle and are taught how to farm, they will be able to take care of themselves. They will live like the Cherokees, Winnebagos, Delawares, and other Indians whom the whites have taught to farm."

"I have heard all this before. Even if my People agreed to what you say, even if we were given cattle and plows, and a mill to make flour, too many days have gone by in anger. We have waited before, but the good white man who was to be sent by the Great Father to teach us never came and the reserve was never provided."

When he finished, Chief Numaga sat quietly with his head bowed as though he were in deep concentration. Two, three, perhaps four minutes passed. Then he stood up, threw off his blanket and hunting shirt, and began to speak in a slow, very deep guttural tone[20] to the interpreter. But as the tempo of his speech picked up, Numaga bypassed the interpreter and spoke in broken English in order to get across his meaning as directly as possible.

"Irishman come—Dutchman come—American man come—China-John come, digum hole—find up money heap—good money find 'um, Paiutes' money, no give 'um Paiutes money!"

He stopped, bent down and scooped up a little pile of dirt, and covered it with his closed fist. Then he held out his other hand with the empty palm turned up to show what the miners did and said. "White man put him hand over money, and no give Paiutes any money—give 'um Paiutes heap God-dam, shake him—beat him—kill him—Big Father help Dutchman—help Irishman—help American man—help China-John man—why no help keep Paiute man? Paiute man heap good long time—no give 'um nothing—Paiute man no kill 'um whites—whitey man kill 'um Paiutes—Paiutes heap fight 'um—Soldier man come—Numaga no sabe! Numaga fight—Numaga die, no care no more."

Lander listened closely to Numaga's fierce, broken sentences, and he heard his warriors' mournful cries as their chief listed the evils the white man had committed against the Paiutes. Lander knew there was really nothing he could say to make things right, for he had already heard even worse accusations of white behavior from Captain Weatherlow and Captain Nightingill. Yet even as he sat and watched Chief Numaga, Lander heard him say that Paiute women had been mistreated by the whites, and he had not fought; that the son of one of his chiefs had been killed by whites at Virginia City, and he had not fought; that herders had driven their ponies and cattle on to Paiute land at Pyramid Lake and he had not fought. But when Major Ormsby and the whites came to kill his People, he had no choice other than to fight.

Chief Numaga rested after his last speech, and he stared into Lander's eyes. Then he said, "I keep the peace for one year. If Smoke Creek Sam kill white man, I will fight him. Numaga is War Chief and will keep the Paiutes mighty good for one year—maybe two years;

whites pretty bad, Numaga wait. Whites mighty bad, Numaga fight."

Colonel Lander listened to this offer of peace. Then he told Chief Numaga that he would send his story to the Great Father at Washington, and that he would try to arrange a treaty between the whites and the Paiutes.

"I will send runners," Numaga said, "to the north for old Chief Winnemucca. We will be at the lower Big Meadows on the Humboldt in the passing of four and ten suns. There we will wait for Major Dodge to come and tell us about this peace treaty. If the Great Father speaks straight, we will bring the women and children away from the dry country of rocks. We will try to learn the white man's ways."

Lander thanked Numaga, and asked if he would go to the soldiers' place by the Carson River, the new place called Fort Churchill, and tell the white warriors that he was now at peace with them.

"I will do this thing you ask. But know this, and tell the Great Father, we will not fight again until the grass is burnt by the glance of next summer's sun. And we will fight no more, for as long as there are stars in the sky, if the white man keeps his promise."

The sky was filled with stars as Chief Numaga finished speaking, and Colonel Lander felt the first chill of the desert evening. Once again, the pipe was brought out, and the men smoked and sat silently as it was passed. When they had finished, Colonel Lander offered Chief Numaga and his warriors more food.

Numaga nodded his thanks, and told Lander that they had already had enough to eat for men who were going to make a long ride. He then pulled his blanket around his broad shoulders and arose from his cross-legged position like a giant golden eagle just beginning to fly. He

bid Lander farewell until their next meeting. Then as
though they had never existed, Chief Numaga and his
warriors stepped away from the light of the campfire and
into the surrounding darkness. They mounted their
ponies, and slowly rode away from the Hot Springs.

The desert wind picked up sand from the movement
of their ponies, but the sound of movement itself was
lost in the noise of the wind. All that had started with
the death of Peter Lassen in the Black Rock Desert and
caught fire at Williams Station had come full circle from
violence to a hope of peace. All that remained was for
men to treat each other with dignity and respect. If
that was possible, there would be no more killing. If
that was not possible, the whirlwind of Paiute warriors
would once again send fear and panic throughout the
Great Basin.

The Return of Seasons

Chief Numaga and his People were home. No longer did they have to live in the land of barren rocks. The endless vision of treeless desert was gone from their minds. Now they looked at the great desert lake, and watched it change its shades of blue as the sun journeyed across the sky. No lookouts were posted on the high mountains, and men prepared for hunting, not for war.

Summer had come and gone in the hot northern deserts. The cries of hunger, the moans of suffering had vanished with the eternal wind. All the talks with Colonel Lander, with the whites at Honey Lake, and with the soldiers at Fort Churchill on the Big Bend of the Carson River were over. It was agreed that Pyramid Lake and the land around it was the country of the Paiutes, and it was agreed that the whites would help the Paiutes to learn how to farm and how to make flour. Best of all, though, the new agent sent to help them was an old friend of the People, a man they respected and trusted as one of their own. The replacement of Major Dodge was none other than Long Beard Warren Wasson. This was a sign, a good sign that the time of killing was over, and the time of living had returned.

Knowing that they were home once more and knowing that Wasson would help them to understand the ways of the whites, the People got ready for the coming of winter. All the karnees were quickly repaired and put back into order, and everyone got ready for the time of icy winds and the long days of little food.

The first scouts returned from the mountains, and they held high a small piñon bough. From it hung a few immature cones. All the People gathered about, and plans were made to gather enough first cones for the pine nut prayer-dance. For the ritual of tasting the first sweet nut meat, of dancing and singing from dusk to dawn, and of asking the People's Father to protect the growing cones from sickness was a ceremony that was older than the most ancient person of the tribe. And when the dance ended, the People knew they would wait until the signs of the season told them that the cones were ripe and that it was time to travel to the mountains and harvest them.

Later, the men would go on antelope hunts. Then, just before the coming of snow, the time of the rabbit drive would take place.

There was much to do. But Chief Numaga looked at the women and children. It pleased him to see them smile again, to hear the women gossip, and to hear the children laugh as they played games. Most of all, he was glad to look at the great lake once more and to watch the water birds as they glided above the surface of the lake in search of food, and to look upward and watch the mountains of clouds run across the blue lake of sky.

The cycle of seasons had returned, and Chief Numaga

was only sad that many of his friends had died in the
whirlwind of hate that had blown across the desert in
a season of sorrow.

2

Between the fall of 1860 and the spring of 1862, Chief
Numaga and the Paiutes had a staunch defender in their
Indian agent. Warren Wasson was a good man in every
sense of the word. He managed to cut through government red tape and obtain food and supplies from the
army stationed at Fort Churchill, and fought to protect
the rights of the Paiutes against white encroachment.
His battle was a constant one, for as he reported to the
Commissioner of Indian Affairs:

> I had great difficulty during my administration to prevent
> whites from settling upon the reservations, and stock men
> from herding stock onto them, to the destruction of the
> grass seeds, one of the principal sources of subsistence
> of the Indians; also to prevent traders and fishermen
> from depriving them of their winter's supply of fish by
> cheating them out of it entirely.[1]

But after Warren Wasson's departure to become a
United States marshal, the Paiutes had a succession of
agents who were incompetent, crooked, or both. Even
the promised reservation at Pyramid Lake remained as
nothing more than an informal agreement subjected to
whatever changes the government might wish to make.

White squatters moved to the "reservation," and they
settled on some of the best ranching land in the area.
Along with this, other Paiute resources were plundered.
The timber that had been set aside for them near Verdi,

Nevada—some 20,000 acres—was taken by the whites in 1865 when the news of the Central Pacific Railroad route became known. All plans for the sawmill that was to cut lumber for the Indians were forgotten, and the value of the timber became much more important than the welfare of the Paiutes. The same attitude prevailed as the tracks neared Wadsworth, Nevada, and once again the Indian lost out to the profit motive as squatters took over the tillable land at the Big Bend of the Truckee River on the Paiute Reservation.[2]

To add to the misery of the Pyramid Lake Paiutes, warfare between the whites and the Nevada Shoshonis broke out along the Overland Road to the east during the years 1861–65. Frightened of Indians and the possibility of Secessionists raids on the Overland Road, the government guarded the central route across Nevada by a line of frontier forts. But trouble was inevitable as the natural food supply of the Indians was either used or destroyed by the overland stage company, railroad builders, and emigrants headed West. When the Indians struck back, the Army's answer was to send the troopers to settle things. And things were *settled* by rifle shots, or by capturing and hanging Indians in the name of "keeping the peace."

Then in the spring of 1865, the Pyramid Lake Paiutes were accused of stealing cattle from white ranchers. Major Charles McDermit, Commander of Fort Churchill, sent Captain Almond B. Wells and Company D of the Nevada Volunteer Cavalry to capture the rustlers.

Early in the morning on March 14, Captain Wells and his troopers charged a Paiute encampment at Mud Lake. Chief Winnemucca and all the young men were away on a hunting trip, and there were no warriors present. But the cavalry did not stop to ask questions, or to take prisoners. Using guns and sabers they killed old men and women, mothers and children in a brutal, bloody massacre. But one person escaped and that was Sarah Winnemucca's younger sister, and she told Sarah what had happened.

> After the soldiers had killed all but some little children and babies still tied up in their baskets, the soldiers took them also, and set the camp on fire and threw them into the flames to see them burn alive. I had one baby brother killed there. My sister jumped on father's best horse and ran away. As she ran, the soldiers ran after her; but thanks be to the Good Father in Spirit-land, my dear sister got away. This almost killed my poor papa. Yet my people kept peaceful.[3]

When Captain Wells returned to Fort Churchill, Major McDermit asked about prisoners. Wells replied he was not able to take any. As this was contrary to McDermit's standing orders he became suspicious about the actions of Company D, and promptly ordered a Court of Inquiry.[4] Yet, as there were no witnesses to give the Indians' version of what had happened, Captain Wells was cleared.

In his report to Governor Blasdel of Nevada, Major McDermit wrote that Captain Wells and his troopers had surprised a camp of Paiutes at Mud Lake and killed thirty-two people, or everyone they found.[5]

Since Major McDermit only had Captain Wells's version of what had happened, it is obvious that he was forced to accept an account of a battle instead of a massacre. Accordingly, in a letter to Brigadier General George Wright at the District Headquarters in Sacramento, California, he wrote:

Captain Wells has returned from Pyramid Lake, where he whipped those Indians badly.[6]

But the days of tragedy had not run their course for the Paiutes. For six years later, War Chief Numaga died of tuberculosis at the Big Bend of the Truckee River.[7] Fearing what might happen to them without their great leader, facing the constant threat of violence and a dwindling food supply, the Paiutes moved northward. Here they joined forces with the Oregon Paiutes and the Bannocks of Idaho. While they attempted to remain isolated from the whites, the increasing presence of prospectors, new mining towns, and ranchers led to sporadic conflicts between the races. And even though President Ulysses S. Grant had officially declared that the Pyramid Lake Reservation be set aside for the Paiutes and all other Indians who might be residing upon it as of March 23, 1874, nobody in the north considered it safe to return.

Their worry proved to be quite realistic. For troopers in the north were sent out to remove them. In 1875, many of the Nevada and Oregon Paiutes, as well as some Bannocks, were interned at the Malheur Reservation in Eastern Oregon. But this was not the end of trouble, for the Indians were again subjected to another dishonest agent. Under the care of W. V. Rinehart, the threat of starvation became more than a possibility, and one of the results of this situation was the Bannock War. This conflict lasted until 1878, cost many Indian and white lives, and used half a million dollars that could have been spent to help the Indians, rather than defeat them in another war.

While the Paiutes wanted no part of this war, the

Bannock chiefs—Egan and Oytes—forced them to leave Malheur with them. Then when the war ended, some of the Paiutes were kept at Fort McDermit, Nevada. Others were sent to the reservation at Yakima, Washington, and were promised that they would be transferred from this overcrowded and very poor reserve to their own homes. But after several years, the transfers had not arrived. The Indians decided that escape and flight was better than incarceration. Thus, in 1883, they forgot about long over-due promises, broke out of the Yakima Reservation and headed for their Nevada home.

Yet one more major event was to shake the Paiute world before the nineteenth century came to an end. This was the revival of an earlier "adventist" movement that combined their own religion with aspects of Christianity. This religious revival was started by Wovoka, "The Cutter," whose father had fought in the 1860 battles near Pyramid Lake as one of Chief Numaga's warriors. At that time, Wovoka was only four years old.

Later, after his father had died, fourteen-year-old Wovoka was given a home by the David Wilson family of Mason Valley, Nevada. This devout white family named him Jack Wilson, and from Mrs. Wilson he learned of the Christian miracles through Bible stories. These stories plus the knowledge that his father had been a Prophet gave Wovoka his initial push toward a career as a Prophet for his People.

He worked very hard at learning the techniques of "creating" miracles, and became capable of entering into self-induced, hypnotic trances. For the downtrodden and dispossessed Paiutes and other Indians from nearby and faraway, his Ghost Dance offered a mystic's hope for the return of the old ways, for the disappearance of the whites, and for the resurrection of the Indian dead. Word of his miracles and of his visits with the Great Spirit and Indians who had been dead for many years quickly spread throughout the West.

Soon there were visits by representatives from other tribes who came to see this new dance of hope, and to hear the words that Wovoka had been told in the land of the dead. Utes, Bannocks, Nevada Shoshonis, and Indians from Northern California were the first to send emissaries to see the Prophet. Then word spread to the Wind River Shoshonis of Wyoming. From there the news traveled to the Cheyenne and the Sioux. All these Indians sent visitors to hear the words and watch the Ghost Dance of the Prophet. And by the spring of 1890, these Indians were all chanting and dancing, and some were wearing "Ghost Shirts" which they believed would protect them from bullets.

But this new hope, this hope born in desperation, this vision of a non-violent man, a quiet Paiute was more than the whites could understand. The army worried about another uprising, another Little Bighorn. The combination of fear and hate found its final fury, its ultimate blood-letting on the icy morning of December 29, 1890, when the 7th Cavalry massacred over two hundred men, women, and children of Big Foot's band of Sioux, and called it the Battle of Wounded Knee. Here in another ruthless chapter in the conflict between whites and Indians, the peaceful dream of Wovoka, the Paiute Prophet, turned into a savage nightmare and a slaughter of innocent people.[8]

3

Shifted from place to place, treated as less than human, humiliated and belittled, robbed of their birthright, the

Paiutes entered the twentieth century as an endangered species, a vanishing race. Yet most Nevada politicians treated the Indians as disenfranchised wards of the state, and looked upon their land claims and water rights as something that did not apply to Indians. Without any doubt, the most powerful enemy that all Nevada Indians had during the period from 1933 to 1954 was the late Senator Patrick A. McCarran. Time after time, Senator McCarran used all the power of his seniority in the United States Senate to try to pass a bill that would have allowed the sale of Pyramid Lake Reservation lands to white squatters without the consent of the tribe.[9] But this anti-Indian attitude was not the province of politicians alone. For as is usually the case, elected officials mirror the prevailing attitudes of most of their constituents. And for many of these voters their attitudes about Indians and most minorities were based upon ignorance, fear, and the need to feel superior.

Even before Senator McCarran's blatant attempt to overlook the rights of the Pyramid Lake Paiutes, another Nevada politician—Representative Francis G. Newlands—shepherded a bill through the United States Congress that has caused a tremendous loss to the Indians and continues to affect their destiny. The result of this bill was the Truckee-Carson Project, which was designed to divert Truckee River water from its normal channel to provide irrigation water for farming land.

In 1905, the construction of Derby Dam and the Truckee Canal drastically cut the flow of water into Pyramid Lake. The lake level began to drop from the 3,860-foot elevation John C. Frémont had noted in 1844 until it reached its present elevation of 3,796 feet. Along with this drop in elevation, Pyramid Lake's vast expanse shrank from some 135,000 acres to 115,000 acres. This reduction in size caused an increase of alkalinity in the water, and an exposed sandbar at the mouth of the Truckee River which prevented the spawning runs of the great cutthroat trout so effectively that by the 1930's they had vanished.[10]

Then in 1948 studies by the state fisheries proved trout could exist in Pyramid Lake provided they were planted each year, for there was no possibility of using the diminished water of the Truckee River for spawning purposes. But while this was good news, one fact remained: the salmon trout that John C. Frémont and his men had hailed as great eating were not to be found. But a year later, a carp fisherman netted some large cutthroat trout in Walker Lake about seventy-five miles south of Pyramid Lake. Then direct descendents of the Pyramid cutthroats were found in two other lakes where the fish had been transplanted at an earlier time. Taking advantage of these finds, the Nevada Fish and Game Commission began a program of restocking Pyramid Lake and of keeping breeding trout and eggs in various hatcheries.[11]

But even a well-organized program of yearly planting cannot prevent the ultimate disaster. For it is an inescapable fact that without a steady flow of sufficient Truckee River water, the great desert lake itself is doomed. And its death appears to be much more than a remote possibility. Most of the Truckee River water is already removed before it has a chance to reach the lake. For in addition to the Truckee-Carson Project, other claims to the river water have developed.

In 1944, the Orr Water Ditch Decree stated that the only water rights that were to be recognized were those for the purposes of irrigation, industrial and municipal use, and power.[12] This, of course, simply ignored the

necessity to keep a steady flow of water into Pyramid
Lake. Now, added to this, there is another threat from
the California-Nevada Interstate Water Compact, which
seeks to allocate more water from the Truckee, Carson,
and Walker rivers and Lake Tahoe between the two
states. The only official suggestion to save some water for
Pyramid Lake has come from the Pyramid Lake Task
Force. But their recommendation, if accepted by the
governors of Nevada and California, will not provide
enough additional water to prevent the ultimate death
of the desert lake.

In all these grabs for water, the moral issue involved—
the fact that the Truckee River water belongs to the Indians and should continue its normal course to Pyramid
Lake—has been neatly avoided by the Department of
Interior. But such is not the case with the Bureau of
Outdoor Recreation, which sees the lake as a great unspoiled natural resource, or with a Senate Hearing at
Pyramid Lake in January 1972, when Senator Edward
Kennedy of Massachusetts and Senator John V. Tunney
of California stated that the Indians had prior rights to
the Truckee River water over all other users.

As a careful study by the Bureau of Outdoor Recreation points out, Pyramid Lake is a legacy for everybody.
It is within thirty-three miles of the heavily populated
area of Reno and Sparks, Nevada; within easy driving
distance of Lake Tahoe, and no more than a half day's
drive from the San Francisco Bay Area.

Not only would this desert lake be of tremendous bene-
fit to all people, it could become a way out of desperate
poverty for the Pyramid Lake Paiutes. For these Indians
who now have substandard incomes, no incomes at all—for
the 70 per cent who are unemployed—and who live in
shacks that are giving way to the weather, the desert lake

represents their greatest economic hope as well as their spiritual home. If the lake were not robbed of its water, if the Paiutes were given the opportunity to develop this magnificent country as a recreational area owned and operated by the Indians, the desert lake could be a lasting monument to all people.[13]

The other choice, the one that is being made every day by upstream users of Truckee River water, is that of an ecological catastrophe. Seventy-three miles of almost untouched, unspoiled shoreline around a body of water larger than Lake Tahoe would slowly become no more than scarred beachlines on the slopes of the mountains, and the bottom of the lake would eventually become a wind-blown, mud-cracked playa. A fisherman's paradise would be reduced to a fading memory. Anaho Island, one of the largest nesting grounds for white pelicans in North America, would cease to exist. But most of all, the ancient home of the Pyramid Lake Paiutes, the land with its ghosts of Chief Numaga and all his brave warriors would become a raw scar in the land where only whirlwinds of dust and sand would carry the memory of this place and its People.

NOTES

PROLOGUE

1. Sessions S. Wheeler, *The Desert Lake: the Story of Nevada's Pyramid Lake* (Caldwell, Idaho: The Caxton Printers, Ltd., 1967), pp. 15–33.

2. Robert F. Heizer and Martin A. Baumhoff, *Prehistoric Rock Art of Nevada and Eastern California* (Berkeley: University of California Press, 1962), p. 14.

3. In the literature of the Great Basin there are many variations for the spelling of Paiute. To avoid confusion, I have used Paiute throughout my text. The only exceptions occur in direct quotations.

4. Wheeler, op. cit., p. 43.

5. Ibid., p. 92.

6. Margaret M. Wheat, *Survival Arts of the Primitive Paiutes* (Reno: University of Nevada Press, 1967), pp. 14–15.

7. Ibid., pp. 9–14.

8. Washo, not Washoe, is the true name of the tribe whose territory included Lake Tahoe, Long Valley Creek, Honey Lake, and upper drainage areas of the Truckee and Carson Rivers. See A. L. Kroeber, *Handbook of the Indians of California* (Washington, D.C.: Government Printing Office, 1925), pp. 569–70.

9. John Bidwell, *Echoes of the Past* (Chico, California: Chico Advertiser, n.d.)

10. John Charles Frémont, *Report of the Exploring Expedition to the Rocky Mountains in the Year 1842, and to Oregon and*

North California in the Years 1843–1844 (Washington, D.C.: Gales and Seaton Printers, 1845), p. 216.

11. Ibid., p. 217.

12. Ibid., p. 219.

CHAPTER 1

1. Asa Merrill Fairfield, *Fairfield's Pioneer History of Lassen County California* (San Francisco: H. S. Crocker Co., 1916), p. 171.

2. Ibid., p. 172.

3. Ibid.

4. Ibid., p. 174.

CHAPTER 2

1. Fairfield, *Fairfield's Pioneer History of Lassen County California*, p. 175.

2. The mystery of who murdered Peter Lassen and Edward Clapper was never solved. Three possibilities were considered: Pit River Indians, Paiutes, or whites. But no proof was ever uncovered.

3. "Statement of Captain William Weatherlow," p. 6, from *Selected Correspondence and Papers from the Utah Superintendency File, 1860–1870*, U. S. Bureau of Indian Affairs, The National Archives, Record Group 75.

4. Located at the base of the Sierra Nevada, almost due east of Lake Tahoe, Genoa is Nevada's oldest town. First named Mormon Station, it began as a small log cabin in 1849. By 1851, it was a regular stop on the California Trail. It was named Genoa in 1858 in honor of Columbus' birthplace.

5. George R. Stewart, *The California Trail* (New York: McGraw-Hill Book Co., Inc., 1962), p. 297.

6. Fairfield, op. cit., p. 176.

7. Ibid.

8. Apparently nobody returned to Black Rock Canyon for Edward Clapper's remains, for no record of this exists.

CHAPTER 3

1. Myron T. Angel, ed., *History of Nevada* (Oakland, California: Thompson & West, 1881), p. 553.

2. Chief Winnemucca's real name was Poito. However, the whites

called him Old Winnemucca. To add to the confusion they called Chief Numaga, Young Winnemucca, and Chief Naana, Little Winnemucca. To avoid this puzzle for readers, I have elected to call only Poito, Chief Winnemucca. My major reason for doing this is that Poito's descendants continue to use the name Winnemucca.

3. Sarah Winnemucca (Hopkins), *Life Among the Piutes: Their Wrongs and Claims,* ed., Mrs. Horace Mann (New York: G. P. Putnam's Sons, 1883), p. 60.

4. Ibid.

5. Adjutant General Raymond White, *History of the Nevada Militia, 1862–1912,* MS., Adjutant General's Office, Carson City.

6. Winnemucca, op. cit., p. 60.

7. Ibid.

8. Ibid.

9. Ibid.

10. No definite history of usage accounts for the term "Captain" as applied to Washo leaders. Possibly, it was copied from its use by wagon train leaders or other whites who so endowed themselves. See James F. Downs, *The Two Worlds of the Washo* (New York: Holt, Rinehart and Winston, 1966), pp. 90–93.

11. See ibid., p. 6, for an interesting discussion of Washo physical characteristics.

12. Winnemucca, op. cit., p. 61.

13. Ibid.

14. Ibid.

15. Ibid.

16. Ibid.

17. Ibid., p. 62.

18. Ibid.

19. Ibid., p. 63.

20. Ibid.

21. No record exists of what happened to this Washo.

22. Winnemucca, op. cit., p. 63.

CHAPTER 4

1. Winnemucca, *Life Among the Piutes,* p. 64.

2. Ibid.

3. For more information on warfare between the Paiutes and Washos, see Downs, *The Two Worlds of the Washo,* pp. 52–54.

4. The first office of the *Territorial Enterprise* was at Genoa, first called Mormon Station. It was moved to Major Ormsby's house on Carson Street on November 12, 1859, where it remained until October 1860. A month later it reopened at Virginia City. See Richard E. Lingenfelter, *1858–1958: The Newspapers of Nevada* (San Francisco: John Howell—Books, 1964), p. 20.

5. Samuel P. Davis, ed., *History of Nevada* (Reno: The Elms Publishing Co., 1913), Vol. I, p. 41.

6. Eliot Lord, *Comstock Mining and Miners* (Washington, D.C.: Government Printing Office, 1883), p. 64.

7. William Wright (Dan DeQuille), *The Big Bonanza*, Introduction by Oscar Lewis (New York: Alfred A. Knopf, Inc., 1947), p. 65.

8. Samuel Young, "Colonel Samuel Young's Journal," Commentary, Notes, and Transcription by Ethel Zimmer, *Quarterly*, Nevada Historical Society, Vol. II, No. 2 (April–June 1959), p. 38.

9. Winnemucca, op. cit., p. 66.

10. Snyder's identity is not very clear. One theory holds that he was a white man who lived among the Paiutes. Another version of his life suggests that he possibly became Sarah Winnemucca's first husband, and that he died during a visit to his home in Germany. See Wright, op. cit., p. 202; and Jack D. Forbes, *Nevada Indians Speak* (Reno: University of Nevada Press, 1967), p. 49.

11. Winnemucca, op. cit., p. 67.

12. As promised, Sarah Winnemucca and her younger sister were taken to the Mission School in San Jose, California, in the spring of 1860. But they were not there for very long. As Sarah later wrote, "Brother Natchez and five other men went with us. On our arrival we were placed in the 'Sisters' School' by Mr. Bonsal and Mr. Scott. We were only there a little while, say three weeks, when complaints were made to the sisters by wealthy parents about Indians being in school with their children. The sisters then wrote to our friends to come and take us away, and so they did,— at least, Mr. Scott did. He kept us a week, and sent word to brother Natchez to come for us, but no one could come, and he sent word for Mr. Scott to put us on the stage and send us back. We arrived at home all right, and shortly after, the war of 1860 began. . . ." Ibid., p. 70.

13. Ibid., p. 67.

14. Ibid., p. 68.

15. Ibid.

16. Ibid., p. 69.

17. Ibid. Sarah Winnemucca wrote that it was a Paiute belief that if a dying person's mother or father were in Spirit-land that his soul would cry out as it entered.

18. Ibid.

19. Ibid., p. 70.

CHAPTER 5

1. Fairfield, *Fairfield's Pioneer History of Lassen County California*, p. 199.

2. Ibid., p. 198.

3. Ibid.

4. Ibid., p. 199.

5. Angel, *History of Nevada*, p. 149.

6. "Statement of Captain William Weatherlow," p. 8, *Selected Correspondence and Papers from the Utah Superintendency File, 1860–1870.*

7. In all his reports, Captain William Weatherlow uses the name Winnemucca. However, in each case he is referring to the Paiute War Chief Numaga, whom the whites called Winnemucca or Young Winnemucca.

8. Fairfield, op. cit., p. 201.

9. Ibid.

10. Ibid., pp. 201–2.

11. Ibid.

CHAPTER 6

1. "Statement of Captain William Weatherlow," p. 9, *Selected Correspondence and Papers from the Utah Superintendency File, 1860–1870.*

2. Ibid., pp. 9–10.

3. Frederick W. Lander was the civilian engineer in charge of the construction of the Fort Kearny–South Pass–Honey Lake wagon road. See W. Turrentine Jackson, *Wagon Roads West* (New Haven, Connecticut: Yale University Press, 1965 edition), Chapter 7.

4. "Letter from Ira A. Eaton to Frederick W. Lander," October 25, 1860, p. 2, *Selected Correspondence and Papers from the Utah Superintendency File, 1860–1870.*

5. Fairfield, *Fairfield's Pioneer History of Lassen County California*, p. 204.

6. "Statement of Captain Weatherlow," p. 10, op. cit.

7. This is a Shoshoni term that refers to an ice-filled winter fog that sometimes forms in the country of northwestern Nevada. See Frederick Webb Hodge, ed., *Handbook of American Indians North of Mexico*, 2 vols., *Bulletin 30*, Bureau of American Ethnology (Washington, D.C.: Government Printing Office, 1912).

8. "Statement of Captain Weatherlow," p. 11, op. cit.

9. Ibid.

10. Ibid.

11. Ibid., p. 12.

12. Ibid.

13. Ibid.

14. Ibid.

15. Ibid.

16. Ibid., p. 13.

17. Ibid.

18. Angel, *History of Nevada*, p. 149.

19. Ibid.

CHAPTER 7

1. Wheat, *Survival Arts of the Primitive Paiutes*, p. 9.

2. Ibid.

3. Ibid.

4. Virginia Cole Trenholm and Maurine Carley, *The Shoshonis: Sentinels of the Rockies* (Norman: University of Oklahoma Press, 1964), p. 8.

5. Winnemucca, *Life Among the Piutes: Their Wrongs and Claims*, p. 16. This gives an account of the symbolic use of the number five among the Paiutes.

6. Angel, *History of Nevada*, p. 151.

7. Ibid.

8. Ibid., p. 150.

9. Ibid., p. 151. This history gives a good account of the animosity that existed between Winnemucca and Numaga.

10. Ibid.

11. Trenholm and Carley, op. cit.

12. The description of Numaga's treatment by his People and the conjecture of what his thoughts must have been during his

ordeal of fasting is based upon various sources cited in the bibliography.

13. This speech is based on Angel, op. cit.

14. Ibid.

15. Ibid.

16. Winnemucca, op. cit., p. 70.

17. For the exact location of Williams Station, see Vincent P. Gianella, "Site of Williams Station, Nevada," *Quarterly,* Nevada Historical Society, Vol. III, No. 4 (1960), pp. 4–11.

18. Winnemucca, op. cit.

19. Ibid., p. 71.

20. Gianella, op. cit., p. 7.

21. Angel, op. cit., p. 152.

22. Samuel S. Buckland was an early settler who ran a trading post about seven miles northeast of Williams Station at the present location of Weeks, Nevada. See Gianella, op. cit., pp. 4–6.

23. The dialogue of the men at Williams Station is based upon what Paiute warriors who were there reported years later. See Angel, op. cit., p. 152; and Winnemucca, op. cit., pp. 70–71.

24. Angel, op. cit.

25. Winnemucca, op. cit., p. 71.

26. The dialogue of the chiefs who recited the wrongs committed against the Paiutes is based upon descriptions in such sources as Angel, op. cit., pp. 148–51; and Effie Mona Mack, *Nevada* (Glendale, California: The Arthur H. Clark Co., 1936), pp. 302–3.

27. Angel, op. cit., p. 151. The account of how Numaga looked at this meeting serves as the basis for this statement in dialogue form.

28. Ibid.

29. Ibid.

30. Ibid.

31. Ibid.

32. Ibid.

CHAPTER 8

1. Lord, *Comstock Mining and Miners,* p. 64.

2. "Letter From Washoe," Sacramento *Daily Union,* April 9, 1860, p. 1.

3. "By Telegraph to the Union . . ." Sacramento *Daily Union*, May 9, 1860, p. 4.

4. Ibid.

5. "Our Washoe Correspondence," *Daily Alta California*, May 15, 1860, p. 1.

6. Ibid.

7. Ibid.

8. Near the western end of the California Trail there were a number of grog shops whose proprietors were true merchants of misery who made their money by cheating the Paiutes, Washos, and trail-weary emigrants. See Mack, *Nevada*, pp. 302–3.

9. George D. Lyman, *The Saga of the Comstock Lode* (New York: Charles Scribner's Sons, 1934), p. 109.

10. "Our Washoe Correspondence," op. cit.

11. Nita R. Spangler, *Letter to David W. Heron, Director, University of Nevada Library*, October 11, 1965, p. 1. Also, Richard F. Pourade, *The Silver Dons* (San Diego, California: The Union-Tribune Publishing Co., 1963), p. 183.

12. Angel, *History of Nevada*, p. 153.

13. Thomas Knott, *Personal Reminiscences*, MS., 1881, p. 10. Quoted by permission of the director, The Bancroft Library, University of California, Berkeley.

14. Charles C. Stevenson, *Biographical Sketch*, typescript, 1888–89, p. 12. Quoted by permission of the director, The Bancroft Library, University of California, Berkeley.

15. Angel, op. cit.

16. Ibid.

CHAPTER 9

1. Samuel Young, "Colonel Samuel Young's Journal," pp. 40–41.

2. Angel, *History of Nevada*, p. 493.

3. William Wright (Dan DeQuille), *Washoe Rambles*, Introduction by Richard E. Lingenfelter (Los Angeles: Westernlore Press, 1963), p. 21.

4. "The Knave," Oakland *Tribune*, July 7, 1957.

5. Samuel S. Buckland, *Indian Fighting in Nevada*, MS., 1879, p. 2. Quoted by permission of the director, The Bancroft Library, University of California, Berkeley.

6. Gianella, "Site of Williams Station, Nevada," pp. 6–7.

7. "The Indian Troubles in Carson Valley . . ." Sacramento *Daily Union,* May 11, 1860, p. 2.

8. Charles Forman, *Statement,* typescript, 1887(?), p. 5. Quoted by permission of the director, The Bancroft Library, University of California, Berkeley.

9. Angel, op. cit., p. 582.

10. Forman, op. cit.

11. Ibid.

12. Knott, *Personal Reminiscences,* p. 10.

13. "Statement of Captain Lance Nightingill," p. 6, *Selected Correspondence and Papers from the Utah Superintendency File, 1860–1870.*

14. Forman, op. cit., p. 6.

15. Ibid.

16. Ibid.

CHAPTER 10

1. "The Fight Near Pyramid Lake," Sacramento *Daily Union,* May 21, 1860, p. 1.

2. Forman, *Statement,* p. 6.

3. "The Fight Near Pyramid Lake," op. cit.

4. Stevenson, *Biographical Sketch,* p. 12.

5. Wheeler, *The Desert Lake,* p. 58.

6. Angel, *History of Nevada,* p. 154.

7. "The Fight Near Pyramid Lake," op. cit.

8. Because of his small stature, Chief Sequinata was often called Chiquito (small) Winnemucca by the whites. In most accounts of the times and in later histories that is the name writers have continued to use.

9. "The Fight Near Pyramid Lake," op. cit.

10. Ibid.

11. Ibid.

12. Forman, op. cit., p. 7.

13. Angel, op. cit.

14. Ibid.

15. Forman, op. cit., p. 8.

16. Ibid.

17. Ibid.

18. Ibid.

19. Angel, op. cit.

20. Ibid., p. 155. This casualty of the battle was Eugene Angel. He was a brother of Myron Angel, the historian and newspaperman; and both of them had come across the vast country of northern Mexico in 1849 on their trip to the goldfields of California. See Ferol Egan, *The El Dorado Trail* (New York: McGraw-Hill Book Co., Inc., 1970), p. 159.

21. Angel, op. cit. The "White Brave" was William Headly, a member of Major Ormsby's Carson City Rangers.

22. Ibid.

23. Ibid., p. 156.

24. Ibid.

25. Ibid.

26. The one-legged man was Captain R. G. Watkins of the Silver City Guards. See Ibid., p. 153.

27. Ibid., p. 157.

28. Ibid.

29. Winnemucca, *Life Among the Piutes*, p. 72.

30. Angel, op. cit.

31. *Daily Alta California*, June 15, 1860, p. 1.

CHAPTER 11

1. "Slaughter of Americans . . ." Sacramento *Daily Union*, May 14, 1860, p. 2.

2. Ibid.

3. Ibid.

4. Ibid.

5. Ibid.

6. Mahlon Dickerson Fairchild, *Pioneer Reminiscences*, MS., Society of California Pioneers, San Francisco, p. 10–4.

7. Wright, *The Big Bonanza*, p. 79.

8. "From Carson Valley," Sacramento *Daily Union*, May 14, 1860, p. 2.

9. Lord, *Comstock Mining and Miners*, p. 70.

10. Wright, op. cit., p. 80. After the war ended, a group of men lit a slow fuse to the loaded cannon, ducked for cover, and watched their great weapon blow up in a shower of splintered wood, pieces of metal bands, and scrap iron.

11. Angel, *History of Nevada*, p. 158.

12. Mack, *Nevada*, p. 348. Bee's Grapevine Line was so-called

because Fred Bee strung the telegraph wire from tree to tree all away across the Sierra Nevada.

13. William C. Miller, ed., "The Pyramid Lake Indian War of 1860," *Quarterly*, Nevada Historical Society, Vol. I, Nos. 1–2 (1957), p. 40.

14. Ibid., p. 41.

15. Ibid.

16. Ibid.

17. Ibid., p. 42.

18. Ibid.

19. Ferol Egan, "Warren Wasson, Model Indian Agent," *Quarterly*, Nevada Historical Society, Vol. XII, No. 3 (1969), p. 6.

CHAPTER 12

1. "Relief Meeting at Placerville," Sacramento *Daily Union*, May 14, 1860, p. 2.

2. Ibid.

3. The concept of local and state militia units had its origin with the first settlers from Europe. Afraid of a standing army, but needing protection, the notion of citizen soldiers became part of our history. Militiamen were called upon to defend the settlements against Indians, insurrection, and invasion. Gradually, the various state militias became the basis for the National Guard. See Dictionary of American History, pp. 403–4.

4. "Relief Meeting at Placerville," op. cit.

5. Edna Bryan Buckbee, *The Saga of Old Tuolumne* (New York: The Press of the Pioneers, Inc., 1935), pp. 83–88.

6. "Relief Meeting in Sacramento," Sacramento *Daily Union*, May 14, 1860, p. 2.

7. Ibid.

8. Ibid.

9. Miller, "The Pyramid Lake Indian War of 1860," p. 48.

10. Ibid., p. 49.

11. Ibid.

12. Ibid.

13. Ibid., p. 50.

14. Ibid.

15. Colonel George Ruhlen (U. S. Army Ret.), "Early Nevada Forts," *Quarterly*, Nevada Historical Society, Vol. VII, Nos. 3–4 (1964), pp. 13–14.

16. Ibid.

17. "Movement of Troops . . ." Sacramento *Daily Union*, May 16, 1860, p. 4.

18. Ibid.

19. Ibid.

20. "Operations In Carson Valley . . ." Sacramento *Daily Union*, May 29, 1860, p. 2.

21. "Correspondence . . ." *The Mountain Democrat*, Placerville, California, June 23, 1860, p. 3.

22. Ibid.

23. Francis P. Farquhar, *History of the Sierra Nevada* (Berkeley: University of California Press, 1965); see footnote, p. 105.

CHAPTER 13

1. I. I. Murphy, *Life of Colonel Daniel E. Hungerford* (Hartford: Press of The Case, Lockwood & Brainard Co., 1891), p. 176.

2. Ibid.

3. Angel, *History of Nevada*, p. 158.

4. Murphy, op. cit., pp. 178–79.

5. John Hays to Alfred Cummings, June 12, 1860, "Report to the Secretary of War," *Senate Executive Document*, No. 1, 36th Congress, 2d Session, p. 89, Serial No. 1079.

6. "Letter from Washoe," San Francisco *Daily Evening Bulletin*, May 26, 1860, p. 1.

7. Anonymous. "A Man of Fixed Principles," *The Argonaut*, Vol. III, No. 25 (December 28, 1878), p. 4.

8. Ibid.

9. "Editor's Table," *Hutchings' Illustrated California Magazine*, Vol. V, No. 1 (July 1860), p. 47.

10. Jacob C. Klein, *Founders of Carson City*, MS., 1883, p. 2. Quoted by permission of the director, The Bancroft Library, University of California, Berkeley.

11. "A Man of Action," *The Morning Call*, San Francisco, May 13, 1883, p. 1.

12. Ibid.

13. *Condition of the Indian Tribes*, Report of the Joint Special Committee (Washington: Government Printing Office, 1867), p. 518.

CHAPTER 14

1. "Correspondence . . ." *The Mountain Democrat*, Placerville, California, June 23, 1860, p. 3.

2. "The Army in Washoe," San Francisco *Daily Evening Bulletin*, June 7, 1860, p. 2.

3. James Kimmins Greer, *Colonel Jack Hays* (New York: E. P. Dutton & Co., Inc., 1952), p. 317.

4. Ibid.

5. The total number of men in this army varies according to which account one accepts. The figure cited here is from the San Francisco *Daily Evening Bulletin*, June 7, 1860. Other accounts run the total to a high of 820, as in the *Territorial Enterprise*, Carson City, June 9, 1860; and a low of 750, as in the San Francisco *Daily Evening Bulletin*, June 16, 1860.

6. "Correspondence . . ." op. cit.

7. "The Army in Washoe," op. cit.

8. Ibid., June 16, 1860, p. 1.

CHAPTER 15

1. "The Washoe War," Sacramento *Daily Union*, June 12, 1860, p. 1.

2. Ibid.

3. "Progress of the Army in Washoe," San Francisco *Daily Evening Bulletin*, June 8, 1860, p. 3.

4. "Statement of Captain William Weatherlow," p. 17, *Selected Correspondence and Papers from the Utah Superintendency File, 1860–1870.*

5. "Progress of the Army in Washoe," op. cit.

6. Ibid.

7. Ibid.

8. Ibid.

9. Angel, *History of Nevada*, p. 569.

10. Ibid., p. 161.

11. "Volunteer Forces in the Field," *Territorial Enterprise*, Carson City, June 9, 1860, p. 1.

12. "The Army in Washoe," San Francisco *Daily Evening Bulletin*, June 16, 1860, p. 1.

13. Ibid.

14. Ibid.

15. "Progress of the Army in Washoe," op. cit.

16. Angel, op. cit., p. 162.

17. "Volunteer Forces in the Field," op. cit.

18. "Correspondence . . ." *The Mountain Democrat,* Placerville, California, June 23, 1860, p. 3.

19. Ibid.

20. "The Army in Washoe," op. cit.

21. Ibid.

22. This dialogue is based upon Buckland, *Indian Fighting in Nevada,* p. 7.

23. Ibid.

24. Ibid.

25. Angel, op. cit., p. 164.

26. Ibid.

27. Buckland, op. cit.

28. Angel, op. cit.

29. Ferol Egan, "The Building of Fort Churchill," *The American West,* Vol. IX, No. 2 (March, 1972).

CHAPTER 16

1. "Letter from Frederick W. Lander to Jacob Thompson, Secretary of Interior, July 22, 1860," p. 8, included in Record Group 48, *Selected Correspondence and Papers from the Utah Superintendency File, 1860–1870.*

2. Ibid.

3. "Letter from the Lander Expedition," *Daily Alta California,* San Francisco, July 15, 1860, p. 1.

4. Ibid.

5. Fairfield, *Fairfield's Pioneer History of Lassen County California,* p. 222.

6. Ibid., p. 223.

7. Ibid.

8. "Letter from Frederick W. Lander to Jacob Thompson . . ." p. 9, op. cit.

9. "Statement of Captain William Weatherlow," p. 20, *Selected Correspondence and Papers from the Utah Superintendency File, 1860–1870.*

10. Ibid.

11. Jackson, *Wagon Roads West,* p. 216.

12. Ibid., pp. 216–17.

13. "Letter from Frederick W. Lander to Captain Hamilton, August 11, 1860," p. 17, *Selected Correspondence* . . . op. cit.

14. Chief Naana was called Little Winnemucca by the whites.

15. ". . . Lander to Captain Hamilton . . ." p. 19, op. cit.

16. "Second Letter to Captain Hamilton, August 16, 1860," p. 21, ibid.

17. "Letter from Lander's Expedition," *Daily Alta California,* San Francisco, September 1, 1860, p. 1.

18. The speeches of Lander and Numaga are adapted from Lander's account of this meeting. "Second Letter to Captain Hamilton . . ." pp. 25–36, op. cit.

19. Ibid., p. 27.

20. This description of Chief Numaga's voice is based upon the report filed by Frank Soulé to the *Daily Alta California,* op. cit., p. 1.

EPILOGUE

1. *Condition of the Indian Tribes,* p. 519.

2. Forbes, *Nevada Indians Speak,* p. 4.

3. Winnemucca, *Life Among the Piutes,* pp. 77–78.

4. Philip Dodd Smith, Jr. "The Sagebrush Soldiers: Nevada's Volunteers in the Civil War," *Quarterly,* Nevada Historical Society, Vol. V, Nos. 3–4 (1962), p. 62.

5. Angel, *History of Nevada,* p. 170.

6. *The War of the Rebellion: A Compilation of the Official Records of the Union and Confederate Armies,* (Washington, D.C.: Government Printing Office, 1897), Series I, Vol. L, Part II, p. 1166.

7. Angel, op. cit., p. 185.

8. For more information about Wovoka, see Edward A. Dyer, Sr., *Wizardry,* n.d., MS., Special Collections Department, University of Nevada Library, University of Nevada, Reno.

9. Forbes, op. cit., pp. 189–219.

10. Wheeler, *The Desert Lake,* pp. 100, 122–26.

11. Ibid., pp. 100–4.

12. Bureau of Outdoor Recreation. *Pyramid Lake Recreation Study Report, Pyramid Lake, Nevada* (San Francisco: Pacific Southwest Regional Office, July 1971), p. 48.

13. Ibid. pp. 56–60.

BIBLIOGRAPHY

Primary Sources

Manuscripts and Letters

Anonymous. *Biography of John Reese*. Salt Lake City? 1884? MS., The Bancroft Library, University of California, Berkeley.

Bruce, A. T., Judge. *Isaac N. Roop*. n.d. MS., The Bancroft Library, University of California, Berkeley.

Buckland, Samuel S. *Indian Fighting in Nevada*. 1879. MS., The Bancroft Library, University of California, Berkeley.

Clayton, Joshua Elliot. *Correspondence and Papers*. 1854–1904. MSS., The Bancroft Library, University of California, Berkeley.

Cradlebaugh, William M. *Nevada Biography*. 1883. MS., The Bancroft Library, University of California, Berkeley.

Dodge, F. *Correspondence*. November 18, 1858; September 28, 1859. MS., University of Arizona, Tucson.

Dyer, Edward A., Sr. *Wizardry*. n.d. MS., Special Collections Department, University of Nevada Library, University of Nevada, Reno.

Fairchild, Mahlon Dickerson. *Pioneer Reminiscences*. MS., Society of California Pioneers, San Francisco.

Forman, Charles. *Statement*. 1887? Typescript, The Bancroft Library, University of California, Berkeley.

Frost, John. *Dictation*. Austin, Nevada. 1885. MS., The Bancroft Library, University of California, Berkeley.

Hays, John C. and Major John Caperton. *Life and Adventures of John C. Hays, the Texas Ranger.* 1879. MS., The Bancroft Library, University of California, Berkeley.

Huffaker, Granville W. *Early Cattle Trade of Nevada.* 1883. MS., The Bancroft Library, University of California, Berkeley.

Klein, Jacob C. *Founders of Carson City.* 1883. MS., The Bancroft Library, University of California, Berkeley.

Knott, Thomas. *Personal Reminiscences.* 1881. MS., The Bancroft Library, University of California, Berkeley.

Lamson, James. *Nine Years' Adventure in California, From September 1852 to September 1861, With Excursions Into Oregon, Washington, and Nevada.* MS., California Historical Society, San Francisco.

Nevers, Samuel A. *Nevada Pioneers.* 1883. MS., The Bancroft Library, University of California, Berkeley.

Roop, Isaac Newton. *Book Recording the First Claims Taken Up in Honey Lake Valley.* MS., The Bancroft Library, University of California, Berkeley.

————. *Letter to Frederick W. Lander.* Susanville, California. June 13, 1860. MS., Library of Congress.

Russell, George. *Biographical Sketch.* 188? MS., The Bancroft Library, University of California, Berkeley.

Salisbury, H. S. *Western Adventures of Don Carlos Salisbury.* n.d. Typescript, Wells Fargo History Room, San Francisco.

Shirley, James Quincy. *Recollections.* 1885. Grande Ronde, Oregon? MS., The Bancroft Library, University of California, Berkeley.

Smith, Grant Horace. *Comstock Notes.* 1859 to 1863, No. 1. MS., The Bancroft Library, University of California, Berkeley.

————. *Papers.* 1859–1863. MSS., The Bancroft Library, University of California, Berkeley.

Spangler, Nita R. *Letter to David Heron, Director, University of Nevada Library.* October 11, 1965. Special Collections Department, Reno.

Stevenson, Charles Clark. *Biographical Sketch.* 1888–89. Typescript, The Bancroft Library, University of California, Berkeley.

Watkins, Richard Gassaway. *Letters to "My Dear Burnett."* Carson City, August 5, 1860; Fort Churchill, September 2, 1860; Genoa City, November 7, 1860. MSS., Special Collections Department, University of Nevada, Reno.

White, Raymond, Adjutant General of Nevada. *History of the Nevada Militia, 1862–1912.* MS., Adjutant General's Office, Carson City.

Winnemucca (Hopkins), Sarah. *Letter to Eli Samuel Parker, Commissioner of Indian Affairs.* Camp McDermit, Nevada, April 4, 1870. MS., The Bancroft Library, University of California, Berkeley.

Wright, William. *Correspondence and Papers.* 1860–1914. MSS., The Bancroft Library, University of California, Berkeley.

Yerington, Henry Marvin. *Correspondence and Papers.* 1864–1950. MSS., The Bancroft Library, University of California, Berkeley.

Books, Government Documents, Journals,
Pamphlets and Periodicals

Angel, Myron T., ed. *History of Nevada.* Oakland, California: Thompson & West, 1881.

Bidwell, John. *Echoes of the Past.* Chico, California: Chico *Advertiser,* n.d.

Bureau of Outdoor Recreation. *Pyramid Lake Recreation Study Report, Pyramid Lake, Nevada.* San Francisco, California: Pacific Southwest Regional Office, July 1971.

Condition of the Indian Tribes. Report of the Joint Special Committee. Washington, D.C.: Government Printing Office, 1867.

DeGroot, Henry. *Sketches of the Washoe Silver Mines.* San Francisco: Hutchins & Rosenfield, 1860.

Egan, Howard. *Pioneering the West, 1846 to 1878.* Richmond, Utah: Howard R. Egan Estate, 1917.

Eno, Henry. *Twenty Years on the Pacific Slopes: Letters of Henry Eno from California and Nevada, 1848–1871.* Edited by W. Turrentine Jackson. New Haven: Yale University Press, 1965.

Frémont, John Charles. *Report of the Exploring Expedition to the Rocky Mountains in the Year 1842 and to Oregon and North California in the Years 1843–1844.* Washington, D.C.: Gales and Seaton Printers, 1845.

The Golden Era. San Francisco: February 3, 1861.

Goodwin, Charles Carroll. *As I Remember Them.* Salt Lake City: Salt Lake Commercial Club, 1913.

Hays, John to Alfred Cummings, June 12, 1860, "Report to the Secretary of War," *Senate Executive Document,* No. 1, 36th Congress, 2d Session, No. 1079.

Kelly, J. Wells. *First Directory of Nevada Territory, 1862*. Introduction by Richard Lingenfelter. Los Gatos, California: The Talisman Press, 1962.

King, Clarence. *Professional Papers of the Engineer Department, U. S. Army*. No. 18, 7 vols. plus atlas. Washington, D.C.: Government Printing Office, 1877.

Knight, William Henry, ed. *Hand-book Almanac for the Pacific States: An Official Register and Business Directory*. San Francisco: H. H. Bancroft and Co., 1862, 1863, 1864.

Knott, Thomas. *Knott Reminiscences of 1881 Including Early History of Nevada in the 1850's*. Edited by H. Hamlin with Introduction by Staff Sgt. H. Svendsgard, and Foreword by Dr. Charles L. Camp. Oakland, California: Holmes Book Co., 1947.

Lander, Frederick West. *Maps and Reports of the Fort Kearney, South Pass, and Honey Lake Wagon Road*. 36th Congress, 2d Session, House Executive Document 64, Serial 1100.

Letters Received By the Office of Indian Affairs: Nevada Superintendency, 1861–1869. Record Group 75. Washington, D.C.: The National Archives.

Lord, Eliot. *Comstock Mining and Miners*. Monographs of the U. S. Geological Survey, Vol. IV. Washington, D.C.: Government Printing Office, 1883.

Miller, William Charles, ed. "The Pyramid Lake Indian War of 1860." *Quarterly*, Nevada Historical Society, Vol. I, Nos. 1–2, 1957.

Post Returns, Churchill, 1860–1869. Record Group 94. Washington, D.C.: The National Archives.

Records of the Quartermaster General: Consolidated Correspondence File Fort Churchill, Nevada. Record Group 92. Washington, D.C.: The National Archives.

Regimental Returns Sixth Infantry, May and June 1860, and Annual Return, 1860. Record Group 94. Washington, D.C.: The National Archives.

Regimental Returns Third Artillery, May and June 1860, and Annual Return, 1860. Record Group 94. Washington, D.C.: The National Archives.

Report of the Commissioner of Indian Affairs, 1859. Washington, D.C.: George W. Bowman, Printer, 1860.

Report of the Commissioner of Indian Affairs, 1860. Washington, D.C.: U. S. Office of Indian Affairs.

Report of the Commissioner of Indian Affairs, 1861. Washington, D.C.: Government Printing Office, 1861.

Report of the Commissioner of Indian Affairs, 1862. Washington, D.C.: Government Printing Office, 1863.

Report of the Commissioner of Indian Affairs, 1863. Washington, D.C.: Government Printing Office, 1864.

Scott, Charles A. "The Nevada Indian Uprising of 1860 As Seen by Charles A. Scott." Edited and annotated by John M. Ellis and Robert E. Stowers. *Arizona and the West: A Quarterly of History,* Vol. III, No. 4, 1961.

Selected Correspondence and Papers from the Utah Superintendency File, 1860–1870. Record Group 75 (including some documents from Record Group 48). U. S. Bureau of Indian Affairs, The National Archives.

Simpson, James H. *Report of Explorations Across the Great Basin of the Territory of Utah for a Direct Wagon Route from Camp Floyd to Genoa, in Carson Valley in 1859.* Washington, D.C.: Government Printing Office, 1876.

Spencer, W. G., Surgeon U. S. Army. *A Report on the Hygiene of the United States Army with Descriptions of Military Posts.* Washington, D.C.: Government Printing Office, 1875.

Steward, Julian H. "Native Cultures in the Intermontane (Great Basin) Area." Smithsonian Institution, *Miscellaneous Collections.* Washington, D.C.: Government Printing Office, 1940.
———. "Notes on Hillers' Photographs of the Paiute and Ute Indians Taken on the Powell Exploration of 1873." Smithsonian Institution, *Miscellaneous Collections,* Vol. XCVIII, No. 18. Washington, D.C.: Government Printing Office, 1939.

Stewart, William Morris. *Reminiscences of Senator William M. Stewart of Nevada.* Edited by George Rothwell Brown. New York: Neal Publishing Co., 1908.

Underhill, Ruth. "The Northern Paiute Indians of California and Nevada." *Bulletin,* U. S. Department of the Interior. Washington, D.C.: Government Printing Office, 1941.

The War of the Rebellion: A Compilation of the Official Records of the Union and Confederate Armies. Washington, D.C.: Government Printing Office, 1897.

Wasson, Warren. *Wasson Reports*. (Photostatic copies of letters sent from Washington concerning the Carson Valley Indian Agency, 1861). Nevada State Historical Society.

Winnemucca (Hopkins), Sarah. *Life Among the Piutes: Their Wrongs and Claims*. Ed., Mrs. Horace Mann. New York: G. P. Putnam's Sons, 1883.

———. "The Pah-Utes." *The Californian*, Vol. VI, San Francisco, July–December 1882.

Wright, William (Dan DeQuille). *Washoe Rambles*. Introduction by Richard E. Lingenfelter. Los Angeles: Westernlore Press, 1963.

Young, Samuel. "Colonel Samuel Young's Journal." Commentary, Notes, and Transcription by Ethel Zimmer. *Quarterly*, Nevada Historical Society, Vol. II, No. 2, April–June 1959.

Newspapers

Daily Alta California. San Francisco, California. May–December 1860.

The Morning Call. San Francisco, California. May 13, 1883.

The Mountain Democrat. Placerville, California. May–June 1860.

The Mountain Messenger. Downieville, California. April 30, 1859.

Oakland *Tribune*. Oakland, California. July 7, 1957.

Sacramento *Daily Union*. Sacramento, California. March–November 1860.

San Francisco *Daily Evening Bulletin*. San Francisco, California. May–June, August–October 1860.

Territorial Enterprise. Carson City, Utah Territory. June 9, 1860.

SECONDARY SOURCES

Books, Pamphlets, and Periodicals

Anonymous. "A Man of Fixed Principles." *The Argonaut*. Vol. III, No. 25, December 28, 1878.

Ashbaugh, Don. *Nevada's Turbulent Yesterday: A Study in Ghost Towns*. Los Angeles: Westernlore Press, 1963.

Bancroft, Hubert Howe. *History of Nevada, Colorado, and Wyoming, 1540–1888*. San Francisco: The History Co., 1890.

———. *History of Utah, 1540–1887*. San Francisco: The History Co., 1890.

———. *Native Races*. San Francisco: The History Co., 1886.

Bandel, Eugene. *Frontier Life in the Army, 1854–1861.* Southwest Historical Series, Vol. 2. Glendale, California: The Arthur H. Clark Co., 1932.

Bartlett, Richard A. *Great Surveys of the American West.* Norman: University of Oklahoma Press, 1962.

Bill, J. H. (surgeon). "Arrow Wounds." *American Journal of Medical Science.* N.S., Vol. XLIV, 1862.

Brimlow, George F. *The Bannock Indian War of 1878.* Caldwell, Idaho: The Caxton Printers, Ltd., 1938.

————. "The Life of Sarah Winnemucca: The Formative Years." *Quarterly,* Oregon Historical Society, June 1952.

Brooks, Juanita. "The Mormons In Carson County, Utah Territory." *Quarterly,* Nevada Historical Society, Vol. VIII, No. 1, 1965.

Browne, J. Ross. "A Peep at Washoe." *Harper's New Monthly Magazine.* Vol. XXII, No. 127, December 1860.

Buckbee, Edna Bryan. *The Saga of Old Tuolumne.* New York: The Press of the Pioneers, Inc., 1935.

Burton, Richard F. *The City of the Saints & Across the Rocky Mountains to California.* Introduction and notes by Fawn M. Brodie. New York: Alfred A. Knopf, Inc., 1963.

Camp, Charles L. *Earth Song: A Prologue to History* (new edition). Palo Alto, California: American West Publishing Co., 1970.

Chorpenning, George. *A Brief History of the Mail Service, Settlement of the Country, and the Indian Depredations Committed on the Mail Trains of George Chorpenning on the Several Routes Between Salt Lake and California from May 1, 1850 to July 1860.* n.p., n.d. Circa 1861.

————. *The Case of George Chorpenning* vs. *The United States: A Brief History of the Facts by the Claimant.* Washington, D.C.: M'Gill & Witherow, Printers and Stereotypers, 1874.

Cline, Gloria Griffen. *Exploring the Great Basin.* Norman: University of Oklahoma Press, 1963.

Conkling, Roscoe P. and Margaret B. *The Butterfield Overland Mail.* Glendale, California: The Arthur H. Clark Co., 1947.

Davis, Samuel P., ed. *The History of Nevada.* Vol. I, Reno: The Elms Publishing Co., 1913.

Downs, James F. *The Two Worlds of the Washo.* New York: Holt, Rinehart & Winston, 1966.

"Editor's Table." *Hutchings' Illustrated California Magazine.* San Francisco, Vol. V, No. 1, July 1860.

Egan, Ferol. *The El Dorado Trail.* New York: McGraw-Hill Book Co., Inc., 1970.

————. "The Building of Fort Churchill." *The American West,* Vol. IX, No. 2 (March 1972).

————. "Warren Wasson, Model Indian Agent." *Quarterly,* Nevada Historical Society, Vol. XII, No. 3, 1969.

Fairfield, Asa Merrill. *Fairfield's Pioneer History of Lassen County California.* San Francisco: H. S. Crocker Co., 1916.

Farquhar, Francis P. *History of the Sierra Nevada.* Berkeley: University of California Press, 1965.

Forbes, Jack D. *Nevada Indians Speak.* Reno: University of Nevada Press, 1967.

Frazer, Robert W. *Forts of the West.* Norman: University of Oklahoma Press, 1965.

Gianella, Vincent P. "Site of Williams Station, Nevada." *Quarterly,* Nevada Historical Society, Vol. III, No. 4, 1960.

Goetzmann, William H. *Army Exploration in the American West.* New Haven: Yale University Press, 1960.

————. *Exploration and Empire.* New York: Alfred A. Knopf, Inc., 1966.

Greer, James Kimmins. *Colonel Jack Hays: Texas Frontier Leader and California Builder.* New York: E. P. Dutton & Co., Inc., 1952.

Hafen, LeRoy R. *The Overland Mail, 1849–1869.* Cleveland: The Arthur H. Clark Co., 1926.

Harrington, J. P. "The Origin of the Names Ute and Paiute." *American Anthropologist,* N.S., Vol. XL. Menasha, Wisconsin: American Anthropological Association, 1938.

Harris, Jack. "The Western Shoshoni." *American Anthropologist,* N.S., Vol. XL. Menasha, Wisconsin: American Anthropological Association, 1938.

Hazen, William Babcock. *Our Barren Lands: the Interior of the United States West of the One-Hundredth Meridian and East of the Sierra Nevadas.* Cincinnati: R. Clarke & Co., 1875.

Heitman, Francis B. *Historical Register and Dictionary of the United States Army, 1789 to 1903.* Washington, D.C., 1903.

Heizer, Robert F., and Martin A. Baumhoff. *Prehistoric Rock Art of Nevada and Eastern California.* Berkeley: University of California Press, 1962.

Heizer, Robert F., and M. A. Whipple. *The California Indians.* Berkeley: University of California Press, 1957.

Hodge, Frederick Webb, ed. *Handbook of American Indians North of Mexico.* 2 vols. *Bulletin 30,* Bureau of American Ethnology. Washington, D.C.: Government Printing Office, 1912.

Hoffman, W. T. "Miscellaneous Ethnographic Observations on Indians Inhabiting Nevada, California, and Arizona." *Tenth Annual Report,* U. S. Geological and Geodetic Survey. Washington, D.C.: Government Printing Office, 1878.

———. "Poisoned Arrows." *American Anthropologist,* Vol. IV. Menasha, Wisconsin: American Anthropological Association, 1891.

Horan, James D. *Timothy O'Sullivan America's Forgotten Photographer.* New York: Doubleday & Company, Inc., 1966.

Howard, Robert West. *Hoofbeats of Destiny.* New York: The New American Library, 1960.

Hunt, Aurora. *The Army of the Pacific, 1860–1866.* Glendale, California: The Arthur H. Clark Co., 1951.

Illustrated History of Plumas, Lassen & Sierra Counties With California from 1513 to 1850. San Francisco: Fariss & Smith, 1882.

Jackson, W. Turrentine. *Wagon Roads West.* New Haven: Yale University Press, new edition 1965.

James, George Wharton. *Lake of the Sky: Lake Tahoe in the High Sierras of California and Nevada.* Chicago: C. T. Powner, 1956.

Kelly, Isabel T. "Ethnography of the Surprise Valley Paiute." *American Archaeology and Ethnology.* Berkeley, University of California, 1932.

Kroeber, A. L. *Handbook of the Indians of California. Bulletin 78.* Bureau of American Ethnology. Washington, D.C.: Government Printing Office, 1925.

Lillard, Richard G. *Desert Challenge, an Interpretation of Nevada.* New York: Alfred A. Knopf, Inc., 1942.

Lingenfelter, Richard E. *1858–1958: The Newspapers of Nevada, A History and Bibliography.* Introduction by David F. Myrick. San Francisco: John Howell—Books, 1964.

Lyman, George D. *The Saga of the Comstock Lode.* New York: Charles Scribner's Sons, 1934.

Mack, Effie Mona. "James Warren Nye and Orion Clemens." *Quarterly,* Nevada Historical Society, Vol. IV, Nos. 3–4, July– December 1961.

———. *Nevada: A History of the State from the Earliest Times Through the Civil War.* Glendale, California: The Arthur H. Clark Co., 1936.

———. "William Morris Stewart 1827–1909." *Quarterly,* Nevada Historical Society, Vol. VII, Nos. 1–2, 1964.

Madsen, Brigham D. *The Bannock of Idaho.* Caldwell, Idaho: The Caxton Press, Ltd., 1958.

Morgan, Dale L. *Jedediah Smith and the Opening of the West.* Indianapolis: Bobbs-Merrill Co., 1953.

———. *The Humboldt: Highroad of the West.* New York: Farrar and Rinehart, Inc., 1943.

Murphy, Ignatius Ingoldsby. *Life of Colonel Daniel E. Hungerford.* Hartford: Press of The Case, Lockwood & Brainard Co., 1891.

Myrick, David F. "Como." *Quarterly,* Nevada Historical Society, Vol. V, No. 2, 1962.

Park, Willard Z. "Paviotso Polyandry." *American Anthropologist,* N.S., Vol. XXXIX. Menasha, Wisconsin: American Anthropological Association, 1937.

———. "Paviotso Shamanism." *American Anthropologist,* N.S., Vol. XXXVI. Menasha, Wisconsin: American Anthropological Association, 1934.

Patterson, Edna B., Louise A. Ulph, and Victor Goodwin. *Nevada's Northeast Frontier.* Sparks, Nevada: Western Printing & Publishing Co., 1969.

Pourade, Richard F. *The Silver Dons.* San Diego, California: The Union-Tribune Publishing Co., 1963.

Preuss, Charles. *Exploring With Frémont.* Translated and edited by Erwin G. and Elisabeth K. Gudde. Norman: University of Oklahoma Press, 1958.

Prucha, Francis Paul, S.J. *A Guide to Military Posts of the United States.* Madison: The State Historical Society of Wisconsin, 1964.

Riddell, Francis A. "Honey Lake Paiute Ethnography." *Anthropological Papers,* No. 4. Carson City: Nevada State Museum, 1960.

Rogers, Fred B. (Colonel, U. S. Army Ret.). *Soldiers of the Overland: Being Some Account of the Services of General*

Patrick Edward Connor and His Volunteers in the Old West. San Francisco: The Grabhorn Press, 1938.

Ruhlen, George (Colonel, U. S. Army Ret.). "Early Nevada Forts." *Quarterly,* Nevada Historical Society, Vol. VII, Nos. 3–4, 1964.

Sanford, George B. (Colonel). *Fighting Rebels and Redskins: Experiences in Army Life of Colonel George B. Sanford 1861–1892.* Introduction and notes by E. R. Hagemann. Norman: University of Oklahoma Press, 1969.

Scott, Edward B. *Saga of Lake Tahoe: A Complete Documentation of Lake Tahoe's Development Over the Last One Hundred Years.* Crystal Bay, Nevada: Sierra-Tahoe Publishing Co., 1957.

Scott, Lalla. *Karnee: A Paiute Narrative.* Reno: University of Nevada Press, 1966.

Smith, Grant Horace. *The History of the Comstock Lode 1850–1920.* Reno: Nevada State Bureau of Mines, University of Nevada, 1943.

Smith, Philip Dodd, Jr. "The Sagebrush Soldiers: Nevada's Volunteers in the Civil War." *Quarterly,* Nevada Historical Society, Vol. V, Nos. 3–4, 1962.

Stegner, Wallace. *Beyond the Hundredth Meridian.* Boston: Houghton Mifflin Co., 1954.

Steward, Julian H. "Basin-Plateau Sociopolitical Groups." *Bulletin 120,* Bureau of American Ethnology. Washington, D.C.: Government Printing Office, 1938.

———. "Nevada Shoshoni." *Anthropological Records,* Vol. VIII, No. 3. Berkeley: University of California, 1941.

———. "Two Paiute Autobiographies." *American Archaeology and Ethnology,* Vol. XXXIII, No. 5. Berkeley: University of California, 1934.

Stewart, George R. *The California Trail.* New York: McGraw-Hill Book Co., Inc., 1962.

———. *Ordeal by Hunger, the Story of the Donner Party.* Boston: Houghton Mifflin Co., new edition 1960.

Stewart, O. C. "The Northern Paiute Bands." *Anthropological Records,* Vol. II, No. 3. Berkeley: University of California, 1939.

Stewart, Robert E., Jr. and M. F. Stewart. *Adolph Sutro: A Biography.* Berkeley: Howell-North Books, 1962.

Sutro, Adolph. *A Trip to Washoe.* San Francisco: The White Knight Press, 1942.

Swanton, John R. *The Indian Tribes of North America. Bulletin 145,* Bureau of American Ethnology. Washington, D.C.: Government Printing Office, 1932.

Swartzlow, Ruby Johnson. *Lassen: His Life and Legacy.* Mineral, California: Loomis Museum Association, 1964.

Trenholm, Virginia Cole, and Maurine Carley. *The Shoshonis: Sentinels of the Rockies.* Norman: University of Oklahoma Press, 1964.

Utley, Robert M. *Frontiersmen in Blue: The United States Army and the Indian, 1848–1865.* New York: The Macmillan Co., 1967.

Watson, Margaret G. *Silver Theatre: Amusements of Nevada's Mining Frontier, 1850 to 1864.* Glendale, California: The Arthur H. Clark Co., 1964.

Wells, H. L. *History of Nevada County, California.* Oakland, California: Thompson & West, 1880.

Wheat, Margaret M. *Survival Arts of the Primitive Paiutes.* Reno: University of Nevada Press, 1967.

Wheeler, Sessions S. *The Desert Lake: the Story of Nevada's Pyramid Lake.* Caldwell, Idaho: The Caxton Printers, Ltd., 1967.

———. *The Nevada Desert.* Caldwell, Idaho: The Caxton Printers, Ltd., 1971.

Wilkins, Thurman. *Clarence King.* New York: The Macmillan Co., 1958.

Wren, Thomas, ed. *A History of the State of Nevada.* New York: Lewis Publishing Co., 1904.

Wright, William (Dan DeQuille). *The Big Bonanza.* Introduction by Oscar Lewis. New York: Alfred A. Knopf, Inc., 1947.

Index

N